Confessions of a 40 (something) Year Old Bachelor

By

Barrington Rose

ISBN: 978-1499246445

In memory of my
Big Brother Jimmy Butler

Foreword

If you wrote a book about your life, would anyone want to read it? Everyone has pondered this question at some point in their life, in hopes of validating their existence and the role they've played on the "big stage" of life. I decided to write this book because my answer to that question was an emphatic, "Hell Yea!"

Sharing the most intimate parts of your life can be a frightening yet exhilarating exercise in human introspection. Years ago, I adopted the phrase "carpe diem" as my mantra and the result has been a lifetime of memorable stories spanning from my crazy college years to dating celebrities, dealing with the loss of my dad, winning lots of cash in Vegas, good times in Brazil, being a black man in America, true Hollywood stories and doing stand- up comedy on the biggest stage in LA.

I hope you will read my story with an open mind and live vicariously through my experiences and my ultimate effort to live the fullest life I could imagine.

Long ago, I read a book entitled *The Road Less Traveled* by M. Scott Peck. The book has been a bestseller for years and serves as a template for how to navigate your life experiences within the context of what is truly possible, and it also attempts to explain why we often fail to reach our highest potential.

After reading this book, as well as many others on self-motivation, I used what I learned and decided to implement it into my daily life. With an insatiable desire for success, love and spiritual enlightenment, I decided to try and live the most balanced and fulfilling life I could dream of.

You will read about my struggles, my wins, my losses, my tears, my pain and my truth. I attest that every word of this book is the absolute truth as I have lived it and recorded it in my mind and now in this book. As a disclaimer, I changed the names of several individuals in my book as a friendly courtesy.

I hope you enjoy the read!

The Chase 1

Freshman Follies 9

Flying High 27

College is a Party 37

Daddy's Gone 53

Back to School 69

The Real World 99

Nouveau Rich 109

Money, money, money... 157

Women do cheat! 163

Tina 171

ATL 187

Go West Young Man 209

LA Hustle 237

Hollywood Burn 251

What Happens in Vegas 261

Hollywood Hookup 267

Mallory 271

Ah Paris! 277

Stand Up for Your Rights 291

Brazil 307

Leilani 315

Celebrity Encounters 337

Stand-Up Comedy 355

Advice for Bachelors 363

The Future 365

Chapter 1

The Chase

As I'm traveling back to my dorm room at East Carolina University circa 1987 in my blue Datsun Hatchback, handed down to me by my sister who was a year ahead of me at Appalachian State; I had the stereo blasting some good reggae music while driving down a two lane country road through a town called Farmville, on my way to Greenville, NC.

I was feeling good because I had toked on a joint before embarking on my trip from my hometown in Winston-Salem, NC. Smoking was a way of making the four hour trek a bit less monotonous and it also helped me to think deeply about my life and where I wanted to go.

My thoughts were suddenly interrupted by the sight of a sheriff's car passing me on the other side of the road and me quickly realizing that I was speeding at least 15 miles over the speed limit. I saw his red lights flash as he was making a U-turn in my review mirror to no doubt come after me.

Feeling panicked and slightly stoned, I decided the most logical thing to do was to try and out run him -- it's amazing how many bad decisions can be made while in a state of herbal bliss.

I checked my rear view mirror again to see the trooper racing in my direction, at which point I decided that I would try to elude him by quickly turning into a residential neighborhood. I checked my rear view again to see the trooper hastily turn into the neighborhood while still hot on my trail.

At this point, my adrenaline had kicked in and all logic had flown out the window, so the only thing I could do was continue my ill-fated escape in my Datsun Hatchback.

As I began to approach a cul-de-sac at the end of the road, I suddenly noticed a dirt road to my right and I deftly steered my car onto the road with the trooper even closer on my tail with his lights flashing and his siren blowing.

While driving along this bumpy dirt road at a high speed, I came upon a ramp-like mound in the road and immediately decided that this was all or nothing; so I grabbed my steering wheel and went airborne for just a few seconds like the *Dukes of Hazzard*!

All the while, the trooper was on my bumper and hell bent on stopping me. Finally I found myself driving through a deserted farm with no way out. Realizing that the chase was over, I slammed on my brakes and quickly put my car in park and then began to slowly step out of my car with my hands up.

The trooper immediately exited his vehicle and approached me with his gun drawn. He started shouting, "Get your hands up! Get your hands up!" Despite the fact that I had just tried to elude a police officer, I wasn't extremely nervous. I guess the adrenaline had taken over and all I could think about was how I was going to get out of this mess.

The officer quickly cuffed me and led me to his patrol car while talking on his radio. As I was sitting in the backseat of the car, I could see through the divider that he was searching my car.

I knew that my car was clean because I had smoked the remainder of my joint and discarded the roach. The officer rushed back to the car, still frantic from the chase and I could see that he was really pissed off. He abruptly asked me in a thick country accent, "What'n hell were you thinkin'?" I didn't really have a good answer but I told him that I was sorry and that I just panicked. I also told him that I was worried about getting another ticket because I already had two other tickets on my record and my parents had threatened to drop my insurance and take my car away.

As we pulled away, I took one last glance at my Datsun which was now covered in mud and dirt. All I could think about was that I would no longer have a car and even worse, the embarrassment of confessing my stupidity to my parents.

On the way to the patrol station, the officer continued talking on his radio. He was explaining to his other officers that he was bringing me in for booking. The trooper turned back towards me and said, "I bet you're from Greensboro huh?" I told him where I was from, but I later realized that he was asking me about Greensboro because it had been a landmark for civil rights protests and the famous lunch counter sit-ins of the 1960's.

So clearly he was a redneck who didn't like black people, *especially* black people who tried to evade his pursuit. Once we arrived at the station, it looked like the old jailhouse from the TV show *Mayberry RFD*. They booked me at the small intake counter and advised me to call a bail bond if I wanted to get out any time soon.

I had never heard of a bail bondsman at the age of 19 and I had never needed one -- until now. They gave me a list of names to call and I immediately picked out a card with a black man's face on it. I called him up and explained what happened. He asked me if I had any money for bail and I told him a little.

Despite the fact that I only had a small amount of money, he said he was on his way to the jail. Once I hung up, they led me to the back and threw me into an old jail cell that reeked with the smell of urine.

The magnitude of my audaciousness began to sink in once I was behind bars. All I could think about was how disappointed my parents would be and how I would explain this fiasco. As I sat on the hard bed frame, my mind began to wonder about Martin Luther King, Jr. and the pictures I recalled of him sitting in a jail cell.

Although our circumstances were dramatically different in terms of how we both wound up behind bars, I began to empathize with what it must have felt like for him to be locked up. I've always had an appreciation for civil rights leaders like MLK, Gandhi and Nelson Mandela; because I know they risked their lives so that others could exercise their right to freedom.

I started thinking about how embarrassed I was for myself as a black man and what the consequences of my actions might mean for me later in my life. I patiently waited for my bail bondsman to arrive, having no idea what to expect or how he might react to seeing me. About an hour later, the trooper returned to my cell and announced that my bondsman had arrived. He unlocked the cell and led me to the front desk where I was greeted by a sharp dressed black man.

He shook my hand, didn't smile and began to introduce himself and explain how the bond process works. He told me that I needed to give him a certain amount of money up front and that he would be responsible for making sure that I showed up for my court date.

Being naïve about the whole process, I thought that I would have to go to trial and have my fate determined by a jury like on TV. He explained to me that I was being charged with evading a blue light and fleeing an officer, each of which were serious offenses.

I nodded to indicate that I understood the charges and then we proceeded to leave the sheriff's station. Once we were in the car, I began to explain to him what happened when he suddenly said to me, "Man you're lucky to be alive, that cracker coulda shot yo' ass out there in that field."

Throughout the ride back to my car, his tone became more fatherly and less business-like. I guess he could see that I was just a young college student who made a really bad mistake. As we approached my car sitting in the deserted farm field, he just shook his head. He couldn't believe that I tried something so daring. I also had a chance to replay the chase in my mind when I saw how far away from the highway I had traveled.

Once I reached my car it started up right away, which was a huge relief. Luckily, there was no major damage to my car. I thanked the bail bondsman for giving me a ride and then I proceeded to continue to my trek back to ECU.

The rest of the trip was obviously a lot different than before, I never exceeded the speed limit and spent a lot of time thinking about my actions. By the time I reached my school, I started feeling a lot better because I knew that I at least had some income from my job at the airport to pay for any fines or fees.

The next week I went to see a top lawyer whose office was located in the tony downtown area of Greenville. When I showed them my citation and explained what happened, they were initially a bit flabbergasted at my story but then they began to laugh about my predicament.

The older attorney was a portly white man who wore suspenders. There was also a younger attorney who was also well dressed. The older attorney said, "Son you got yo' self into quite a pickle." He paused and sighed, "But the good news is that I know the judge over there in Farmville and I'll see if I can work somethin' out."

I was very relieved to hear those words. I let out a huge sigh of relief and then I began to chuckle. "So how much are you going to charge me?" I inquired. The older attorney replied that since I was a student, he was going to give me a special rate of $100. I couldn't believe that he was helping me for such a small amount. I was expecting him to quote me at least $500.

We all smiled and laughed a bit more about the situation. When I left, they shook my hand and set up an appointment for me to return to their office for an update.

As I walked out the door, the portly attorney said to me, "Hey don't get in any more trouble now." I nodded and happily exited their office.

A couple of weeks went by, I was trying to get back into my normal groove of work and school while still thinking about the consequences of my situation, when I suddenly received a call from the older attorney. He told me that everything had been taken care of and the charges had been dropped. I was especially elated to hear the good news because I didn't even have to pay a fine, and most importantly -- I wouldn't have a record.

I felt fortunate to be able to resolve this fiasco without having any major long term consequences. I think the fact that I was a college student helped quite a bit. Greenville is a small college town that has always had a reputation for looking out for students.

My parents never found out about the incident, but I admitted to my mom a couple of years ago that I had been arrested in college, and proceeded to provide details of the chase to which she simply laughed along with the story.

Chapter 2

Freshman Follies

My college life was simply epic. I can recall my first night·on campus as a freshman. I was hanging out of my fourth floor dorm window in Scott Hall listening to some old school beats, when I spotted a sexy, young, dark skinned girl with a bangin' body wearing "short shorts" and strolling along the sidewalk. I yelled out to her, "Hey wassup!?" -- which was apparently an original opening line for a young and horny freshman. She looked up and replied, "Hey not much, wassup with you?" To which I replied, "Just chillin', I saw you and I just wanted to say wassup."

We chatted for a couple of minutes and then I boldly decided to invite her to my room. She said, "Sure!" and began to make her way into the dorm. I hopped back inside and began to make plans for her arrival. I was excited about the thought of meeting this girl and what might happen with her once she arrived.

I was fortunate because I didn't have a roommate at the time. Soon a knock came upon the door and I rushed to open it, still excited to see this fine young chocolate "sista." Once I opened the door, I was even more impressed with her and also proud of myself for having the guts to get her up there.

She sauntered into the room and began to check out my pad. As she walked in, I began to check out her amazing body. She wasn't particularly cute but she was far from ugly -- all that didn't matter because she had a great shape and a sexy attitude -- two things that drive most men crazy.

We both laughed about the spontaneity of our meeting and wasted no time getting down to business; it was almost as if we were reading each other's minds and we knew that this encounter would be fun. We started kissing and I began to explore her body, feeling even more excited and aroused at how quickly everything was taking place.

Within a few minutes, we were on my bed and I was struggling to get her clothes off -- until finally she was nude and at which point I was completely aroused. As we began to embrace, I could feel how soft and warm her curvaceous body was against mine. I could tell that she had lots of experience and that she knew what she was doing, which made it even more intense because she had a sexual energy that simply exuded from her pores.

We began to have passionate sex and all I could think about was the fact that I had just met her twenty minutes ago outside of my window. We explored each other for quite a while then we both came to an intense climax. Exhausted from our love session, we both laid in bed staring at the ceiling and talking about freshman stuff. I knew at that moment, that college was going to be a very fun experience for me.

Once we were done with our lovemaking, she began to get dressed and gathered up her things. We hugged and kissed a bit more before she left, we didn't exchange numbers because she was also new on campus and during that time nobody had cell phones.

After she left, I was ecstatic about the serendipitous encounter and I went back to staring out my window and into the crisp night air with a smile on my face.

Life as a new student college student was transformative and enlightening on many levels. All of sudden there was a whole new world of new friends and opportunities to grow and learn.

I grew up in a predominately white neighborhood on the outskirts of Winston-Salem, NC. Most people who lived in the city referred to the far out areas as the "boonies" and that's exactly what it was -- it was a remote area with a few middle schools, several brick laden Baptist and Moravian churches and lots of long winding country roads.

Our neighborhood was a mix of middle to upper-middle class families and a few families who obviously had a lot more than most.   They were mostly southern white people and a sprinkling of black families, so my opportunities to date black women were limited to just a couple of girls in another nearby neighborhood. Throughout high school, I really didn't date much until I was a junior, which also coincided with me getting my first car, a 1967 Chevrolet Malibu which I hated.   I wanted a stylish, preferably foreign car to make up for the previous years I felt I had lost by not having the access and ability to date women outside of my neighborhood.

Ironically, today a 1967 Chevrolet Malibu in top condition sells for about $20,000, but that's not something a teenager contemplates when he's trying to impress young ladies.

Dating white girls wasn't really an option because this was the South and most parents didn't want their daughters dating black guys.   However, there were a few white girls who liked to secretly mess around but interracial dating was certainly not a common thing back then.

I recall an older black friend of mine from my neighborhood named Darnell, who told me that he had recently knocked on the door of an attractive white girl that he had befriended in school and how her father came to the door, threatened him and told him to stay away from his daughter.

There were also a couple of occasions when we first moved into our house when a group of rednecks would ride by our house in a jeep and shout, "Niggers get outta here!" I remember standing in our large fenced-in backyard with my dad on one of these occasions. I was completely shocked, I glanced at my dad and he seemed unfazed. He never reacted and I only heard him speak about it casually with my mother and some family friends afterwards.

I had seen these guys before and I knew where they lived, I also knew that their younger sister rode my bus and went to my junior high school. I never forgot that incident and I recall asking her on the bus one day if her brothers were part of the KKK. She was very timid and simply responded, "No." She didn't bother to elaborate, but I knew that she was embarrassed for herself and her family.

I discovered years later that one of the wealthiest families in my nearby neighborhood *were* members of the KKK and their dad was rumored to have been a Grand Wizard. The ironic thing about that revelation was that my youngest brother Jack was best friends with their youngest son and they loved having Jack around their house.

They were big in the construction industry and had an enormous lake, boats, trampolines, tennis courts and motorcycles. I only remember visiting their house a couple of times to play tennis and jump on their trampoline but I always felt that something just wasn't kosher about me being there.

Prior to moving to the "boonies," we lived in the city in a black neighborhood but once my mom and dad started making better money, my dad who was raised on a farm -- longed for a more rural setting. However, this new setting was both a blessing and a curse for me. I had my own spacious room downstairs and I had a sense of privacy as well but my interactions with black people were limited, except for the few that lived in my neighborhood and nearby.

When I arrived at ECU, even though it was a predominately white school there was a large population of black students. This was something that was very new for me and I quickly began to make new friends. I was especially excited about having the opportunity to date smart, attractive black women from different places. I had never really had a steady girlfriend in high school because of my lack of transportation and my remote location, so seeing all these voluptuous and intelligent women on campus was definitely an eye opener.

There were a few girls that I immediately singled out who lived in an all-girls dorm across the way. There was a crew of "sistas" from the Raleigh area who decided to all live together in the same dorm. I would become friends with them and eventually met a few of their homeboys. We all seemed to be a big, happy, horny crew of party loving students.

Thursday night was always a big party night and somebody in our crew always had drinks in their room, mainly cheap vodka to start the weekend off right. A couple of the college bars also offered ten cent beer night on Thursday which made it *really* difficult to get to class on Friday.

Figuring out which girls in our crew were available wasn't really all that difficult, especially when there was alcohol involved -- but women also have a way of letting you know if they're interested and apparently I had a couple of early suitors. One of the girls that I started messing around with was a girl named Josie. She was tall and light skinned with a cool laid back style about herself.

Josie and I never really got serious, but she would often come over to my dorm room to hang out, drink and have sex. She was very passionate and we really enjoyed each other but I also knew that she was seeing someone else in our crew as well, a tall guy from Greensboro known as Slam.

Josie had another friend named Leona who was a cute brown skin girl with a sweet personality. Leona let me know that she was interested in hooking up with me but she wasn't sure about what was going on with me and Josie. They must have had a conversation because one day Leona showed up at my dorm room with a real sly smile on her face. She tried to play it cool but I knew what she was there for.

Leona and I hooked up a few times and we all still continued to hang out as a crew and no one seemed to really have any issues with the arrangements. I knew that some of the other guys were also hooking up with them because they had known each other since high school. They also had another friend named Kim who was kind of meek. She was cute but she wasn't vivacious like the rest of her friends. Kim would occasionally drop by and just watch soap operas with me but then her visits became more frequent and I finally figured out her motives, but we never slept together (at least I don't think we did).

This was the first time in my life that I had so much access to young available women and it felt invigorating because I've always had a strong sex drive and this situation seemed to be ideal for making up for lost time in my high school years. The energy on campus was electric, especially whenever there was a big football game. Back then, ECU was known for playing big schools like Penn State, Miami and Auburn, and occasionally we won which meant that the energy on campus was even more electric.

I lived in the athlete's dorm which was always buzzing with action. Girls were constantly visiting the dorm and hanging out with the football and basketball players. One of the guys that became a friend was Blue Edwards, ECU's all-time scoring leader and 12 year NBA veteran -- let's just say that Blue was a quiet storm both on and off the court.

I was a very productive receiver and running back at my high school, West Forsyth and my plan was to walk on at ECU even though I had been offered a scholarship to Lenoir Rhyne, a small school in Hickory, NC. I chose ECU because I saw a football calendar in my coach's office one day with pretty girls on it and I knew that ECU had a reputation for being a party school, so I figured what better place to play football.

I had played football and basketball for most of my childhood and I was a pretty good athlete and I'm still competitive to this very day, especially in basketball. When my senior year rolled around, I started receiving letters from lots of schools including Wake Forest, ECU, UNC, Maryland, Georgia and a few others. I was a really good receiver who usually caught anything that was well thrown, which was not that common in high school, but I also had speed to make up for our quarterback's lack of accuracy.

I was extremely confident in my abilities as an athlete but I was also insecure in other areas like dating and socializing. All of that began to dissipate when I arrived at college and started expanding my circle of friends and gaining more experience in the dating world.

Josie and I continued to see each other but things got awkward when I started hearing rumors that Slam wasn't too happy about me hooking up with her. We eventually cooled things off and I started meeting other girls outside of our crew to hang out with. One of those girls was a sweet, country girl named Sonya who I was immediately smitten with upon meeting her. The bad thing was that she also lived in the same dorm as my other female friends. I remember telling her the first time I saw her that I was going to make her my girlfriend. She seemed extremely flattered and began flirting with me with her pretty brown eyes. We went on a couple of dates during which I discovered that she was a virgin.

I wasn't really sure how to approach that situation but I knew that I wanted to be with her. During a last minute road trip to Raleigh with another couple, I sensed that she wanted to have sex but I wasn't very confident in taking her virginity because I had never been with a virgin and I didn't feel worthy of her "flower."

We messed around a few more times but I still couldn't convince myself that I was worthy of her because I didn't want to considered a "bad guy" if things didn't work out with us. We eventually drifted apart and never had sex but I later found out that she hooked up with a guy named Rick who was an asshole and most definitely took her virginity.

As my freshman year continued to unfold I began to socialize a lot more. As a young dude growing up in a remote area, I wasn't accustomed to living in close quarters with so many different types of people. I didn't know anyone at ECU when I first arrived but by my sophomore year I started meeting some cool people who became really good friends. One of those people was a guy named Charles; he was different from most students because he apparently came from a wealthy family. I think his dad owned a couple of Hardee's restaurants in his hometown and he also had a really nice condo that he owned off campus.

Charles didn't seem like a regular student because he had a new car and a house and he also seemed like a cool guy that could possibly introduce me to some cool chicks. Charles was also very much into Prince and I think he had a weird fascination with being as much like him as possible. He never wore outlandish clothes or anything like that but he was definitely a big fan.

Most people in those days were big Prince fans, so it didn't seem very odd for a guy with money to emulate his idol. I remember hanging out with Charles one day on campus when he spotted a girl that I had also seen before a few times. She was simply radiant, she had smooth, pecan brown skin, curly jet black hair and crystal clear eyes that looked like pearls. Her name was Darlene and she was from D.C., which made her even more attractive for a couple of country boys with swagger.

I remember Charles saying how bad he wanted to meet her and how sexy he thought she was. I was also enamored with Darlene but I had never gotten up the courage to ask her out because she was a year ahead of me and probably wasn't interested in dating a younger guy. One day I ran into Darlene in the hallway of one of our Political Science buildings and I got up the nerve to talk to her and began telling her about my friend Charles who really wanted to meet her.

She seemed interested in meeting Charles, although I was secretly wishing that she would say she was more interested in hanging out with me. Darlene seemed like the kind of girl who would date a guy with a nice car but not a sophomore who lived on campus like me. So I gave her Charles's number and later informed him that he should be getting a call from her.

A few weeks went by and I ran into Darlene again on campus and she stopped me and said, "Hey I went out with your friend Charles." I replied, "And?" She went on to tell me that Charles was a little weird for her taste. She told me that she went to his house and he had neon lights and smoke rising up from his bed like Prince did in his concerts. We both immediately busted out laughing!

We laughed so hard that I almost cried because I knew that he was a big fan, but I had no idea that he had taken it *that* far. Darlene and I started hitting it off after that encounter. We were spending a lot of time together and she eventually became my first love.

We were both Political Science majors which was great because we took some of the same classes and helped each other study for tests. Darlene was everything I could want in a girlfriend, she was smart, she was pretty and she also had a really nice chest. She also taught me how to play the game of chess; she loved baseball and also introduced me to jazz artists such as Michael Franks, George Howard, Phyllis Hyman and Jonathan Butler. In return, I taught her how to roll the perfect joint.

We had great sex and whenever we smoked beforehand it always made the sex even more enjoyable. We both had roommates, so finding a place to have sex sometimes was a challenge. I remember one night, we snuck into the gym at night after it was closed and made our way into the men's locker room. We were both scared of getting caught but that made it even more exciting.

There really wasn't a comfortable place for us to have sex in the locker room so she wound up straddling me on a bench. It wasn't ideal but it was perfect for our little rendezvous. We were both nervous about getting caught to really let loose in our lovemaking but after a few minutes we both were satisfied and began to sneak our way out of the building. Later, we laughed about our little secret encounter and how much fun it would be to do it again.

We always looked forward to the weekends when her roommate was out of town so that we could have uninterrupted sex and enjoy each other's company. It felt good to have a steady girlfriend and for the first time in my life I was in love and I felt that we had a bright future together despite the fact that we were both very young.

After we had been dating for a while, Darlene thought it was a good idea for me to meet her mother who lived in the D.C. area. She had told me a lot about her mother and they seemed very close. She told me that her mom had been married twice and was contemplating marrying her current boyfriend, who Darlene wasn't exactly crazy about.

One weekend, Darlene and I packed up her car and headed up to meet her mom. It was about a five hour drive from Greenville, so we took turns driving and stopping along the way. I had only been to D.C. a couple of times prior to our visit and I was excited about seeing the city and experiencing the culture. When we finally arrived at her house, her mom instantly came out to greet us.

She had features like Darlene and seemed well kept for her age. She greeted me and welcomed me into their house where I also met her boyfriend, John. John was kind of nerdy and seemed to be a bit uptight. He would randomly spout out statistics to support whatever point he was trying to make during a few of our conversations. I was given my own room next to Darlene's room, which wasn't a surprise considering that most parents would not allow their daughter's boyfriend to share a room with their daughter.

I was kind of nervous because I could sense that her mom was trying to belittle me by making little snide remarks about where I was from. She thought that I was just some country bumpkin with no ambition who wasn't good enough for her daughter.

I recall telling a story about a time when I called Darlene at work and identified myself as her boyfriend and her mom rudely interrupted me and said, "You told them you were her boyfriend?" -- as if that was somehow unprofessional. I shrugged and continued my story but I knew from that point that she didn't like me and my stay at her house wasn't going to be fun.

I tried to simply be a nice guy and impress her folks but I was still a bit uncomfortable in their house. One night, her mom was baking a large piece of salmon and asked if I could help cut it. She handed me a large knife and I began to carefully slice the fish when the knife suddenly slipped in my hand and gashed my thumb which started bleeding profusely.

I felt like such a klutz because I was bleeding in their kitchen and apparently was unable to simply slice a piece of fish. I'm sure that incident didn't sit well with her mom either, she probably chalked it up as one more strike against me.

Darlene and I had stopped at the liquor store before heading to her house. I picked up a bottle of cognac which was not something that I drank at the time, but I thought it would impress her mom. So before we had dinner, we had a round of drinks and her mom was impressed with the cognac. Darlene was sure to tell her that I purchased it, which I think made me seem more mature.

All went well at dinner with no more major snafus and afterwards we small talked until everyone was ready to retire. I remember laying in my bed thinking about Darlene in the next room and how I couldn't wait to be with her.

The next day her mom was up early and off to church. Darlene and I said we were tired from our travels and that we had decided to stay home, besides we had already talked about spending our morning together. After her mom left we couldn't wait to get it on, she came into my room wearing her night clothes and started undressing. I was still somewhat sleepy but very eager to get her clothes off.

We made love for a while and then chilled out on the bed. She told me how happy she was I came with her and not to worry about her mom. We laughed about me nearly cutting my thumb off with the knife and about how corny John's stories were.

The rest of the trip was pretty cool; we hung out in different areas of the city. My favorite spot was a jazz club in Georgetown called Blues Alley where we saw the late George Howard. He was magnificent and put on a great show and he also had a surprisingly witty sense of humor.

I felt good on our return trip back to school. I started feeling like Darlene and I were soul mates, as if we were simply meant to be together.

Chapter 3

Flying High

Everything else was going well, including my job at the airport where there was no shortage of drama and good times. I worked as a ramp agent at the small commuter airport in town called the Pitt-Greenville Airport. That was a great job for a college student because it paid fairly well and offered me a chance to interact with lots of different people, including celebrities.

Michael Jordan would hold his annual golf tournament in Greenville and that event always brought a lot of celebrities into town; although many of them didn't seem happy that they had to fly on the small commuter planes to reach town. I wasn't a big fan of those planes either because they weren't pressurized and gave me excruciating headaches whenever I would travel back home.

One of the frequent visitors to Greenville was Kenny Smith, former UNC and NBA basketball player and now currently long time host of *NBA on TNT*. Kenny was a really cool guy who I once tried to emulate my game after when I was younger. We would often chat when he came to town; we talked about basketball and about the state of the NBA during that time. He was dating a very pretty girl in town who was a local news reporter, but I'm sure he didn't know that my good friend also named Kenny was seeing his girl when he wasn't around.

Kenny Smith had a bought her car and I remember my friend Kenny driving it quite a bit, so that was interesting but Kenny was a celebrity who traveled a lot, so I'm sure he had other women as well.

I remember there was a time when Kenny had flown in late and left behind a bag that included his wallet and some other miscellaneous stuff. One of my coworkers and I discovered the bag and quickly realized that it belonged to Kenny. We knew it was his bag because we checked the ID inside the wallet and also noticed that he had a lot of money, including large checks written out to him.

My coworker and I were both college students and he jokingly suggested that we take the money and discard the wallet. I told him that wasn't a good idea and besides, I had too much respect for Kenny to do that -- so we decided to hold on to the wallet until he returned. About an hour later, he returned to the airport appearing a bit frantic. He asked if we had seen his bag with his wallet and we immediately told him we had it.

He was very relieved and after receiving his returned wallet he offered us each $100 for our trouble. At first we both refused his offer but then he said, "Alright drinks on me then?" -- to which we happily accepted his money as a reward.

I remember seeing Kenny a few years later after graduation at an NBA All Star party in Charlotte, NC. I was hanging out with one of my buddies and we had finagled our way into the exclusive party where I ran into Blue Edwards who was hanging out with Kenny and some other ball players. They both greeted me warmly and then I introduced them to my friend who was very impressed that they knew me because we were both big basketball fans and both came from a town with no big celebrities.

The job at the airport was exciting, especially when we were under pressure to get the flight out on time. I was mainly a ramp agent but we had to also do reservations, security and make boarding announcements which was always fun because people would often tell me that I had a professional sounding voice.

There was a lot of time between arriving flights at a small airport so I had time to study and sometimes goof off on the luggage cart. I really enjoyed my job and I thought about making a career of the airlines as a marketing or sales executive, even though that was a rare position for an African-American to have during those days.

I worked with some really interesting characters, a few of them were college students, some were aspiring pilots and there were a couple of older people who simply enjoyed working for the airlines. I'm pretty sure I was the first black person they had ever hired and I felt an obligation to represent myself well.

There was one girl who worked there named Valerie. She was a beautiful tall blond with blue eyes from Virginia and her parents apparently had wealth. I had never been with a white girl as pretty as Valerie and I just assumed that she probably wasn't interested in me. I also recall a time when she was giving me a ride home and as we were leaving the parking lot, she nearly hit a car driven by a black guy and she screamed, "Hey watch out nigger!" I was shocked, but her comment didn't seem to register with her at all, it was as if I wasn't black or even in the car with her.

She just continued driving and talking as if everything was normal. I didn't say anything because she seemed oblivious to what she had said and I didn't want to have any racial beef with a coworker.

As Valerie and I began to work together more, we would often flirt with each other. I knew that she didn't have a boyfriend and her male roommate, Dereck, who also worked with us, told me that she was a virgin --

which really piqued my interest. Sometimes I would go over to their place and hang out with them to drink and play games.

One day Valerie invited me over when her roommate wasn't around and I happily said okay, even though I knew it was risky having a girlfriend and being seen with her. We were hanging out and drinking and I still couldn't believe that she was really interested in me, until she started to flirt while we were alone.

I didn't get the impression that she wanted to go all the way but I knew she wanted to mess around. After a couple of drinks and some casual conversation, she started to get that look in her eyes as if she wanted me to make a move on her. I was still dating Darlene at the time and we had been seeing each other for a few months, so I was hesitant to do anything with her.

I saw Valerie as potential trophy sex because she was new to me and the thought that she was possibly a virgin was very enticing. I'm still not sure how true that part of her story was but I couldn't bring myself to get involved with her because we were coworkers and I also still had a girlfriend.

There were some other interesting characters that I worked with as well, one of them was a really cool guy named Nick. Nick was supposedly an aspiring pilot but I never saw him actually taking flying lessons. He also had a roommate who worked with us and they always seemed to have the best weed and they were very generous with their stash.

When I first started working at the airport, it was well known that someone had stolen a bunch of tickets at some point not long before I started and everybody assumed it was Nick. The more I got to know Nick; I also assumed that he was the culprit. In those days, a lot of tickets were simply handwritten on carbon paper, so anyone who had a blank ticket could essentially write out their destination to anywhere USAir flew.

There were constant whispers that Nick could be arrested at any time but they could never actually pin the theft on him, but it didn't seem to affect his demeanor or his performance at work. Nick was always jovial and lighthearted, he would often come by my house to hang out and play cards. He started coming by so much at one point that Darlene started calling him "Nick at Night."

I never asked Nick about the ticket caper and he never bothered to admit his guilt but we both knew that he and his roommate were the culprits. Nick could sometimes be a bit reckless and carefree on the job as well. There was a time when we had just unloaded a plane and I was riding on the back of the luggage cart as Nick drove like a bat out of hell towards the luggage carousel.

He was driving way too fast and almost caused some of the bags to dislodge from the cart. I glanced at the bags, quickly turned around again and nearly hit my head on a brick wall. I instantly ducked my head to avoid an awful impact that would have seriously injured me or much worse, kill me!

I started screaming at him in disbelief that he was so careless. He kept apologizing profusely and begging forgiveness. I eventually calmed down, but even to this day I thank God I wasn't seriously injured in a potentially gruesome accident.

The airport was always buzzing with passengers and crew members including pilots and pretty flight attendants, constantly shuttling back and forth through the terminal. One of the other characters I met was a pilot named Ron. Ron was known as "Whitey" and not because he had a full head of completely white hair. Ron was a cokehead and small time dealer. I had tried coke when I was in high school a couple of times but I wasn't a frequent user because I knew the consequences of forming a habit.

Apparently there was a very small circle of employees who knew the real meaning behind Ron's nickname and I had heard that they sometimes scored small amounts of coke from him whenever he was in town. Ron was such a cool operator, he always wore his hip aviator shades and he was always flirting with the flight attendants. He looked like a guy who might live on a boat and wear shorts year round.

He befriended me right away, I guess because I was new and the only black person working there. After meeting him a couple of times, he asked me one day if I wanted to do some "blow" in the bathroom. I said okay and we proceeded to the men's bathroom where he quickly dispensed a couple of hits onto a tiny spoon. I snorted a couple of hits and wiped my nose and then he proceeded to do the same. I also rubbed a little bit on my gums as well to get that numb feeling.

Once we had our fix we walked out of the bathroom and acted as if everything was normal. He began to make his way back to the plane and I started helping load the plane. I was often the ramp agent with the neon sticks who guided the planes to a stop and also upon departure -- that was a really cool part of my job that I always looked forward to.

As Ron taxied the plane away from the gate, he gave me a big thumbs-up and I gave him a salute in return as he steered the plane towards the runway. Being high on coke was intense and it gave me a tremendous sense of confidence and energy. The high usually didn't last very long which is probably why so many people get hooked. In order to maintain a high, you had to keep snorting which was not something I really enjoyed.

I never had an addictive personality and I knew that I would never develop a habit to any drug, not even to marijuana. The times when I would get high were typically hanging out with friends or when I was listening to music. I was always into sports so I never worried about the effects of any drug on my body because I knew that I could sweat and burn off any effects.

One night I went by Ron's hotel room to hang out and when he opened the door, I was shocked to see sweet, innocent Valerie sitting on the bed with a wry look on her face. He welcomed me into the room as I gave Valerie a sly smile. She chuckled a bit and we all sat down and chatted for a little while, while getting high. It was really strange to see her doing drugs; I always thought she was so demure and conservative.

I started thinking back to around the time that she and I were alone and how wrong I was about her intentions. She was the *last* person at my job that I thought would be hanging out with "Whitey." I wasn't sure if they were sleeping together but I wouldn't have been surprised because most women would not have gone to a man's hotel room to get high and not have sex.

When I left, he followed me into the hallway and said, "Hey listen don't tell anybody about this, ok?" I assured him that his secret was safe and not to worry, which made me think that he was *definitely* sleeping with her.

Chapter 4

College is a Party

One of the most interesting characters I met while in college was my long time roommate Edwin. Ed was also a Political Science major, so we took a lot of the same classes and we both were known for being outspoken in some of our classes. It wasn't uncommon for Ed and I to have open discussions in class about politics and race, which always made the class a lot more interesting (at least for us).

Ed was also a member of a black fraternity called the Sigmas. He was a fairly short guy with a stocky build and he was known on campus as the hardest stepper on the yard. I remember going to step shows at a little amphitheater on the north side of campus and seeing Ed stomping and shouting like he had been possessed by a spirit that had taken over his body. He was sweating and pumping his legs and arms so hard that I thought he was going to pass out.

People were always excited to see Ed step, he really knew how to captivate the crowd and put on a great show. I was never really into the Greek life but I had been invited to pledge by all of the black frats, including the Kappas, Q's, Sigmas, the Alphas and even the Groove Phi Groove, which only had one member who was a really cool brother who liked to discuss politics.

It always seemed to me that the guys who pledged fraternities were the guys who didn't get a lot of attention in high school and they obviously needed to be part of something to make themselves feel important and prestigious.

I was the captain of my high school football team and I played multiple sports while in school and I never really had a problem getting girls so I didn't see the attraction of getting my ass beat to join a group of guys who I didn't really admire all that much. Although today, I have lots of friends who are Greek and very active in their communities – which I greatly admire.

Ed and I decided to be roommates and we quickly found a place off campus called Kingston Apartments. It was a large apartment complex off campus with really nice landscaping and amenities. The apartments were huge, fully furnished and typically about 2000 square feet with a large living space and bedrooms. We both had good jobs and worked a lot, so we decided to start throwing parties. Ed was a manager at a large grocery store and I would often swing by and get the major hookup from him on groceries and beer. Our frig was always stocked with choice meats and cold beer.

Ed seemed to really enjoy his job. He had a big personality and was always chatting with his customers and making them feel special. I remember one time while shopping there, he was feeling so good that he started giving away bottles of champagne to a few customers. I think he was just showing off, trying to show people that he was the black man in charge, but what he was *really* doing was giving away the store's merchandise.

Our first party happened almost by accident, we were hanging out at a Delta party off campus and it was just sort of lame so I suggested that everybody come back to our house and hang out because we had a cold keg of beer that needed to be tapped.

Once we arrived back at our house, almost everybody from the Delta party had shown up. We had a large keg sitting in a cold bucket of ice in our kitchen and everybody just started drinking and having themselves a good time. I was always really good at mixing up beats, so I put on one of my special mix tapes and then the party really started to rock. As the vibe in our new place started to take on the feeling of a nightclub, Ed and I just looked at each other, laughed and said, "Here we go!"

The crowd started to grow when word got out that we were having a party. Even our neighbors started coming through and hanging out -- there's something about a cold keg of beer that draws college students in like flies. One of our upstairs neighbors was a girl named Emily Procter, she's now a major Hollywood actress starring on *CSI Miami*. She and her female roommates were fun and always loved to party.

They would often flirt with us because after a while, we had become the party boys who knew how to put on a good time. Almost every other weekend we would have a big party in our apartment and as our reputation began to grow we started noticing random people entering our place as if it were a dance club. We always had plenty of free beer, liquor and lots of sexy ladies at our place, so I'm sure that had something to do with the growing crowds.

One of the guys who showed up one night was Keith Gatlin, former University of Maryland college basketball player who was a teammate of Len Bias when he overdosed on cocaine shortly after being drafted by the Boston Celtics in 1986. He showed up with Blue Edwards and they both towered above the rest of crowd and gave the party a sense of celebrity.

Keith and I became friends and would often play ball together and go to Denny's and destroy their all-you-can-eat buffet. We never talked about the Len Bias incident because I'm sure he was tired of talking about it. Whenever we would hang out, random people would approach him and give their condolences, even two years after Len's death.

He seemed to have a sadness about the situation sometimes but I think he just resolved in his mind that he would forever be linked to such a controversial story.

Other jocks would eventually come through such as Jeff Blake, former NFL quarterback and current record holder at ECU. A lot of athletes started showing up to our many parties and word began to spread like wildfire that Ed and Barry's was the place to be on the weekend.

The parties started getting so popular that I couldn't go out to other parties without people constantly asking me about our next party or if they could come by later and hang out. It wasn't uncommon for us to go out to a party and return back home with a small crowd of people.

The feeling of throwing a really great party was simply nirvana. I really enjoyed the way people would seem to let go of their inhibitions when they were partying with us. Our extra-large living room often became a huge dance floor where Ed would sometimes step at the delight of everyone there. I would also join in with a cool, funky kind of flow that was always a hit with the ladies.

Run DMC, MC Hammer, Tribe Called Quest, Eric B and Rakim could always be heard thumping through the loud speakers that I had hooked up, complete with strobe lights that really gave the setting a club-like feel.

We could have charged money at the door and made a nice profit but the fact that it was free made the vibe even better. I remember walking across campus one day and one of the most beautiful girls I had ever seen, stopped me and asked if she could come to one of our parties soon.

Her name was Dana and she was half Indian and half white. I knew she was on the swim team in school and I had seen her a few times on campus with a couple of basketball players. She was fairly tall with a slim but shapely athletic build, nice tan, short and sexy haircut and the most beautiful eyes I had ever seen. I couldn't believe that she was asking to come to my house because I knew that she had a boyfriend. I simply said, "Of course, you don't have to ask my permission. You should just drop by like everybody else does." We both laughed and she said that she would definitely stop by sometime. I don't recall Dana ever coming to one of our parties but little did I know that our introduction that day would not be our last encounter.

Darlene and I had been dating for almost a year at this point when she decided to move to an apartment far from campus. We were still seeing each other but not quite as much as before. She was in her last year of school and she was focused on preparing for graduation. I, on the other hand was focused on working, studying and partying.

Darlene came to a couple of our parties but she stopped coming after she saw how many people were coming to our house, especially the women. I had been faithful to Darlene for almost a year and only flirted with other women occasionally. Darlene wasn't crazy about seeing so many women hanging out at my house. I knew she trusted me but I'm sure any woman would feel "some kind of way" about her man entertaining dozens of women at his house.

Halloween is usually a really fun time on most college campuses and ECU was no exception. Ed and I had planned on having a big party at our house which had become a very popular destination by now. We wanted to have an outdoor party in the parking lot in front of our house so we rented a large beer cart with three spouts on each side for six different types of beer. We invited a few of our friends and expected a much bigger than normal crowd.

I remember getting off work late that night and pulling up to the entrance of my apartment complex and seeing a line of cars backed up all the way to the street. I couldn't believe what I was seeing; I even saw a black limousine pulling into the complex. I just shook my head in amazement.

When I finally got to my house it was complete insanity, there were people everywhere dressed up in outrageous Halloween costumes drinking and dancing wildly. Once I found Ed, we looked at each other in amazement that so many people had shown up. It seemed like there were at least a thousand people standing in front of our apartment. Shortly after I arrived, the beer cart had suddenly run out of beer and the natives started to get restless.

There was a group of white guys who were pissed that the beer was gone, so they started shaking the cart and trying to tip it over. I knew at that point that things could easily get out of control, so Ed and I rushed over to calm things down. Everyone eventually calmed down and blended back into the crowd as we gazed around at the spectacle that was taking place. It seemed like everyone who had ever come to one our parties was there along with a *lot* of other guests that our neighbors had apparently invited.

We all partied hard until the early hours when people started to thin out and make their way home. After everyone had left, we surveyed the parking lot which looked like a hurricane had come through. There were bottles, cans, cups and other trash strewn everywhere, thankfully the beer cart was still standing because we had to return it and retrieve our deposit soon.

Ed and I started cleaning up as much as we could -- in light of the condition we were in. We laughed and smiled the whole time about how ridiculous the party had gotten. The next day we slept in late but when we finally made it out of our house, our neighbors who were still hung over, congratulated us on throwing an epic party.

After every party there were always a couple of girls who didn't make it home or just wanted to stay over at our place. Till that point I had not hooked up with any of the girls who came by, but there was a sexy Filipino girl who was built like a brick house that stayed over one night. I remembered seeing her driving a sporty little red car around town. I can't recall her name but she stood out because there weren't many Asians in Greenville and she was definitely attractive. I hadn't been with any other girls since seeing Darlene and I kind of suspected that she might have started secretly seeing someone else. In my mind, I kind of wanted her to be seeing someone so I wouldn't feel guilty about cheating with another woman.

I think we had reached a point where we knew that our relationship was changing and we also had an understanding that we wouldn't stop seeing each other because of another person. I was still in love with her and I always thought we had a future together, but this time temptation took over.

I recall my new Asian friend casually hanging out the next morning in her panties with her other cute girlfriend, who my boy Ed was all over. They were lounging on the couch and laughing when I prompted Ed to take his girl to his room, which he hastily did. Once Ms. Asia and I were alone we started having more drinks, even though it was early in the morning. We were listening to music and dirty dancing with each other. She looked at me and seductively said, "You're a bad boy." I looked at her and replied, "I sure am baby and I wanna show you how bad."

So we proceeded to my room where we started kissing and groping each other. I kept caressing her nice round ass; I had never been with an Asian girl and definitely not one with a nice round derriere. The heat of the moment and the alcohol started to take over and we couldn't take our hands off each other. She had me so turned up that I knew there was no turning back. I hadn't been with another woman in quite a while and I was excited to explore her.

She reclined on my bed drawing me in closer; I easily complied and began to slide her panties off. She had on a sexy bra and panty set that looked like Victoria's Secret and I was anxious to discover *all* of her secrets.

Once I put on my condom, we embraced and began to slowly enjoy each other. She moaned and started playing with her hair. Staring down at her, I couldn't believe this beautiful girl was giving herself to me so freely. I didn't want to rush so I took my time and enjoyed every rhythmic stroke with her.

We were both buzzed and feeling the excitement and warmth of each other which made the sex almost tantric-like. I wasn't a "minute man," but all guys have had experiences where they just got too excited and couldn't really enjoy the moment.

Whenever I felt like I was about to explode, I closed my eyes and thought of something else to avoid climaxing, like a Statistics test that I had to take soon. It started working and then I reached a point where I just didn't want to stop. We continued our love making for at least an hour or more, taking breaks only after a couple of intense orgasms to refuel our drinks.

Once we were physically exhausted and drained from enjoying each other we sprawled out on my bed and simply listened to the music playing in the background. I asked her why she stayed, she told me that she had seen me around but I was always with my girlfriend. I've always suspected that women are attracted to men who are in relationships, it seems that there's something very instinctive about women that attracts them to seemingly stable men in relationships. Maybe its jealousy or maybe it's just a basal instinct that draws them towards a man that's already taken. I've heard so many stories of broken relationships caused by a close friend or simply "the other woman."

I once saw Chris Rock perform and he said that 90 percent of the women were dating ten percent of the guys. I must say I have to agree with him. An attractive woman is not going to settle for a guy that she's not extremely attracted to, which means that a certain type of male will almost always have more than his share of available women. This is simply a fact of life that's been going on since the beginning of time, just like the lions of the jungle -- the dominant male will always have his choice of lionesses to mate with.

I may not have been every woman's cup of tea but I started to get a lot of attention from various women who I had only seen sporadically on campus. I remember there was a pretty blonde girl who was friends with a beautiful black girl who was, Ms. Black ECU for homecoming. Yes, we had black and white homecoming queens, usually because the black vote wasn't divided and we typically all voted for the one black girl that was running for the title.

She approached me one day and told me that she had a friend who wanted to meet me. I said, "Oh really?" She went on to describe her friend and I couldn't believe it was the pretty blonde that I would sometimes see her with. She gave me her friend's number and suggested that I call her. Feeling very intrigued by this mysterious encounter, I imagined how people would act if they saw me out with this blonde beauty. Not forgetting that this was the South and that interracial dating wasn't very common, I knew I had to be discreet (not to mention that I also had a girlfriend at the time).

So I called up her friend who seemed delighted to hear from me. We chatted for a bit about school and at the end of our conversation, she surprisingly invited me to come by her house soon. I was flattered to receive the invite and quickly jotted down her address.

A couple of days later I went by her house, which was actually a trailer located not too far from campus. She opened the door when she saw my car pulling up and invited me inside. She was extremely beautiful; she had a baby doll face with big blue eyes, long lashes and big hair. I was bit mesmerized by her beauty, despite the layers of makeup she was wearing. She was a true southern belle in every sense.

It was a little strange to be in her place and I couldn't help but wonder why she was living in a trailer by herself. She gave me a tour of her narrow trailer and then we ended up in her bedroom. I thought to myself, "Wow this could be much easier than I imagined." I sat down on her bed as she slid next to me and started showing me a photo album filled with pictures of her in various beauty pageants. I also noticed that she had several trophies on her dresser as well.

She told me that she was recently a runner-up in the Miss North Carolina beauty pageant and that she was preparing for another competition. I remember her telling me that she had received a full academic scholarship to attend school at ECU, which definitely made an impression on me -- she obviously had brains *and* beauty.

As she continued to talk about herself, I started to wonder how far she might go and if the night would end with us all over each other. I was curious to know why she wanted me to come over to her house if she wasn't going to have sex. I told her that I thought she was beautiful and smart. She blushed and quickly gazed into my eyes for a moment. "Sooo, what's going on? Your friend said you were interested in meeting me." I said.

She laughed a bit and said, "Yea I told her that if she saw you, to give you my number." I replied, "Oh really?" She told me that she thought I was cute and that she wanted to get to know me. I was flattered that she had been keeping a secret crush on me. We chatted for a bit more and I started to realize that she was not game for a quick hookup, at least not that night.

I hung around for about another thirty minutes and then decided that it was time to leave. She escorted me to the door and gave me a hug, but no kiss. As I walked away, she batted her big eyelashes and in her sweet Southern accent said, "Thanks for coming by, I'll see ya' around." I bid her farewell and began to make my way home. On the way home, I was trying to figure out what had just happened, the whole experience seemed so surreal. I was full of myself when I started to contemplate how pretty she was and how much she seemed to like me.

I've never been the type of black guy that chases after white women, just because they're white. I've always seen the beauty of all women, but white women like her seemed to be off limits. I never saw a black man with a white woman that beautiful when I was growing up, so her flirtation was definitely intriguing. I never met up with her again but I would see her around campus occasionally and we would simply smile at each other and continue on our way.

Darlene and I were still seeing each other but not quite as much, her apartment was on the outskirts of town and I was busy working and trying to keep up with my schoolwork. Despite all of the distractions and shenanigans that were a part of my life, I still managed to keep my grades up. I started to excel in a few classes, particularly Social Science and International Politics classes that required lots of writing and analysis.

Some of my professors complimented me on my writing and encouraged me to pursue an advanced degree. My goal was to apply to law school once I completed my undergrad degree. Ironically I would later have an experience in my life that absolutely felt like I had attended law school and had become a capable litigator -- which I will discuss later in this memoir.

Chapter 5

Daddy's Gone

Things were going well, I was making money, had plenty of friends, a beautiful girlfriend and my classwork gradually became a bit more interesting -- till one day when I was at work and one of my coworkers shouted out that my mom was on the phone. I knew right away that this was odd because my mom didn't even have my work number. There've only been a couple of times in my life when I've heard my mom sounding so frantic and this was unfortunately one of those times. I answered the phone and I could immediately hear the distress in her voice. I said, "Hello," and I could immediately hear the distress in her voice as she shouted, "Your daddy's gone Barry!" She began to repeat herself, "Barry, your daddy's gone!"

My heart dropped and everything that I thought was real, suddenly became a mystery. My dad was young and fit; he was built like a farmer, which had been in our dad's family for generations. He was sturdy and easy going (most of the time). I never thought that he would be gone so soon. I remember telling her that I was on my way home and not to overly stress herself. I slowly hung up the phone feeling like I had just been hit with a boulder. All of my coworkers could tell that it was not good news; I simply told them that I had to go because I had just lost my dad.

They wished me well and offered me condolences and comfort. As I drove back to my apartment, I began to think about everything that this meant to my family, my mother, my sister and my two younger brothers. We were a close knit family growing up, we had our typical sibling struggles but we genuinely loved each other. Once I arrived home, I told my roommate and best friend Ed what happened. He just kept saying, "Barry are you serious?" We were both in disbelief.

I started packing my clothes in preparation for my trip; I also called Darlene to let her know the news as well. Once I was packed and dressed, Ed wished me well and I started walking to my car. Just before I reached my car, a single light post that had never lost power and had never been out, suddenly flickered off for a few seconds and then it suddenly came back on. I knew right away that it was him letting me know he was there, it couldn't have been anything else but a sign that he had crossed over.

I had never had a moment of such intense clarity in my life until that moment; it gave me strength and helped me to face what was going on at home. The flight home was an opportunity to think deeply about the future and prepare myself for my arrival. Once I arrived at the airport in Winston-Salem, I was greeted by Mr. Cain, our good family friend. Until that point, I had maintained my cool but when I saw him, I just busted out into tears. He offered me a hug and gave his condolences.

As we were riding back to my house, he gave me encouragement and offered his assistance. When we finally got to my house, I rushed up the stairs and into the house to see my Aunt Lea and a few other relatives gathered in the living room. I quickly shouted, "Where's my mom!?" They told me she was in her bedroom. I dashed to the back of the house towards her room and discovered her sitting on the edge of her bed surrounded by my siblings. Her eyes were swollen from crying and she looked a bit dazed. We all quickly embraced as she told us she loved us and encouraged us to pull together as a family to make it through our father's loss.

I had only heard a little bit of what had actually happened to my dad but she began to explain that he was crossing a bridge in his tractor-trailer when another truck suddenly swerved and hit him head-on in Virginia. I could only imagine how lethal that type of impact could have been with the force of two behemoth trucks barreling towards each other.

She began to rock back and forth, looking off into the distance as if she were searching for him. My parents had been married for quite a while and at one point during my early years had gotten divorced and then remarried. They had a great relationship, they both worked hard to make sure that we had everything we needed, including paying for me and my sister's tuition while we were simultaneously enrolled in college.

My parents had surprised me a few months earlier with a brand new Ford Escort GT that I absolutely loved. It was a sporty silver color with cool looking side molding and wide tires. It definitely fit my personality and also helped to increase my rapidly growing profile on campus. My mom said that my dad wanted me to have it because he was proud of me and wanted me to have the best.

My dad and I did not have the best relationship; we were just two completely different people. I was into sports and my dad was only a casual watcher of sports, he was more into landscaping and mechanical work. He always made sure that our yard was immaculate, planting beautiful flowers every season and fertilizing our lawn to give it that plush deep green color that made the flowers pop whenever you drove by.

I remember one day, he decided to get fancy and started cutting diagonal lines on his riding mower across our front yard and then reversing and cutting in the other direction to give it a blended baseball field type of design. I thought it was unique and people would sometimes honk their horns when they drove by to acknowledge how neat our yard was.

I would often cut the yard when he wasn't home but I also knew that he took pride in cutting the grass and probably looked forward to putting his touch on his prized landscape. My dad was a full time truck driver but we also used to mow lawns on the weekends for extra money. I remember loading up our stand-up mower into my trunk and looking forward to collecting sometimes $200 on the weekend just cutting grass.

It was hard work but it taught me discipline and an appreciation for earning an honest dollar at a very early age. Till this day, I cherish hard work and I know that almost anything is possible if you work your ass off for it.

Over the next few days, cards and flowers continued to show up at our house. I remember a bouquet of flowers that was sent to me by my coworkers. I will never forget how good that made me feel to know they were thinking of me. My family began making arrangements for my dad's funeral with the help of Russell funeral home. They were very supportive and professional about our loss and offered us great comfort.

I was talking to Darlene one day and she told me that she, Ed and her good friend Jennifer were going to come to the funeral. I was excited about seeing them and I knew that their presence would make things a bit livelier and easier to manage.

Once they arrived into town, our family friends, The Cains, who lived down the street had made accommodations for them to stay in their house, which had plenty of space since their only child Randy had already shipped off to college.

I remember hanging out in their basement and playing ping pong and darts with Darlene, Ed and Jennifer. I told them how much I really appreciated them coming so far to pay their respects to my family. Having Darlene there was great because she had been my girl for quite a while and we had become very close.

The day of the funeral came and I had decided that I would say a few words about my father despite all of the sadness that I had been feeling. We held the funeral at our family church and it was packed with family and friends showing their respect.

After a few relatives and family friends had said a few words, I was invited up by our family minister Rev. Robinson who had also been my high school counselor. Initially, I was a bit overwhelmed while choking back tears but then I began to become more confident in my remarks.

I spoke about how proud I was of my dad and how much we would miss him. I began to recite a very popular poem entitled *Footprints in the Sand*. I described my dad's journey over the thousands of miles of highway that he had traveled and how he must have felt out there on his own. I concluded with a message that was analogous to the poem, which states, "The times when you have only seen one set of footprints, is when I carried you."

I stated that although my dad had traveled thousands of miles across many highways, I knew that God had carried him across many of those miles. I thanked everyone in attendance on behalf of my family and encouraged them to pray for our welfare.

When I returned to my seat, I was warmly greeted by my grieving family. Everyone felt that my remarks were uplifting and congratulated me on having the wherewithal to deliver my words under such dire circumstances.

I remember our close family friend, Alma Cain approaching me afterwards and saying, "Son you can be whatever you want to be, don't ever forget that." That meant a lot to me because I had great respect for her, as she was like family to us.

Once we had fellowshipped in the dining hall of the church, we headed out to our family limousines en route to my dad's family church in Shelby, NC, which was about an hour and a half away. The trip down to Shelby was somber and mostly silent. I remember seeing cars pulling over along the long country roads to pay their respects. That's always something I appreciated about the South, the humanity that common people had displayed in our time of grief.

When we arrived at the church, it was already packed with family and well-wishers. Both of my parents came from large families, so there were a lot of relatives anxiously awaiting our arrival.

The ceremony began after they somberly wheeled my dad's casket, adorned with beautiful flowers to the podium. The choir began to sing and I could see well-dressed family members waving church fans and occasionally shouting, "Glory Halleluhah!" By this time, I think my mom had become more settled and seemed to be holding up very well.

When the service was over, the funeral directors began rolling his casket out to the cemetery located behind the church. It was a beautiful day and I could hear the birds chirping in the distance. The assembly slowly carried his casket towards the burial site followed by a procession of close family.

Once the casket was placed atop the burial site, our immediate family began to fill into the few rows of chairs under the tent. The preacher said a few more remarks and I remember glancing at my grandmother who was distraught and overcome with emotion and realizing that she had just lost her first child.

When the service was over, my grandmother shouted out, "I wanna go with Bobby! Take me lord! Oh take me lord!" It was heartbreaking for everyone, the tears and weeping began to get louder as the finality of his ceremony began to sink in. My grandfather who had not said very much at all during the entire funeral, yelled out, "Bobby preached his own funeral! Yes he did."

After the funeral we all hung out in the parking lot as numerous family members greeted us and told us many stories about their encounters with my dad. I love coming from a big family, it makes those unfortunate occasions like funerals seem more like a family reunion.

As the sun began to fade, we collected ourselves and retreated to the awaiting limos to take us back home. Initially, the mood on the ride back was silent and reflective as we contemplated our life without him, but then my always outspoken cousin Delphine decided it was time to shake off those blues and crank up the radio.

She's always been a fun and outgoing person to be around. "Well Bobby liked to party and have a good time, so I think we should too!" she said -- and with that, the ride instantly became much more enjoyable. We were blasting the radio with whatever pop song was on and waving our hands in the air (like we just didn't care) and laughing about good times.

The mood was much lighter once we arrived back home and everyone seemed to be in good spirits. I've always said that when I'm dead and gone, I hope there won't be any sad songs at my funeral. I hope there will be a DJ and bright balloons to celebrate my life the way I lived it.

After a few days, I returned to school and to work. I was more focused than ever on my future. There's something about losing a parent that makes you more cognizant of your own mortality. I started thinking about how long I would live and how my fate might find me one day.

Lots of my friends at school expressed their condolences to me for the loss of my dad. Getting back into school life was a bit challenging at first and I remember a good friend of mine asking me why I was back at school so soon. I didn't really think about it, I just knew that I had to go on. I knew that my father would want me to finish my education and become successful.

My father and I were often at odds with each other and we didn't really talk very much. He never had a man-to-man talk with me and we rarely sat and talked "mano e' mano." There were times when we almost came to blows during an argument which made me question my own sanity. I knew that I couldn't hit my dad because I knew that one of us probably would not have survived a fist fight.

So I took his punishment and internalized it, which made me hard and bitter towards people sometimes. I think he was taking his disappointments with his own life and his relationship with his father out on me. I wasn't like him and he knew that. My father was raised on a large farm owned by my grandfather who probably had over 1000 acres at one point. I remember riding on his industrial size John Deere tractor and thinking how awesome that gigantic green and yellow tractor looked out in the fields.

As kids we would sometimes spend our summers with our grandparents on their farm, where they had acres and acres of apples, green beans, okra, watermelons, corn, lettuce and lima beans. We also helped our grandfather pick his crop during harvest season along with a gaggle of first cousins who were close to our age.

It was hard work but it was also fun because he would let us drive his tractor and his trucks even though I was only 13 or 14 years old at the time. He also had a few horses that he would sometimes make us ride so that we would not be afraid of them. I always enjoyed galloping at full speed on our family horse named Carolina. She was a beautiful brown Palomino with a white streak running the length of her nose, and it always seemed like she would run like the wind whenever I was on board.

I remember watching my grandfather "break in" in his new horses. He would wrestle with the horses and slam them to the ground in an effort to break their spirit and domesticate them to farm life. He certainly wasn't "The Horse Whisperer," he was "The Horse Wrestler."

My grandfather was a domineering type of person who challenged his own kids to be successful but not always in the most positive of ways. He often overreached into their lives and placed restrictions on their activities which blunted some of their talents and abilities. My father was the first son and the oldest of his seven children, so he probably bore the brunt of his abuse the most -- this was the same thing that my dad was doing to me but I didn't realize it until much later in life.

I was just a kid who wanted to be great at something, whether it was sports, business, writing, music or film it didn't matter -- I just wanted to matter. I knew I had talent and if I had had a supportive father, I probably would have achieved a lot more in my life thus far.

My grandfather didn't want my dad to move away from the farm when he married my mom; according to the stories I've been told. He was suspicious of city folks and felt that the "big city" of Winston-Salem would corrupt his boy. Winston-Salem has a population of about 250,000, so I guess that seemed like a huge metropolis to my grandfather who had lived most of his life on a farm.

When I was growing up, I never saw my grandfather drink and never heard him cuss. Only in the past few years have I begun to hear about his drinking, his cussing and his other kids! Parents back then seemed to have a special talent for hiding their indiscretions from their children. My sister Carol recently informed me that she had met a guy at the family reunion who turned out to be an uncle.

Apparently my grandfather had a couple of kids outside of his marriage and very few of us actually knew about them until recently. It wasn't until my college years that I discovered that I also had a brother named Jessie who my dad had fathered when I was about ten years old.

I remember my mom being ticked off at him one day while we were having our evening dinner. She started hinting at the fact that we were not our dad's only kids and I could see my dad start to become irate. He tried to play it cool but it was clear that my mom had struck a nerve with him. He kept saying that she was just kidding; he gritted his teeth and told her to stop talking.

I never really thought about that episode much afterwards because I didn't know what to think. I had never seen pictures of this mysterious brother and had never heard his name mentioned. It wasn't until after my dad passed away, that we all had a chance to meet Jessie, who looked a lot like my dad.

I think the fact that my dad had a secret child prevented him from being able to honestly communicate with me. I recall a time once when I was home from school and I tried to bring up a conversation about girls and dating. He seemed really uncomfortable simply talking about dating. He murmured, "Yea you gotta be careful," and went back to reading his paper.

I always promised myself that if I was ever fortunate enough to have a son, I would bestow upon him everything that I know about the world and how it works, especially dating. One of the reasons I don't have kids now is because I never wanted to be in a situation where my kids would suffer due to my past transgressions. I think it's the responsibility of every generation to help their kids evolve and prepare them for the challenges of the world.

I've been lucky in some instances that I didn't have children with some of the women that I was dating, because I never wanted to repeat the mistakes that I've seen so many men make, which is becoming a reluctant father with a woman that they're not in love with or planning to marry.

Single parenthood seems to be the norm nowadays, but it may not always be the best situation to raise a child. I believe that kids need nurturing from both their mothers and their fathers in order to have a well-balanced childhood. In cases where there are two mothers raising a boy, which is also becoming more common; the boy typically will have a male role model to shape his identity as a man. If he does not have a positive male role model in his life then he may spend his whole life searching for a father figure or in some cases he may adopt his mother's mannerisms and choose a different orientation.

My dad was a great provider but he was not an ideal father for a kid like me, who needed someone to invest time into my talents and make sure that I was mentally and spiritually prepared to take on the world. He taught me strength through his discipline and hard work, but he never attempted to have a real relationship with me even though we lived in the same house.

My idea of becoming a man was a bit warped because I knew that I didn't want to be like my dad. I wanted to be *better* than him in the sense that I could one day raise a loving family that talked about everything and didn't use physical force as a means of punishment or intimidation.

I recently posted on my Facebook account that kids are lucky these days because they get timeouts whereas we used to get "belt outs." I'm certainly glad to see a paradigm shift in how kids are disciplined over the past twenty years.

Chapter 6

Back to School

Settling back into school became a lot easier when I returned to be greeted by close friends who encouraged me to stay strong. After a few weeks, things seemed to return to normal so Ed and I decided to have another party. At this point I was a fourth year junior and I could sense my college years coming to an end. We didn't have very many parties after my dad's death but I remember on one night, Darlene's friend Jennifer showed up to our house.

I was kind of surprised because I had never seen her at any of our parties. Jennifer was a brown skin girl with a nice shape who usually wore nerdy looking glasses. She never had a boyfriend that I recall and I remember a friend telling me to watch her because they thought she was after my girlfriend.

I didn't take their advice very serious and never saw her as a threat to my relationship with Darlene. I was never really attracted to Jennifer but this night seemed to be a different vibe. We were both drinking and dirty dancing together, which I'm sure raised a few eyebrows from some of our guests.

 As the night went on, we kept running into each other and it just seemed like we had an unusual connection. After the party began to wind down, she was still there hanging out and drinking. As she was about to leave, I offered to walk her to her apartment which was not far from my place.

We were both tipsy as we walked slowly towards her place. Once we arrived at her door, she invited me inside for a minute. I complimented her on her place and took a seat on her couch. She asked me if I wanted another drink, I said sure and accepted a glass of wine from her.

The next thing I know we were hugging on the couch but we weren't kissing. It felt strange because I had never thought about Jennifer in that way. She was attractive but not as pretty as Darlene, so there was no imminent attraction between us. As we continued to caress each other, things started to get heated and in my inebriated state of my mind, I probably got a little too aggressive and things changed quickly. She started becoming rambunctious and sternly said, "I can't believe you would try and do this to me!" At that moment, everything changed. I replied, "Do *what* to you? You invited me up here!"

She replied, "You know what you tried to do!" I just shook my head and told her that I was leaving. As I made my way down the stairs, I knew that Darlene would find out very soon. I couldn't believe that I had gone that far with Jennifer, even though she had willingly invited me to her place and seductively seduced me.

When I returned home, I immediately told Ed what happened. In disbelief he said, "But Barry she was here all night shaking and grinding her booty on you, like you were her man." I agreed with him but I knew that this situation was about to become explosive. I went to my room and sat on my bed to try and calm my mind and prepare myself for the storm that was about to come.

I started questioning my actions and what may have motivated me to try and hook up with Jennifer. Sometimes people will subconsciously try to sabotage a relationship as a means of getting out. Darlene and I were still seeing each other but a distance had grown between us. She was preparing to graduate and I was focused on moving forward after my dad's departure. I also couldn't help but sense that there was someone else in her life. Most people in a relationship can instinctively tell if things are not completely kosher with their lover.

I had not been completely faithful to her but I recall being at her apartment one day and discovering pictures in her kitchen drawer of her mother's recent wedding. I noticed that there was one guy that always seemed to show up in the pictures. I asked her about him and she quickly replied that he was just a family friend, but my spider senses told me that was not the complete truth. I never really said much else about it, but I had a feeling that they had been seeing each other on her return trips home.

The next morning I got a call from Darlene sounding upset and frantic. She said that Jennifer had called and told her that I tried to have sex with her last night. It was the moment that I had dreaded and I couldn't really explain my actions. I knew that it was a no-win situation, even if I tried to blame the whole episode on Jennifer. She began sobbing and saying, "How could you do this to me? My *best* friend?" We talked for a few more minutes then she angrily hung up on the phone on me.

Sensing that our relationship was over and that I may never talk to her again, I tried to pull myself together. The magnitude of everything seemed to come crashing down on me. I had just lost my father and now I was about to lose a woman that I loved. I began reviewing my actions and honestly asking myself if I had intentionally created a situation that would cause a rift between me and Darlene. Neither of us were completely sure about what was going to happen when she left to return home after graduation.

I was also still dealing with the emotions of losing my dad and I think that my behavior gradually became more risk oriented. People have different ways of dealing with grief, I think my grief manifested into an attitude of defiance. I was trying to find my way and I had a lot of bottled up emotions about my lack of a relationship with my dad. Life started to feel unfair and my reaction to those feelings was to shut people out of my life and deal with my troubles in a very matter-of-fact kind of way.

A week or so went by and I had not talked to Darlene at all. It felt strange to not speak with her sense we were so used to talking every day. One night Nick decided to drop by to have a couple of beers and play cards with me and Ed. While we were playing cards, Darlene's name came up and Nick immediately said, "Oh yea I saw her today at the grocery store with some other guy." I was floored but I didn't let on that I was incensed. I replied, "Oh really?" Nick said, "Yea she was with some dude, I don't think she saw me." I didn't react; I just kept playing cards and swigging on my beer.

At that moment, all of my suspicions had come true. I knew there was another guy and I knew *exactly* who he was. I didn't know his name but I knew he was the guy from the pictures. The night grew older and we all seemed a bit tired. Nick bailed out and Ed retired to his room but I was still buzzing about the news that Nick had just delivered.

I knew that Darlene was a proud person and that she didn't like the idea of people on campus knowing that I allegedly tried to sleep with her best friend. So I think her initial response was to call the other guy in her life and have him come down to Greenville, so she could show the world that she was not hurt.

I tried to get some sleep but my mind kept wondering about Darlene and this other guy -- so I popped up out of bed, it must have been around 4am and decided to drive over to her apartment. When I pulled into her parking lot, I immediately noticed her car and I also noticed another car parked next to hers with Maryland tags on it and I knew straight away that he was there.

I pounced up the stairs full of adrenaline and began repeatedly ringing her doorbell and pounding on her door while shouting, "Darlene come to the door!" I continued berating her door for at least an hour as the sun began to rise and her neighbors started to peak out their windows.

I was determined to see for myself what was going on. Finally, I decided to go back down the stairs and climb up on to her second floor balcony. Still juiced up on adrenaline, I deftly climbed up on to the balcony and began banging on her patio door. By this time, I knew that whoever this guy was, he knew that I was not going to stop until we had a confrontation, even if I had to break her door down.

Finally after banging on her patio door for another 30 minutes, she wistfully came to the door and slid it open for me to enter. I was steaming mad and I was anxious to see who was inside. She kept saying, "What are you doing!?" I replied, "I know somebody is here!" Then I darted towards her bedroom to see the guy from the pictures looking terrified at the sight of seeing me standing in the doorway.

He was still in the bed and started shrieking and fidgeting as if he wasn't sure whether to run or charge me. I wasn't sure if I was going to fight him, but I was hurt at the sight of seeing him in her bed. It all made sense at that moment, everything that I suspected was true. I turned towards Darlene who looked mortified; she had tears in her eyes and a look of astonishment. Suddenly I heard a police officer's voice shout, "Is everything ok!?" He was knocking at the front and asking to come in. Darlene hastily let him in. Upon entering he looked at me and said, "Is everything alright in here?" I replied, "Yea I just caught this guy with my girlfriend," pointing towards her other lover who was now standing in the hallway.

I think initially he wanted to arrest me for domestic disturbance but when I told him why I was adamantly trying to get into her house, the officer seemed to sympathize with me and decided not arrest me. He surveyed all of us and surmised that no one was hurt and decided to simply leave us alone.

After the officer left, I just looked at Darlene and shook my head. I was hurt and bewildered that she would invite this guy to her place so quickly after our fall out. I decided to leave abruptly. I had made my point and I could tell that they were both ashamed and embarrassed that I caught them.

I had hooked up with a couple of girls since I started seeing Darlene but that was during the times that she would return home for the summer. I never slept with Jennifer that awful night but Darlene's response to my indiscretions was probably what I needed to clarify what was really going on with her and this mysterious other guy.

Both of us had cheated but she seemed to have had an ongoing relationship for quite a while. I knew that she loved me but I guess she still had feelings for this guy and they would see each other when she was home, which was probably encouraged by her mother who I knew didn't like me.

After that episode, Darlene and I didn't speak for a couple of weeks. I thought about her often and decided to call her one day just to make sure she was okay. She seemed happy to hear from me. We chatted for a little while and near the end of our conversation, she invited me over for dinner later that night. I was more than happy to accept Darlene's invite because it had been a while since I had seen her.

When I got to her house, she opened the door with a sheepish look on her face. I was instantly greeted by the aroma of the meal she was preparing. She invited me in and told me that dinner would be ready shortly. I followed her into the kitchen as she started fiddling with her pots and pans, at which point I grabbed her by the arm and said, "I missed you." She seemed relieved to hear those words.

She finally cracked a smile and gave me a big hug. At that moment, I was just happy to have her back in my arms. Everything that had transpired before then didn't seem to matter. We both cracked up about how ridiculous the last few weeks had been. We sat down and enjoyed our meal together and it seemed as if we hadn't missed a beat. Darlene and I had been together for almost two years and it felt like there was nothing that could tear us apart.

Ironically, it seemed as if our fallout had made our relationship stronger. There were no more secrets between us and it made me think seriously about getting married. We both knew that her time at school was nearing an end and we had talked about me moving to D.C. after I graduated so we could be together.

Things slowly began to return to normal and our close friends seemed happy to see us together again. Her relationship with Jennifer had changed quite a bit, I know they stopped hanging out for a while but I think they eventually reconciled their differences.

I had started working a lot of hours and it felt like I was a full time employee taking part time classes. I was motivated to have money and to not be a typical broke college student -- and if that meant taking a bit longer to complete my degree, then so be it.

At one point Ed and I had started up a carpet cleaning business called Magic Carpet Cleaners with the carpet cleaner machines from his grocery store. I was so motivated to make the business a success; I went out and put up signs on telephone poles advertising our great service and low rates. I started getting a few calls and I was also getting work from some of the people at the airport to clean their planes and their homes.

I had read about a guy named Barry Minkow who had started a carpet cleaning business when he was 19 and had built a 100 million dollar company within just a couple of years. I figured if he could do it, then why not me! I didn't realize till years later that Minkow was actually running a Ponzi scheme and fraudulently inflating the value of his company stock.

I remember going on a sales call to a motel in town to do a demo of our cleaning service. I showed up on time and was excited about the possibility of landing a contract with the motel owner. The owner was a fairly young looking, Middle Eastern guy who promptly escorted me to a room that he wanted to have the carpet cleaned in.

I immediately noticed that the carpet was filthy and old. Feeling a bit skeptical about the task I was about to take on, I unloaded the heavy machinery from my trunk and hauled it into the motel room. After a few minutes of shampooing and scrubbing specific areas of the carpet, it started to look a lot better to my surprise.

I decided to go over some of the trouble spots on the carpet again, just to make sure that it looked a lot better than before. Once I finished cleaning the old worn out carpet, I loaded my machine back into my car and called the owner into the room to have a look.

Upon entering the room, he said. in his Middle Eastern accent, "Tis not bawd but I cannot tell if eetz clean because eetz still wet." I couldn't believe this guy was trying to tell me that the carpet I had just thoroughly cleaned was not actually clean. "I'm pretty sure this carpet is about as clean as it's going to get sir." I replied.

He looked the carpet over again once more and said, "Mmm..I dunno, eetz still wet so I cannot say for sure if I want you to clean the others." Realizing that this guy was full of it, I hastily packed up the rest of my gear and gave him my business card. I left the motel feeling a bit down about being suckered into cleaning this jerk's room for free but I was also encouraged by the fact that I had the guts to go after a large account and I knew that there were dozens of other motels in town.

I've always been a very ambitious person (sometimes too a fault) but as a young entrepreneur, I learned a very valuable lesson that day -- *Always do your best and let the chips fall where they may.*

I think my main motivation was to prove to my late father that I was capable of being an extremely successful person. I never received any type of real encouragement from him. There was a time when I informed my parents that I had received a football scholarship from Lenoir Rhyne College but the school would not cover the entire cost of my tuition.

While heatedly discussing the matter, my father point blank told me that he didn't think I was good enough to play college football, despite the fact that he had only attended one of my games during the two years I played in high school.

I was a bright student in high school and I enjoyed learning. I remember him asking me one day, "What makes you think you're so smart?" All of these things weighed heavily on my conscious and made me question my abilities and my future aspirations, so I decided to use his criticism as motivation to succeed by all means necessary.

During my final college years, I was also involved in selling Amway. I was introduced to the company through a friend of mine named Kevin. He and his girlfriend had met this older couple who lived in town and began to tell me about the earning potential of being a successful Amway rep.

Being only 21, I quickly picked up the sales pitch and managed to recruit a few fellow college students and locals while I was still in school. I was so motivated to become a top producer that I became almost obsessed with recruiting new members, and if you've ever had friends that sold multi-level marketing -- the constant selling and proselytizing can be a bit much.

I once attended a huge Amway rally in Greenville along with a few of my sponsors and new recruits. It was held in a large convention center and people seemed to be genuinely excited about what they were selling. Everyone was well dressed and all of the speakers constantly bragged about how much money they were making and what a good life they had since joining Amway.

During the time that I was selling Amway, they had a partnership with the now defunct MCI telephone company whereby, every Amway rep who signed up a new MCI customer would receive 10 percent of their bill as long as they were a customer. That was the most exciting aspect of the entire program for me, because I had managed to sign up a few new customers and I was aggressively selling the benefits of MCI during my off hours. When I wasn't studying or working or spending time with Darlene, I was knocking on doors and trying to sign up more customers.

In order to be successful selling door-to-door you had to be extremely confident. Whenever I got nervous about selling I would recall the inspiring speeches I had heard from my sponsors and from the convention. I eventually honed my sales pitch down to a succinct 10 minute door step presentation that usually got a good response regardless of whether or not they signed up.

During that time, I was also selling ethnic T-shirts to a lot of the black college kids on campus. This was during a time when black consciousness was a popular thing among a lot of my African-American friends. I found a black owned T-shirt printing company in D.C. and I would make trips up there to buy large quantities of T-shirts from them wholesale.

I would always have T-shirts with me when I was on campus and people would sometimes stop and ask me what type of shirts I had that day. Selling T-shirts was fun and it was also less strenuous than cleaning carpets, so I eventually let the cleaning business go and focused on expanding my T-shirt business.

Every year there would be a big event on campus at North Carolina A&T College called Aggie Fest. It was their homecoming celebration and I decided to print up a lot of T-shirts and load up my brother's new truck and set up a booth. Our T-shirts were selling like hotcakes and Darlene was there with me as we hustled for two days and eventually sold every shirt that we made, including the one on my back!

After a long two days of selling T-shirts, Darlene and I headed back to my parent's house and started counting up the money that we had made. We were both excited as we counted our loot, I think we had made about $2000 -- which was great considering we were both still college kids.

I remember initially being reluctant to give Darlene any of the money that we had made. I explained to her that I had to cover my expenses to which she replied, "Well you have to pay your employees as well." I chuckled and then gave her a fair amount of the money that we had made. That's one of the things that I really loved about Darlene, she always stood up for herself.

Things were going very well for me despite the numerous business ventures that I had going on. I was working a lot, studying, and spending my free time with Darlene so I didn't have a lot of time for parties. I decided that I wanted to move into a nicer place, so my mom who had received a large chunk of insurance money from my father's accident offered to pay my rent in a new apartment and also buy me some new furniture.

I found a really nice apartment complex a bit farther from campus and closer to my job. I decided to roommate with another friend of mine named Norwood, who was a big jovial guy who loved to eat and was once a pretty good athlete. The apartment complex we lived in was a mix of senior college students and local professionals.

One of our next door neighbors was a lady whose husband worked for the university and she was a nosey stay-at-home housewife. Sometimes she would randomly knock on our door just to see what was going on in our apartment. There weren't a lot of black college students that lived there, so she was probably trying to figure out if we were drug dealers.

Ironically, our neighbors on the other side were actually drug dealers. There was a young black dude who lived next door to us who drove a brand new white BMW. It was obvious he was a drug dealer because Greenville was such a small town and people like him stood out. One day I saw our nosey, conservative looking neighbor leaving their apartment. She seemed startled to see me. I just smirked and kept walking down the stairs. I don't think she was doing anything inappropriate, most likely just being curious about her new neighbors.

They always had an interesting mix of people visiting their house. I recall seeing two of the prettiest black girls on campus, Lawanda and Tasha going into their apartment. I was kind of shocked because they didn't seem like the type of girls that would hang out with drug dealers. They seemed a little surprised to see that I lived next door.

A few days later, I ran into Mr. Drug Dealer and I asked him how he knew those girls. He shook his head and said, "Man I never thought that I would hook up with a girl that fine." I knew then that Lawanda and Tasha weren't the good girls I had imagined. Money has a way of seducing people into vulnerable positions that you wouldn't expect, which is something I would soon learn first-hand.

Graduation day was soon approaching for Darlene and I decided that I wanted to buy her a ring. I wasn't quite ready to ask her to marry me, but I wanted to buy her a nice token of my appreciation. I picked out a nice ruby colored "friendship" ring and waited until graduation day to present it to her.

We were all gathered in the lounge area of the Sheraton hotel, having a post- graduation gathering for Darlene. Her mom and grandmother were there along with a few other relatives. Darlene's mom had given her a ring box with a key inside to a new car, which was symbolic of her mom intending to buy her a new car. Darlene wasn't too surprised as she had already told me that her mom was going to buy her a car.

After everyone had congratulated her, I also presented Darlene with a ring box and a card. Her mother seemed a bit perturbed that I was seemingly "stealing her thunder" on Darlene's graduation day.

I handed the ring box to Darlene who seemed quite surprised. Her family also seemed quite interested in my gift to her. Darlene hastily opened up the box and let out a gasp, "Oh baby thank you so much!" I had bought her a ruby red ring with a really unique design. She was always classy and hip, so it really fit her style. Her mother leaned in to take a really good look at the ring and said, "That's not an engagement ring is it?"

I simply smiled and said, "No it's not an engagement ring, I just wanted to buy her something nice." Her mother seemed quite relieved. Darlene gave me a big hug, "Babe its beautiful thank you!" She slipped the ring onto her finger and proudly showed her grandmother how nice it looked on her hand. Her grandmother who didn't really say much, nodded and said, "Yes that's very nice."

I don't recall how much I paid for the ring but it certainly wasn't cheap. I wanted her to have something to remember me by because I knew that we would be far apart. Darlene and I had been dating for almost three years at this point, so her graduation day was bitter sweet for both of us.

It took me a few weeks to adjust to life without Darlene on a daily basis. I was committed to being faithful to her for a couple of months but as most long distance relationships go, circumstances change. There were a couple of girls who I had flirted with while I was dating Darlene, who seemed to take a new interest in me now that I was seemingly available.

I was still in love with Darlene but neither of us knew how often we would be able to see each other. We had a very good sex life and the idea of going without sex just wasn't going to satisfy me; besides I wasn't 100 percent certain that she was going to be faithful to me. I guess I really wasn't too concerned if she was seeing someone else because I wouldn't have had any way of knowing.

It would be almost another year before I graduated and I couldn't expect her to be completely faithful to me. The times that she came to visit me after graduation were very awkward. I recall a time when Darlene was visiting, and as I was taking the trash out, a young white girl who lived nearby was making her way up the stairs to my house.

My heart started racing when I saw her because I knew that she was headed to my house. I can only think that it was divine intervention that I ran into her because I would not have been able to explain to Darlene why this girl was coming to my house. I quickly shooed her away and told her that my girlfriend was in town.

There was also another time when she visited that she found condoms in my trash can -- that's probably the dumbest thing that any guy can do, who's cheating on his girlfriend! I'm not sure if I forgot to throw them away or maybe subconsciously I wanted her to find them. During that time, I had a king size black lacquer waterbed and a king sized libido to match.

I was kind of surprised that she didn't make a huge fuss about it. She slyly presented me with the used condom wrapper and said, "Someone's been busy." I felt like such a fool but I was also kind of relieved that she knew the truth.

I'm sure she had her suspicions; I also knew that she still had friends on campus who probably gave her updates on my activities. There was also a time when a girl she knew from D.C. named Tammy (a.k.a. Big T) due to her height and her massive 44 double D chest, dropped by to pick up some T-shirts from me. Tammy was fly and very shapely. She stood about 6 feet tall and she wore a geometric cut like the girl from Klimaxx. She had a strong D.C. accent and she had also dated a guy named Todd who was part of our clique for a while.

She and her friend were selling some of my T-shirts and making a little extra money on the side. I knew that Darlene didn't really trust Tammy around me and probably suspected that we were sleeping together. I was attracted to Tammy but we had too many common friends, which made things awkward for us. Tammy and I *did* eventually hook up after a last minute road trip to Virginia Beach with a few other friends.

We had flirted with each other during the whole trip and when we returned to Greenville, she decided to spend the night at my place. I had always wondered what it would be like to have sex with her. She was tall with fair skin and those huge set of knockers that all the guys talked about. We were laying on my waterbed and groping each other as I was anxiously trying to undo her bra strap. The constant motion of the waterbed made it difficult to undo. Finally, I was able to set them free and I was not disappointed. She had perfect round breasts that spilled out of her bra as I watched her toss her bra aside.

Feeling like a kid with a brand new toy, I sunk my face deep into those double D's and began kneading and kissing on her perky nipples. She said, "Slow down baby." I was so aroused to be with her that I was probably a little *too* anxious. I slowed down my pace as I continued to suckle on her chest and caress her body.

I got up to find my condoms and glanced back at her long naked torso sprawled out on my bed. She was built like an Amazon woman with perfect curves and smooth skin. I found my condoms and maneuvered myself back on to the bed with her, which caused us both to sway with the motion of the bed.

Feeling even more aroused, I positioned myself on top of her and began to kiss her neck and make my way back to those lovely breasts while at the same time slowly sliding myself into her. We both let out a gasp as if we had both been waiting for this moment at last.

She was quite a handful, I had never been with woman of her physical stature before which made the sex a bit more exciting, but the constant motion of the bed made it difficult to get into a firm position to where we could both enjoy each other. We continued sloshing around on the bed and embracing each other but it wasn't magical like I had expected. She wasn't loud and energetic like I had expected and when I exploded, she was sort of nonresponsive as if my climax was no big deal to her.

Tammy was always laid-back but I never thought that she would be that way in bed. Sometimes when you've visualized having sex with someone for a while and then you finally get to be with that person and the sex is kind of disappointing, it just feels like a letdown.

After we were done, we both passed out pretty quickly -- tired from our travels. Waking up next to her the next morning was a bit odd because there was no chemistry between us and the sex that we had the night before seemed more like a conquest than an actual connection.

Tammy and I never had sex again and our long flirtation with each other had finally come to an end. I recently talked to her briefly and she told me that she was still living in Maryland and that she was a single mother with two kids.

I was in my last year of school and I was also still working my job at the airport which had become a bit more stressful due to a new manager named Nancy who had taken over. Nancy was bad news for everybody; she and her husband also managed a UPS store in town. She had her favorites and it seemed like she wanted to fire everybody else.

Confessions of a 40 (something) Year Old Bachelor 91

I knew I was leaving soon and I really didn't want to deal with the stress of this job while also trying to focus on graduating and preparing to leave Greenville. There was always something peculiar about Nancy, she was married but she became really close to this girl who worked with us named Lisa who was a lesbian.

Her other favorite was this really creepy guy named Brian, who was also married but he was extremely effeminate and always made sure his hair was starched with not one single hair out of place. He also wore a cheesy pencil thin moustache to complete his ridiculous persona.

Together it seemed like they had hatched a plan to get rid of everybody who wasn't gay. I loved my job because it fit my schedule and it paid pretty well but I had seriously thought about quitting; but there were also additional benefits like free hotel vouchers. Whenever a flight was canceled, we would give the passengers a voucher to stay at the Sheraton overnight for free.

Sometimes I would use the vouchers so that Darlene and I could enjoy a night together in a classy hotel room for free. They weren't actually free and I shouldn't have been using them but I was a risk taker and it didn't seem like a big deal until one day I decided to use a voucher to throw a party in one of their suites.

A couple of friends of mine had encouraged me to have a party since it had been a while since the days of our crazy house parties. So I decided to do it big and have a party in their penthouse suite. When I reserved the room I was well dressed, wearing a suit and looking like a hotel guest.

I was praying that no one at the hotel would recognize me. Once I received the keys, I called up a few of my friends and invited them over to the room. The room was really nice, it was the size of three of their rooms and was a great place to have a small party. I decided that we needed to have good music so I lugged my home stereo up a few flights of stairs to avoid detection from the hotel staff.

I asked people to park in the back and enter the hotel through the rear door to avoid alerting any of the hotel staff. A couple of hours later, there were about 20 people in the room and they were drinking and some were smoking which became the unraveling of our evening.

The party had just begun to get cranked up when I got a call from the front desk about complaints of marijuana smoke coming from the room. They asked me to come down stairs and talk with the manager and at that point I knew that the party was over.

I told them that I would be down right away and hung up the phone. As soon as I hung up I shouted, "Party is over folks, we gotta go!" I started gathering my stereo equipment as my guest reluctantly filed out of the room. A few people asked me what was going on but I didn't have time to explain to them that the room was not paid for and I was about to be in a lot of trouble.

I hastily gathered up as much stereo equipment as I could and made it to the end of the hallway without being seen by their staff. Once I was in the stairwell and making my way down, I couldn't believe that I had done something so risky. I had a good reputation at work and I knew that my job was now in jeopardy.

After finally making it to my car, I was able to load up some of my equipment but I still had other stuff up in the room that I needed to get. I quickly darted back into the hotel entrance only to be confronted by one of their employees.

"Are you Mr. Rose?" he said. I replied, "Yea that's me." "Our manager would like to speak with you." He then escorted me to the manager's office. Along the way I ran into a few of my friends who stopped and asked me if everything was okay. I told them that I just needed to go talk to the manager about something.

I was too embarrassed to tell them the truth and besides it really didn't matter. Once I arrived at the manager's office, he gave me a stern look as if he recognized me. "Don't I know you? Don't you work at the airport?" he said. I replied, "Yes I do." He invited me into his office to have a seat. He was a young looking guy and he seemed to gloat about the fact that he had caught me.

"So you know you're in trouble, right?" he said. Realizing that the game was up and instead of pleading with him for mercy, I calmly leaned back in my chair, looked him square in the eyes and said, "Yep you got me." I think he was a little surprised at my cavalier attitude, considering everything that was at stake. I told him that what I did was stupid and that if he wanted me to pay for the room, I would.

As he sat and listened to me I think he began to empathize with me, he was probably in his early 30's and most likely had his own share of college shenanigans. He asked me how long I had worked for the airport, I told him for about two years. He seemed impressed that I was working and going to school full-time. I began to feel less fearful about the consequences of my actions and at the end of our conversation; I said, "So are you going to tell my job about this?" He smiled at me and said, "Naw don't worry about it, just make sure that the *next* time I see you, you're a guest."

We both stood up and I let out a huge sigh of relief as I shook his hand. I left his office and headed back up to the suite to get the rest of my equipment. Once I had loaded up the rest of my stuff, I made my way back to my house and even though I had escaped the worst possible scenario -- I was still concerned that somehow my job would find out.

My attitude towards life during that time was very much laissez-faire. I think I was still dealing with the grief of losing my father and also subconsciously worried about losing my life at an early age. Weird thoughts go through your mind when you lose a parent, especially when they're gone too soon.

I had a "no fear" attitude that served me well during certain times but also became a detriment as well. The only way that I could deal with everything that was going on in my life, was to keep working hard and keep moving forward. I've always had a very strong work ethic which has helped me get through some pretty rough times.

When I returned back to work, a couple of my coworkers quietly pulled me to the side and told me that they had heard about the hotel incident. Luckily, they were really cool friends who were just looking out for me and promised not to tell the manager. No one at the time liked our new manager Nancy, so I wasn't worried about being ratted out.

As I began to approach my graduation day, Darlene and I would still talk on the phone frequently but we didn't see each other quite as often. She was preparing for grad school at Howard University and I was preparing for the next chapter in my life. I had also begun to count down the number of days I had left at work as well. I was happy that I was going to be leaving soon but I knew that I would miss all of the friends that I had made at work. Many of my coworkers were not college students and they depended on a regular income from their job at the airport, whereas I was a full-time employee who was about to graduate and go on to pursue my dreams.

I think there was some resentment from the new manager Nancy about me leaving on my own terms. She probably wanted to fire me just to show me that she had the power. She had methodically gotten rid of almost everyone that she didn't like. I only had a few weeks left before graduation day, when one day as I was sitting on a table in the security area after the flight had departed; Nancy approached me and said that she needed to talk to me.

I was a little nervous that she was going to tell me that she had heard about the hotel incident, but as she began talking I realized that she had no idea about the hotel voucher scheme and that she was explaining to me why she was going to fire me.

I had been very outspoken recently about some of the changes that were taking place at work. I had seen some good friends fired over very petty incidents and I guess my way of getting back at her was to complain.

While I was sitting on the table with my feet planted on the ground, Nancy surprisingly positioned herself in a sexual manner onto my knee as she was still explaining to me why she was going to fire me. I could feel the warmness of her crotch on my knee as she continued to talk to me. It was very bizarre because I was being sexually harassed and fired at the same time!

I can't recall specifically what her reasons were for firing me but it probably had something to do with being late a few times. I was baffled by her actions because I knew that she was married, I also knew that she was probably having an affair with Lisa the Lesbian but I had no idea that she was sexually attracted to me. I was a little bit hurt that I was fired but I knew that it was her sick way of pleasing her ego and sending me a salacious message at the same time.

When graduation day finally came around, a lot of my family members including my grandparents had made the long drive to Greenville to see me graduate. I just remember the whole ceremony being rather short and me being anxious to hit the road the next day in my already packed moving truck.

As I made my way back to my hometown, I reflected on all the good times and bad times that I had in college. It had taken me five years to complete my degree and I think my final grade point average was 2.8, which wasn't bad but I knew that I could've done better.

I really enjoyed college and I loved learning new things and it also prepared me for the world that I was about to encounter.

Chapter 7

The Real World

Life after college was very interesting and I was anxious to discover what life as a new grad and full-fledged adult was like. I didn't waste any time finding a new job, I had put together a really good resume and cover letter, emphasizing my eagerness, my work experience and my strong work ethic. I decided to drop by the administrative offices of USAir in the Greensboro airport with my resume in hand.

I made sure that I was impeccably dressed, wearing a conservative blue suit with a red tie and shiny black shoes. I looked like I was applying for a job on Wall Street instead of a position at the airport. Once I reached the door where their office was located, I paused for a second and said a little prayer -- then confidently opened the door and began to approach the receptionist who was seated just a few feet away from the door. "Hi I'm Barrington Rose, I just stopped by to see if you were hiring for any positions at the airport."

The receptionist seemed a little stunned at my presence and a bit bewildered at the site of an articulate and well-dressed black man asking about a job. She gave me a fake smile and said in her southern accent, "Oh I dunno know, we might be hirin' for some ramp agents but we're only lookin' for people that have experience." I replied, "Oh that's great, I have almost three years of experience working as a ramp and reservations agent."

She seemed surprised to hear that I had experience working at an airport. As we continued to chat, her demeanor became more positive towards me and I got the impression that she would recommend me for a job. I knew that she was kind of racist but I think my confidence and my attitude convinced her to give me a chance.

After quickly scanning my resume, she said that she would pass it on to the manager and that he would probably call me the next day. I thanked her for her time and left the office feeling elated about the prospect of working at a much bigger airport and being around the big jumbo jets that I loved to see soar through the air.

The next day I received a call from the manager who told me that he had reviewed my resume and wanted me to come back in to meet with him about a job as a ramp agent. I told him that I was excited about the opportunity and that I looked forward to seeing him the next day.

I returned the next day, still impeccably dressed (in the same suit) but different tie. The receptionist who had greeted me so coldly the day before seemed happy to see me. She told me to take a seat and that the manager would be out soon to see me.

As I sat in the waiting area, I glanced around to see if there were any other black people in the office. There were only a few people who worked in the office but they were all white and probably had gotten their job through a referral from someone who worked there.

I tried to pretend like I was interested in the magazine that I was reading, but I was a little nervous like most people are before an interview and I tried to calm my nerves by recalling all the times that I had knocked on people's doors and tried to sell them Amway -- and all the other crazy business ventures that I was a part of while in college.

Finally, the manager came out and greeted me. He was a middle aged guy with dark hair and a bit on the short side but he seemed sincere to meet me and then we proceeded to his office. Once we arrived at his office, I took a seat and he started asking me about my experience working at the Greenville airport.

I told him that I enjoyed it and that it was a great job for a college student but I was really interested in working at a bigger airport and possibly becoming a sales executive in the industry at some point. He seemed impressed with me and as he began to tell me about the position I could tell that he was not from the South -- he didn't have a southern accent which meant that he wasn't a redneck and *that* meant that my chances of getting the job were pretty good.

Unfortunately, early in my career I had interviewed with white guys from the South who clearly had no intention of hiring me and probably just wanted to document that they had interviewed black candidates. This guy seemed different, I didn't know where he was from but we both hit it off and he wound up offering me the job at the end of our conversation. I gladly accepted and he told me that they would be in touch once they had completed my reference checks.

I had provided them with a couple of names of my former coworkers but I did not give them Nancy's name as a reference for obvious reasons. A few days later, I received a call from the manager telling me that everything was okay and that I would be starting my new job soon.

The only bad part about the job was the hours; I had to be at work by 5am for an eight hour shift. I've never really been a morning person but I was so excited about this new job that I would get up early and make sure that I was on time. I was happy to have the job but there were some mornings when it was hard to stay alert.

One morning while driving the ramp cart loaded with baskets of U.S. mail along the runway and towards the plane, I had forgotten to tie down the baskets and as

I was driving -- I started to hear the sound of mail flying around in the air.

I slammed on the brakes and jumped off the cart to see a trail of mail scattered everywhere. Luckily, I was far enough away from the plane that no one else saw me, so I quickly began to gather as much mail as I could in the pitch dark of the cold morning before anyone noticed. Once I had gathered as much mail as I could find, some of it now wet from the morning dew -- I secured the baskets tightly and finally made my way towards the plane without any further mishaps.

Working around the big jumbo jets was definitely more exciting than the small propeller planes I was accustomed to in Greenville. I was always anxious to taxi in the big body jets with their loud and powerful engines. With my neon sticks and ear muffs, I would be responsible for safely directing the mammoth planes into the gate area.

However, one day while loading bags for a departing flight, I accidentally bumped the wing of the plane with my luggage cart. I guess I was having a bad day because I could have avoided hitting the wing but I was probably tired and a bit frustrated. The pilot and my coworkers saw the accident and immediately started checking out the wing.

I knew that this was no small incident as the pilot continued to survey the impacted area. He eventually called over my supervisor who also took a look. He asked me what happened and I explained to him that I was having a hard time maneuvering the cart around the wing. My supervisor was very disappointed and started instructing everyone to stop loading the bags.

The pilot hopped back on to the plane and apparently started telling the passengers that the flight had been canceled. Once I saw the passengers looking upset and getting off the plane, the impact of my recklessness began to sink in. Even though I had only nudged the wing with the cart, the pilots were required to cancel the flight until further inspection.

A few minutes later, I was called into the manager's office to explain what happened. When I arrived at the receptionist's desk, she greeted me with a scowl as if she couldn't believe that she had given this black guy a chance and now he had screwed it up. I was already embarrassed but her reaction made me boil inside but I calmly waited to see the manager and explain to him what happened. Once I got to the manager's office, I was afraid that he was going to fire me on the spot. Airlines lose a lot of money whenever a flight is canceled and I knew that this was no small matter.

He was surprisingly calm as I told him my story and when I was done, he said, "You know this could have been avoided, right?" I replied, "Yes sir." "I'm going to have to suspend you for one day and I also need you to write up a report of the incident." I was kind of relieved that he only suspended me for one day because I knew that it could have been much worse.

The next day I sat at home and thought about what a foolish mistake I had made. I also began writing up the report that he had requested. I tried to paint as concise of a picture as I could (without fully implicating myself of course) about what happened that day. I really had no excuse other than the fact that I was tired, but the truth was, I was having a very stubborn moment and simply slammed the cart into the wing out of frustration.

The next day when I returned to work, some of my coworkers seemed surprised to see me. They kidded me about being a "screw up" and for being suspended. I worked with a lot of free spirited characters and I remember hearing one of the funniest dirty jokes I've ever heard in my life that day.

There was a slightly older white guy who had worked there for a while and he was always cracking jokes and having fun. We were loading up the spacious cargo bin of a jumbo jet when he said, "Hey Rose, you wanna hear a funny joke?" I said, "Go ahead Chief." "Well there was this little girl who was picking roses out of her garden one day and she got a thorn, like a prick in her finger. So she ran inside and started yelling 'Mommy, mommy give me some cider to put my finger in!' Well her mom said, 'Where'n da world did you hear that you should put your finger in cider?' Well the little girl replied, 'From big sister, she always says whenever she gets a prick in her hand, she can't wait to put it inside her.'"

I howled with laughter! I had never heard such a funny joke and he seemed to have *lots* of them. Suddenly I got a call on my walkie-talkie asking me to report to the manager's office. I had turned in my incident report earlier that day, so I had no idea why I was being summoned to his office. When I arrived at his office, I was expecting bad news but when I saw him, he actually had a smile on his face. He told me to come into his office and have a seat, which I promptly did.

"How's everything?" he said.

"Oh everything is good." I replied.

"Good, ya know I was reading over your incident report and I gotta tell ya -- that's one of the best reports I've ever read."

"Really?"

"Yea you did a really good job of describing everything that happened and it was really easy to read."

"Well thank you, I appreciate that." I politely replied.

At this point, I couldn't believe that the wing debacle had now turned into a positive situation. The same manager that I thought was going to fire me just a couple of days earlier, was now gushing over my writing skills. I think the fact that I was black also had a lot to do with his adulation, he probably wanted to say, "Wow you're a good writer for a black guy."

Being a ramp agent didn't require good writing skills but the fact that I *could* write made a huge impression on him. So from that point on, he had a new found respect for me which made the whole incident seem more like an opportunity and less like a debacle. It's strange sometimes how a bad situation can turn into such a blessing.

I really enjoyed my job at the airport and I had big plans to matriculate into an executive position within the airlines in a few years. Occasionally, I would see black pilots and I would always be proud to see them because they were a rarity -- back then there weren't a lot of African-Americans who worked in operations and probably none that worked in executive sales.

There were rumors that USAir was about to have layoffs and sure enough, I received a call early one morning before I left for work, notifying me that I had been laid off. I was shell shocked. I didn't expect to be let go from a job that I had just started a few months earlier. It seemed kind of unfair at the time but it taught me a very valuable life lesson: *Never assume that your job is permanent.*

Chapter 8

Nouveau Rich

I didn't waste any time looking for a new job. On my way back from picking up my last check, I stopped by my dad's old company Roadway Trucking to fill out an application. A couple of days later, I received a phone call from a manager who asked me to come in for an interview. I had applied for a manager trainee position and I knew that it paid fairly well, so I was excited about meeting with them.

When I arrived for the interview, I was well dressed as usual and met with one of their hiring managers. He was a short, stocky guy who kind of reminded me of a cop. He never mentioned the fact that he knew my dad and I was reluctant to bring it up until we got to a point during the interview that I felt that he wasn't going to give me the job.

The hiring manager had asked me about my career plans and I responded that I wanted to work for the company and also possibly go to law school. His response

was, "Well I wouldn't come to an interview and tell my
potential employer that I wanted to go to law school."

I was *definitely* taken aback by his response and I
got the impression that he was trying to talk me out of
the job. I thought that by mentioning my aspiration to
study law it would impress him but he was a good ol'
boy who probably wouldn't have hired me if my dad had
not worked and died for his company. So I looked him
square in the eyes and said, "You know my dad used to
work here, right?"

He seemed a little surprised at my comeback. He
replied, "Yea I know he did, he was one of our best
drivers." I was glad to hear him say something positive
about my dad but I still got the sense that he really didn't
want to hire me and was only meeting with me out of
obligation.

I eventually got the job but I never forgot about the
way he treated me that day. My family was really proud
that I had gotten a job there and they were excited for
me and my career. Working at Roadway was definitely a
drastic change from working at the airport. The airport
was always exciting with the roar of the big planes and the
constant commotion of passengers shuttling through the
airport. Roadway was a drab outdoor truck dock that
accommodated about 100 trucks and was open 24 hours
per day.

As a manager trainee, I was responsible for checking each trailer to make sure that they were evenly balanced during the loading process. A truck that's unevenly loaded could potentially become a hazard in an adverse situation. I had a hand held computer that I used to enter the information about each trailer as I inspected them.

The extent of my job was to walk the entirety of the cold, hard concrete dock which was about the circumference of an outdoor track and then return to the tiny outdoor dock office and upload the data. It didn't require a lot of skill to do this job and it wasn't very challenging either, but somehow this was considered training for management. My shifts were long, typically from 5am to 5pm; four days a week and there were many cold nights when my feet would start to go numb from the walking and the weather.

It was a challenge sometimes to stay awake during those long hours and I always looked forward to quitting time. I had gotten into the habit of stopping at the convenience store and picking up a six pack for the 40 minute drive home with the intent of only drinking a couple of beers to ease away the pain of the day –- but I would occasionally drink the *whole* six pack by the time I reached home.

I had enjoyed drinking beer but I had never drank to get rid of my aches and pains before, and I knew that the stress of this new job was causing me to drink *way* more than I was accustomed to. I wasn't becoming an alcoholic but the beer seemed to be a good reward for a hard day's work and it helped take my mind off the troubles of the day. Usually by the time I arrived home, I would be very tired and very buzzed from the beer and more than ready to fall fast asleep.

Most of the guys I worked with were about my father's age and had been with the company for a long time. Most of the management trainees were young college grads like me, which created an interesting mix of clean-cut neophytes and hardcore older dockworkers working side-by-side. Occasionally some of the older black guys would stop me and tell me stories about when they used to work with my dad. They seemed proud that I was working there and I knew they had a lot of respect for my dad.

The dock was a male dominated environment but there was one girl who was a management trainee and she was very pretty. She was a fairly tall, light skin black girl with pretty green eyes. She had Caucasian features but you could tell that someone in her family was black. Her name was Lisa and she seemed to relish the fact that she was the only girl who worked on the dock.

She had sort of a tomboyish type of attitude but she was also classy. Everyone would flirt with Lisa, even the older married guys -- and there were constant rumors about who she was sleeping with. She seemed to enjoy the attention but she always remained professional which was probably difficult considering that she was the only girl working with a bunch of horny guys.

Lisa and I became friendly but we never flirted with each other while we were on the job because of the environment that we worked in. We would talk on the phone sometimes and she would tell me about all the crazy things that she had heard at work. She was a very cool girl but I could tell that she was very ambitious about climbing up the ladder at Roadway, which at this point was not something I was contemplating.

My mom had filed a wrongful death lawsuit against the trucking company that was responsible for my dad's accident and she had recently told me that a big settlement was coming soon. So I was biding my time to figure out whether or not I was going to quit this unfulfilling job once I received my settlement. The job paid very well but I wasn't happy and I knew that if I quit, my family would be disappointed.

One day while talking to Lisa on the phone, she invited me over to her house to hang out. We had been flirting with each other for a while and I was anxious to spend some time with her. She was very sexy and I was hoping that she and I would have some type of chemistry outside of work. When I arrived at her apartment she looked a lot different than she did at work. At work we all wore dark khakis, sweaters and work boots which didn't really accentuate her body or her sexuality.

She looked fresh and relaxed; her hair was still wet from her shower as she greeted me at the door. She seemed happy to see me and invited me into her place. Her apartment was bright and neat and it gave me a chance to see her in a different light, outside of the drab loading dock environment that we worked in.

We sat on her couch and watched TV for a little while but the sexual tension between us eventually took over. I could tell from the oversized sweaters that she wore to work that she had a nice size chest and I couldn't wait to get my hands on them. We started kissing and making out on her couch. I could tell that she had not been with a guy in a while; we both worked really long hours and the days off didn't seem like sufficient time for dating. We continued kissing and caressing each other until we were both worked up into a passionate frenzy. Suddenly, she pushed me away and tried to gather herself while pulling her hair back at the same time.

I had been rubbing between her legs and I could tell that she was starting to get hot. We took a break from our foreplay and relaxed on the couch for a little bit to cool ourselves down. I wasn't expecting her to have sex with me, the fact that we were making out was satisfying enough for me at the time.

She seemed just as curious about me as I was about her but being coworkers still made things a bit awkward. We didn't really have great chemistry and it seemed like our mutual attraction was one of convenience. She was the only attractive girl at my job and there didn't seem to be any other eligible guys that she could date at Roadway.

We hung out and watched TV a little while longer and made out a bit more before I left. She made me promise that I wouldn't tell anybody about our secret affair. We both knew that the guys at the job were big on gossip, which was quite surprising. I didn't learn a lot while working at Roadway but I did discover that grown men have a tendency to gossip like giddy schoolgirls in a courtyard.

Whenever I saw Lisa at work, we just pretended like we were platonic coworkers, however, sometimes when we were alone in the office we would sneak and mess around. The job really didn't get much better and I started to loathe the long hours which was usually from sun up to sun down. Sometimes the only thing I looked forward to was seeing her at work but that wasn't enough to keep me around.

My mom called me up one day and happily said, "The lawsuit is over, they're going to settle with us next week." I replied, "How much?" She said, "A million dollars." I was more than thrilled to hear those words, I knew that my mom had been under a lot of stress since my dad's death and she was working diligently with our attorneys to get a generous settlement.

Once my mom told me the good news, I started looking forward to my last day at Roadway. I wasn't sure how this was going to change my life but I was happy for my mom and for my siblings because we had been through a lot since my dad passed.

She told me that we had to drive up to Virginia soon to attend a settlement conference with a judge who would decide how the money would be divided among our family. A few days later, we were headed up near the Richmond, Virginia area which was apparently where the trucking company that was responsible for my dad's death was based. My mom had used some of the money from her insurance policy to buy a new white Cadillac a few months earlier and we all cruised up in her car along with my Aunt Viola, who was my mom's older sister.

Once we arrived at the courthouse we were greeted by a young and pretty attorney representing the law firm that my mom had retained to adjudicate our wrongful death lawsuit. She was blonde and wore a blue business suit and greeted all of us enthusiastically, which may have had something to do with the fact that we were about to receive a million dollar settlement.

She escorted us into a huge court room with tall ceilings and long rows of wooden pews. Once we were all seated she took a seat in the row in front of us, positioning herself directly in front of me which I thought was curious. She started asking me and my sister about school and other types of small talk. All of us were a bit anxious and I think she was naturally trying to allay our fears about the process.

A few minutes later, the judge walked into the cavernous courtroom and we were all directed to stand up as the court bailiff introduced the judge to the podium which seemed like it was a mile away from us.

As we were standing, my mom whispered out loud to my Aunt Viola, "You see that girl flirtin' with Barry?" I looked over at her and just chuckled because I was thinking the same thing. It was my first real taste of how money can seemingly make you more attractive. I had no doubt that she was flirting and the fact that my mom noticed was both funny and embarrassing.

The judge urged us to take a seat and immediately began to articulate the day's proceedings, including our lawsuit which he addressed right away. The attorneys for the trucking company were seated on the other side of the courtroom and they seemed anxious to get the matter resolved. The judge went through a few procedural things and then he finally got to the reason why we were all there --- the money.

He stated that as a result of a settlement with the trucking company we were to receive an amount of $1 million. He then began to discuss the disbursement of the money within our family. The judge indicated that my mom would receive a total of $600,000 and that myself and my three siblings would each receive $100,000. He asked our family attorney if we were okay with the arrangement and she indicated that we would accept the terms. The attorneys for the trucking company also indicated that they were in agreement with the final settlement.

We were all elated to finally bring this chapter of our journey to an end. However, out of the blue, a young looking attorney with Hispanic features and dark hair accompanied by a 13 year old boy who looked a *lot* like my dad burst into the courtroom and demanded that the proceedings be halted until his client was able to make a claim against my father's estate.

We were all in shock! The courtroom became a bit raucous once they arrived and everyone was curious to know who they were. It didn't take long for me to figure out what this disruption was about. The boy whose name was Jessie sat quietly as his young looking attorney explained to the judge that Jessie was my father's child out of wedlock and he had come to lay claim to his part of the settlement.

My family was flabbergasted. I didn't understand why someone would wait until the 11th hour to claim a part of their father's estate whom they had never met. His attorney explained that Jessie had planned to seek out his father but because of his untimely demise, he would no longer be able to meet him and therefore should be entitled to compensation.

After a few minutes of deliberation, the judge decided that he would indeed grant Jessie and his attorney a portion of the settlement. He decided that he would give Jessie $35,000, which meant that we would all receive a slightly lesser amount than we had just been informed.

Once the hearing was over, Jessie and his attorney awkwardly approached us as we were leaving the courtroom and introduced themselves. Despite the last-minute theatrics, my mom was very gracious. She smiled and introduced herself and the rest of our family to our newfound biological brother. He seemed relieved that we didn't appear to be upset. His attorney also seemed relieved and offered me a handshake which I refused because I felt that he had disrespected our family during our time of celebration and closure.

I simply shook my head at him and gave him an icy stare as we continued to exit the courtroom. I wasn't upset with Jessie because I knew that he was not to blame. Typically, whenever someone wishes to lay claim to an estate, they make their case known in advance of the hearing but his attorney for whatever reason decided to disrupt the proceedings at the very last minute. Supposedly, he had just found out about the hearing and drove up to the courthouse just in time, but I had my suspicions about his story –- it seemed a bit farfetched. Whatever the case may be, the lawsuit was over and we had a chance to meet our mysterious brother that we had only heard about sporadically.

On our ride home, my mom seemed happy that everything was over. She mentioned that she couldn't believe how much Jessie looked like our father to which we all agreed. After a long and very emotional day, I was looking forward to getting home and contemplating the next phase of my life.

The next few days at work were really tough because I knew that I would be receiving $90,000 in a few days and I had already made up my mind that I was going to leave my job at Roadway. I knew that my family would be a bit disappointed but ultimately I had to make a decision that was in my best interest.

About a week later, we were called to our attorney's office in downtown Winston-Salem to receive our settlement checks. I was anxious to receive my check and had already made plans to buy a car and get a new apartment. My sister and I were sharing a condo near Hanes Mall and I was looking forward to getting my own place.

Once I left the attorney's office, I went directly to the Wachovia bank branch across the street and deposited my hefty check. The banker was a sharp looking black lady who seemed quite surprised that someone so young was depositing $90,000. "I hope that you invest your money wisely, a lot of people never see this much money in their life." She said with a smile and a slight hint of admiration.

I assured her that I would be smart with my money and left the bank office feeling like a new man. I was only 22 years old and excited about what the world had to offer. Like any young man with a windfall of money, I decided to treat myself to a fancy new car. I had looked at a couple of cars before I had even received my check and I was excited about getting a new ride.

One day I decided to drive up to the Mercedes dealership near my house and casually walked into the huge showroom to see several sales guys sitting at their desk. The first guy was black and he quickly ducked his head to pretend as if he didn't see me. Then another sales guy who was white strolled right past me in the middle of the showroom and didn't even speak. Finally, a tall white haired and sharply dressed white guy stood up and approached me with a friendly smile. He shook my hand and welcomed me to the dealership.

"So what brings you in?" he said.

"I saw a white Mercedes outside that I want to test drive." I replied.

"Oh yea, the E series…she's a beautiful car. Let me go get the keys and we'll take her out for a drive." he said with a smile.

The salesman hustled away to find the keys as I stood standing in the middle of the showroom. I glanced around at a few of the cars and noticed the other two salesmen that had ignored me, curiously checking me out. They probably thought I was some young kid with big dreams and no money who was there to simply waste their time.

The friendly sales guy returned with the keys and escorted me outside towards the car. As we got closer to the car, I had already made up my mind that I was going to buy it. It was a gleaming white E series sedan with grey trim and it had grey leather seats that felt like butter. The sales guy jumped behind the wheel and pulled the car out of the parking space so that I could take the wheel.

Once I got behind the wheel, I was even more impressed –- it had a wood grain steering wheel and wood grain accents in the dashboard and gear box. I eased the car towards the exit as my heart began to race at the thought of buying this car and driving it every day. We merged onto a two lane road away from the dealership as I gradually began to give it more gas and it responded with a burst of horsepower and precision.

"Yea I like this." I said with a big smile.

"Oh yea she's got a lot of power, don't be afraid to open her up."

I couldn't believe how casual he was about the whole test drive. He seemed like he wasn't concerned at all about me driving fast or getting caught by the police. So I punched it! The car felt like it was gliding along the long country road and hugging every curve. As I continued driving at a high rate of speed, a car coming from the other direction suddenly swerved onto the yellow divider and then quickly darted back into their lane. I pressed the brakes for a potential collision and I was amazed at how the car responded.

"Wow I can't believe that fool almost hit us!" I said. The salesman who seemed unfazed simply said, "Well if he had hit us, he'd uh been in a lot worse shape." At that moment I was sold, I knew this was the car for me. The salesman's confidence and my high speed test drive had clenched the deal.

We returned to the dealership and went to his office to discuss the price. I think they had listed the car for $28,000, it was a year old and had low mileage on it; but I knew I wasn't going to pay their sticker price.

"So you like the car huh?

"Yea it's nice, but I don't know about that price."

"Well, we might be able to work something out but it depends on how you were planning to pay."

"Oh I'm paying cash." I said with a smile.

The salesman seemed impressed.

"Well cash is always good." he said with a chuckle.

"Are you ready to take the car home today?"

"Yea, if the price is right."

"Alright let me check with my manager on what we can do with the price…hang tight I'll be right back."

"Okay no problem."

"You want anything like a soda or a coffee or something?"

"Naw I'm good, appreciate it."

"Okay sit tight I'll be right back."

While the salesman was away I started thinking about all the fun I would have in my new ride. I knew that this car would instantly upgrade my profile and my status; it was certainly a big step up from the Ford Escort GT that I was driving at the time.

The friendly sales guy returned to his office a few minutes later with a smile on his face.

"Well I've got some good news for you Mr. Rose."

"Okay."

"We're willing to drop the price on the car to $27,000...how's that sound to ya'?"

I was kind of disappointed at their offer and it suddenly took a bit of the excitement from my expectations. Car salesmen are very good at using their customer's enthusiasm to their advantage. Once they see that a customer is sold -- hook, line and sinker -- they immediately begin to try and stick them with an overpriced car.

I had always been a tough negotiator and even though I was excited about getting a new car, I wasn't prepared to be stiffed either.

"$27,000? That's only a thousand off the sticker price."

"Yea but we've got a lot invested in this car and it's really the best price that we can offer."

"Well I'm not going to pay that price for the car...I tell you what, I'll bring you a check for $25,000 and then we'll have a deal?"

He leaned back in his chair to ponder my counteroffer.

"$25,000? That's not going to be enough for that car Mr. Rose."

Feeling like we were at an impasse, I suddenly decided to stand up and walk out.

"Well that's all I'm willing to pay for the car. You have my number if you decide to meet my price." I said as I exited his office.

The sales guy was shocked that I had simply walked out. He seemed dismayed that I had turned the tables on him. I had effectively used his enthusiasm against him. I knew that he was anxious to sell the car and that my offer was too good to turn down. So I abruptly left the dealership and jumped back into my Ford Escort GT and headed back home. My GT was still fairly new and I didn't really *need* a new car but the idea of having a luxury car was too enticing.

I drove back to my house and within a few minutes of walking in the door my phone began to ring. I quickly answered the phone; it was the sales guy sounding very excited.

"Mr. Rose I think we have a deal!"

"Oh yea?"

"Yea I talked to my manager and he agreed to sell you the car for $25,000."

"Alright sounds good, I'll come by tomorrow with a check and pick up the car."

"Sounds good Mr. Rose, we'll have her cleaned and ready to go for ya."

I hung up the phone and shouted, "Yea!!!" I was excited about getting the car but I was also proud of myself for being a tough negotiator. The sales guy probably assumed that I was young and naïve and would probably cave in to his sales pressure like every other customer had probably done.

I learned another valuable lesson that day: *Always be willing to walk away from the deal.* It has helped me throughout my life and my sales career.

The next day I arrived at the dealership around noon to pick up my new car. Once I walked into the dealership, the first person that greeted me was the same black guy who had ignored me the day before. He introduced himself and starting asking me questions in an attempt to figure out if he knew me or my family somehow.

I politely chatted with him for a few minutes until I noticed my salesperson approaching with a big smile on his face. He greeted me and escorted me towards his office. As I walked away, the black sales guy said, "Hey it was nice meeting you." I nodded my head in reply, sensing that this guy was kicking himself for passing up an easy sale. It was my first major encounter with how poorly black customers are treated sometimes, even by our own people.

The one thing that impressed me the most about my salesperson was that he was completely nonjudgmental. He never gave me the impression that he was concerned about me wasting his time, which I really appreciated. He was a really cool guy who decided to take a chance on me and treated me with respect throughout the process.

He asked me if I brought the check. I quickly whipped out my checkbook and began to nervously write out the sale amount. The whole experience seemed surreal -- I couldn't believe that I was actually paying cash for a new car. I didn't have a lot of experience writing checks for $25,000, so I took my time and made sure everything was correct. Once I was done, I proudly handed the check to the sales guy who quickly inspected it and said, "Alright looks good...we just need to verify the funds with your bank, which shouldn't take very long."

The sales guy left the office for a few minutes and then returned and said, "Ok Mr. Rose everything looks good, congratulations on your new car." I smiled as he handed me my keys. Once I had completed all of the paperwork, I headed outside to jump into my new car. On the way out, the manager stopped me and introduced himself and congratulated me on buying the car.

I was all smiles as I left the dealership. I decided to leave my GT at the dealer for a few days until I could make arrangements to pick it up. I quickly hit the road and took my new Benz for a ride up the highway. It didn't take long to notice a few admiring glances along the way. Winston-Salem was not typically a place where you see young black guys driving Mercedes, so I'm sure I was an interesting sight to quite a few people.

When I arrived home, I was anxious to show off my new ride to my sister. She was very impressed as she was also in the market to buy a new car as well. While we were outside checking out my car, one of our neighbors, a very cute white girl who had a curvaceous body like a gymnast -- pulled up. I had admired her since we moved in but I never really made a move on her. We would sometimes hang out and watch TV together but we never messed around, probably because we were next door neighbors.

"Hey nice car." she said exiting her car. "Thanks!" I replied. "Oh this is *your* car?" "Yea I just got it." She seemed baffled by the sight of me in a fairly new Mercedes. I could tell that she was a bit envious and also a bit more attracted to me because of my new wheels.

Now that I had the car I wanted, my next goal was to find myself a sweet bachelor pad. I had seen a new gated apartment complex not far from my house that I was interested in checking out. So one day I dropped by to take a tour and hopefully find a place that I liked. The leasing agent took me to a brand new apartment that had just been completed. It was a huge one bedroom apartment with a sun room and a washer and dryer.

The brand new smell and the spacious living room were enough to convince me that this was the right place for me. The leasing agent escorted me back to the office so that I could complete the rental agreement. Once I had completed the paperwork, I whipped out my checkbook once again and wrote her a check for my first six months of rent. She stared at the check for a few seconds in disbelief. She had seen me arrive in a Mercedes and there was no doubt that she was wondering how I had so much money.

I had put on my application that I still worked for Roadway, which I did at the time but I could tell that she was curious about my seemingly wealthy status. When we were done, she handed me my signed lease and scheduled a time for me to move in.

I was definitely looking forward to having my own place, especially in a ritzy neighborhood because I knew that I would meet other affluent people and possibly some well-to-do single ladies.

After I had purchased my new wheels and signed off on the lease for my new apartment there was only one thing left to do to complete my transformation –- quit my job at Roadway. I had given this a lot of thought and despite the fact that I didn't love my job; I was still making very good money for a recent college graduate.

I considered toughing it out in hopes that the job would become more meaningful but I knew that I had no interest in working in the trucking industry. So I decided that I simply had to go to work and inform them that I was leaving. I had a lot of mixed emotions on my drive up to the dock but as I got closer, I started feeling more confident about my decision. The idea of not having to work on a cold, concrete dock at 5am was certainly something that I looked forward to.

When I arrived, I found the manager's office and thanked him for giving me the opportunity and promptly informed him that I was leaving. He seemed a bit surprised that someone my age would be quitting such a coveted job. I shook his hand and made my way towards the dock where I said goodbye to a few of my coworkers.

One of the first people that I ran into was Lisa, she couldn't believe that I was quitting. She said, "Boy you must've gotten a lot of money." "I'm not rich but I'm okay." I replied. She kind of shrugged her shoulders still in disbelief that I was leaving.

Apparently a few of my dad's friends at work had heard about the settlement and wished me well before I left. Once I had said my goodbyes, I jumped in my Mercedes and hit the highway -- feeling elated about the future.

Having money in the bank and being able to buy just about everything that I wanted felt exhilarating and like most people who receive a windfall of money I was ready to spend. One of the first things I bought was a telephone for my car, which was a fairly new technology and not something that most people would have installed in their car.

I went to Circuit City and had them install a sleek-looking pushbutton phone into my armrest. I didn't really need a phone in my car but it gave my ride a James Bond type of effect and it was always amusing to see people staring at me while at a stoplight and talking on my phone.

I remember taking a road trip to Raleigh to hang out with some old friends and I decided to call up an attractive girl named Dawn who I had gone to school with but never dated. She was surprised to hear from me and quickly asked me where I was calling from. I proudly replied that I was calling her from my car, which she could not believe that it was possible to call someone from your car.

I knew that she would be impressed but we didn't talk very long because she was concerned about the dangers of me driving and talking on the phone at the same time -- which of course it was.

One day I decided to drop into a furniture store near the mall that I had briefly worked in prior to taking the job at Roadway and paid cash for some new furniture for my new bachelor pad. I bought a Carolina blue and white striped sofa set and a big screen TV for my lounging area. One of my good friends called my place the "Dean Dome" because of the blue and white theme, but that wasn't intentional -- although I was a huge Tarheel fan, the color scheme was exactly what my placed needed, a relaxed beach type vibe (even though I was miles away from any beach.)

I still had my ridiculous black lacquer king-size waterbed in my bedroom, so I purchased a comfortable black leather chair for my seating area. It didn't take long for my place to come together and it would soon become a true bachelor pad as I began to meet attractive new ladies.

I had never really had problems getting dates in the past but having a nice car and a luxury apartment certainly helped increase my profile as a young mover and shaker. I lived in a building filled with young, attractive professional females and of course, I was the only guy. I had plenty of opportunities to sleep with some of them but I was leery about messing around with a neighbor because of the close proximity, although I would sometimes hang out in their apartments where the temptation was sometimes hard to bare.

However, there was an older couple who lived next door to me and they had produced two of the most naturally beautiful daughters I had ever seen. They were in their early thirties and they both looked like the type of girls you would see on the cover of a *Dark and Lovely* box. One of them lived in the complex, one building over from her parents and her name was Vanessa. Vanessa was vivacious, she had a flirtatious and straightforward attitude which I loved, but she also had a live-in boyfriend who was white.

Vanessa and her sister would often visit their parents and afterwards invite themselves over to my place. I certainly didn't mind seeing these two beautiful and statuesque black queens dropping by unexpectedly. Whenever they were in my apartment, there was always a bit of sexual tension between us. They were always playful and often teased me with flirty winks and long passionate hugs before they departed, even though they were both in relationships.

There were times when I felt that it was definitely possible to have a threesome with them but the fact that they were both in relationships probably prevented that from happening. However, one day Vanessa knocked on my door and told me that she had a really cute friend named Melissa that she wanted me to meet. She began to describe her friend as someone who was attractive, well-educated and also had a small son. I had never dated a woman with a child at that point but I knew that her friend had to be a special lady based on everything she shared with me, including her pending divorce from a former NBA basketball player.

Vanessa gave me her friend's phone number and suggested that I call her soon to set up a date. I reached out to Melissa a few days later and we had a great conversation so we decided to meet up at a Chinese restaurant down the street from my apartment. I was excited about meeting her and when she walked through the door, I was definitely impressed.

She was about 5'5 with amazing curves, light skin tone and piercing green eyes. I was immediately smitten with her looks and her demeanor. We greeted each other cheerfully and sat down to order some delicious Chinese food. We chatted a bit about our backgrounds over egg rolls and Wonton soup. I was impressed to learn that she had just completed her Master's degree and was in the process of working towards her doctorate. I've always been attracted to really intelligent women; I think my dream woman would be someone with the intellect of Michelle Obama, a body like Naomi Campbell and the sex appeal of a Scarlett Johansson.

Melissa had a very sweet demeanor and we seemed to hit it off right away. After we finished our meal, I was tempted to invite her back to my place for drinks but she seemed like a classy, mature lady and I didn't want to risk making a bad impression. So we agreed to go on a second date which I was very much looking forward to. Melissa was about five years older than me and I had never really dated an older woman until I met her. Not only was Melissa a few years older than me but I knew that she was accustomed to having money. She had come from an affluent family and she was currently separated from a former NBA player who was now a coach.

I knew that there wasn't much I could do financially to impress her but it was refreshing to be with a woman who didn't seem to care about how much money I had. Getting someone to babysit her young son was sometimes challenging, so our next date was actually at her house. She invited me over to her house to watch a movie after her son had fallen asleep. She had a very nice brick home near a lake on the other side of town and she was also in the process of building an even bigger and brand new house next door. We lounged on her couch and drank a couple of glasses of red wine while pretending to be interested in the movie we were watching. Once the wine started to kick in, we snuggled closer together and began to kiss and caress each other.

Her body felt so amazing. She was voluptuous and curvy with soft hair and mesmerizing green eyes. We both started to get excited from our foreplay and continued our exploration of each other on her couch. The moment became so intense that we quickly decided to retreat to her bedroom. We both staggered up from the couch, still a bit tipsy from the wine. She grabbed my hand and led me towards her room and I willingly complied. As I followed behind her, I just shook my head at the sight of her nice round hips swaying as she led me towards her spacious bedroom.

Once we were on the bed, she quickly mounted me as I cupped her plump round ass with both hands and felt the fullness of her hips and her curves. We started kissing passionately while she hovered over me with her firm breasts dangling in my face, inviting me to suckle on her bosom. I started sliding down her sweatpants and caressing her big soft bottom while playfully stroking her. I started thinking about how my status as a young, seemingly wealthy guy had played a part in me getting to this moment with this beautiful lady. I felt like a rock star who was hooking up with his first groupie, but she was clearly no groupie and she was probably attracted to the fact that I wasn't concerned about her wealth.

We continued our intense foreplay until we were both nude and lying on her bed. I could feel how wet she had become and I had also become fully aroused and anxious to explore her. I quickly slipped on my condom that was in my jeans and slowly made my way on top of her as she began to moan. I could tell that she had probably not had sex in a while since she was going through a divorce and raising a child at the same time. She seemed anxious to pull me inside as we embraced and felt the sensation of our bodies coming together. I felt a rush come over my body as I began to gently stroke her. She had a pretty conservative demeanor but when we started to make love, she started to let loose.

Everything started to make sense. She had probably asked her friend Vanessa to introduce her to a young eligible guy with the intentions of fulfilling her sexual needs – and I just happened to be that guy. I stared down at her while continuing to gently stroke her, trying not to climax too fast but then I found my groove and started to thrust myself into her -- feeling her body gyrate and convulse in response. I was so attracted to her, which made the love making even more intense. Looking into her eyes and feeling her warmth was simply electric. The times when I've had the best sex is when I'm completely enamored with the woman I'm with. It could be her attitude or her body or even her personality that sets me off into a zone where I want to just ravage her body all night long – and that's exactly what I did!

We enjoyed each other for quite a while, resting in between our intense and sweaty sex marathon. I was completely satisfied and as I lay on her bed, I started thinking about what it would be like to have her as my girl. She was much more mature and educated than I was and she had already started a family, so I wasn't sure if we were a perfect match but we certainly had sexual chemistry, which was a good start. Also her pending divorce weighed a lot on my outlook. Getting divorced from someone doesn't mean that they're out of your life, especially if there are kids involved. So I wasn't sure if I was ready to take on that kind of responsibility at the age of 22 and also deal with any potential drama from her son's famous father.

Melissa had mentioned that she suspected that her phones were tapped at some point and she thought it was her ex spying on her during their separation. That revelation certainly caused me some concern as well and I didn't want to get involved in the middle of nasty divorce with someone I had just met. After we finished our love making, I headed out. I knew that I couldn't spend the night with her despite the fact it was early morning by now because she had a son who didn't need to see a stranger roaming around in their house early in the morning. I kissed her goodbye and walked towards my car feeling exhausted and elated about my night with her.

Melissa and I went out on a few more dates afterwards and we began to develop a close friendship but there was always a distance between us because of her personal situation and my reluctance to get too heavily involved. I'm sure that she and Vanessa had talked about our dates and probably about our sexual encounters because one day I received a call from Vanessa out of the blue, sounding very seductive on the phone. She told me that she heard "good things" about me from Melissa and she wanted to come over and find out for herself. I was a little bit surprised but not completely caught off guard because she had been flirting with me since I moved in despite her live-in boyfriend arrangement.

"Are you going to give me the Magic Johnson treatment?" she said.

"The what!?" I replied.

"You know, the Magic Johnson treatment. A condom."

I chuckled a bit and said, "Sure." Magic had recently announced that he had HIV and I'm sure she was also concerned about getting pregnant by a neighbor that she was planning on having an affair with.

Vanessa was very attractive, she reminded me of a young Robin Givens. She was a natural brown skin beauty with a nice booty, who stood about 5'8 and she always seemed to have on tight fitting track pants whenever I saw her. I didn't hesitate to invite her over even though I was a bit leery about being caught by her boyfriend, whom I had met a couple of times. She assured me that he was out of town and that we had nothing to worry about.

A few minutes later she arrived at my door with a look on her face as if she was ready to get down to business. She had on a pair of those tight fitting track pants and I was looking forward to "crossing the finish line" with her. We started kissing and groping each other almost as soon as she walked in the door. I led her to my bedroom where she quickly took a seat on the edge of my bed and started pulling down my pants while I was still standing. She immediately started giving me head while holding my hips and shoving my penis into her mouth.

"I love sucking cock." she said with a sexy smile.

"I see...that feels good baby." I replied.

She continued pleasuring me with her mouth while I stared out the bay window in my bedroom at the trees, thinking about how great my life was. Vanessa had recently introduced me to one of her best friends and now here she was in my bedroom giving me head like she was a porn star. I started thinking that this must be what it feels like to be an NBA player or a movie star; beautiful women wanting to have sex with you, even though you haven't taken them on a date or spent any money on them.

Vanessa had gotten me to a point where I was about to explode and then she pushed me away and started removing the rest of her clothes. Meanwhile, I had secured my condom and was ready for action. We reclined on my waterbed and slowly acclimated to the rhythm of the bed as I climbed on top of her and eased myself inside. She grabbed my face and started kissing me.

"Oh baby! Fuck me good baby, fuck me good!" she screamed.

Her moaning and screaming got me even more excited as I started pumping and thrusting so hard that I could feel her ass hitting the bottom of the waterbed. Vanessa was a screamer and a talker, which didn't surprise me since she never seemed to be at a loss for words. We didn't make love for a long time but we both had intense orgasms. When she came, she locked her legs around my back and started shaking and convulsing and

I could feel the flow from her vagina engulfing me as we climaxed at the same time.

Sex with Vanessa was amazing, but I knew that this was only temporary. She had a man and I wasn't interested in breaking up their relationship. We both apparently had a strong sexual desire to be together and she took the first step in making that happen. We never had sex again but a couple of months later, she dropped by house and told me that she had broken up with her boyfriend and that she was interested in having a relationship with me. I didn't really know quite what to say. The truth of the matter was that I was attracted to her but I didn't really trust her. She had introduced me to her best friend who I had slept with and then she had sex with me while still in a relationship -- not exactly the makings of a great relationship; so I just told her that I was seeing someone and I wished her the best.

I had some good friends that lived in the Raleigh Durham area and I started spending a lot of time there hanging out with them and going to clubs. One of the clubs that we would frequent was called Fevers. It was a huge club and I typically didn't have problems meeting women there, especially when they saw me in the Benz. I would often run into my former classmates from ECU at the clubs in Raleigh. One of the people that I was surprised to see was Dana, the half white and half Indian swimmer that I met on campus during our wild partying days at school. She was hanging out in the club with some black girls who had played basketball at ECU. She seemed happy to see me even though she and I had never really talked very much while we were in school.

"Hey you're still looking good I see." I said.

"Thanks, you too."

"So you still have a boyfriend?"

"No, what about you? Do you still have a girlfriend?"

"Naw we broke up a while ago, so I guess I'm just living the single life."

We both gazed at each other for a moment and then I said, "You wanna dance?" She said yes and we both headed off to the dance floor. This was during a time when young people would actually dance together instead of the twerkin' and booty grinding that takes place now in the clubs. We danced a couple of songs and I pulled her in close so that I could finally feel her amazing body that I had admired for so long. Dana was an exotic looking girl; she had a Halle Berry style haircut with flawless skin and a nice physique. She was the kind of girl that other girls admired.

We went back to the bar and I ordered a round of drinks for her and her friends. We sipped on our drinks and chatted about good times in school as the night grew older. Just talking to her and looking in her eyes I could tell that she was ready to leave with me; so I asked her if she wanted to go and she said yes. We quickly finished our drinks, she told her girlfriends that she was leaving with me and then we proceeded to make our way to the door. As we were leaving together, I could see some admiring glances from a few people. Dana was the prettiest girl in the club and she was going home with *me*.

Once we got to her place things started to heat up as soon as we got into her house. We were both still a little bit buzzed from the drinks and anxious to get our hands on each other. After a few minutes of small talk and foreplay on her couch, she stood up and led me to her bedroom. She had such a sexy walk; she seemed to glide like she was on a runway. Dana was not only beautiful but she was also athletic and her body seemed fit for a good workout – and that's exactly what we did. She was not very vocal or energetic in bed but she was so stunning that it didn't seem to matter that much. There's an old theory that suggests that beautiful women are not as good in bed because they know they don't have to try as hard. I tend to agree with this theory for the most part, but there are also exceptions such as Brazilian women, which I will talk about later in this book.

I will never forget how clean and fresh she smelled even after hanging out at a club all night. Her fresh scent and her exotic looks definitely enhanced our love making session. We enjoyed each other for a while and then we collapsed into a post coital stupor as we cuddled and spooned each other. Sometimes after a spontaneous sexual encounter, I would consider leaving but I was in no hurry to leave her side, being with her made me feel good. There's something about being with a beautiful woman that makes a man fill proud and masculine. A pretty woman can melt the heart of the coldest man and make him sing lullabies and bring her flowers for no reason. It's been this way since the beginning of time, we're programmed to attract those which will make good mates and have strong offspring. I certainly thought about what our kids would look like, which is something most couples often contemplate.

Dana and I started seeing each other frequently on the weekends. She lived in Raleigh and I still lived in Winston-Salem which was about two and a half hours away but I didn't mind driving to Raleigh to see her. I always loved the way people would glance at us when we were out. Dana had a very calm demeanor, she was very laid back and she always had a smile on her face. She was also a bit aloof and sometimes a bit of an airhead, but I couldn't hold that against her. After all, she was easy on the eyes and she had a positive attitude.

I was hesitant to get too involved with her because I also knew that she was easy game. Dana had dated a couple of high profile football and basketball players in school, so I knew that she had a thing for black men and she just seemed to freelance between different black guys. Sometimes she would come to Winston-Salem to stay at my place and have sex all weekend and after a while, she started developing feelings for me. It was kind of awkward to be in a relationship with a pretty woman who most men would have flipped out over. I didn't want to get serious with her because she wasn't intellectually stimulating. It's the great conundrum that many men face; deciding between brains or beauty. Most successful men wind up "settling" for beauty because it's the easy choice. I personally like an intelligent woman. Intelligence is sexy. Although, it's rare to find a woman whose intellect exceeds her physical beauty. There's an old joke about a guy who couldn't decide which woman he wanted to marry. He had his choice of three different women, each of them beautiful and smart which made his decision even tougher, so he simply chose the one with the biggest breasts.

The great thing about Dana was that she was always willing to have sex. We had great sexual chemistry and spent a lot of our time together in bed enjoying each other. I remember one weekend that she came to stay with me and we were having sex and the next morning she started complaining about pain in her vagina. She couldn't figure out why it was hurting so bad but I had a pretty good idea. The night before we had one of our most intense sessions together and I recall being so horny that I couldn't stop drilling her with all-of-my prowess. She was in so much pain that she went to see a local doctor the same day. I kind of chuckled because I knew what the problem was -- I was too big for her. I wouldn't say that I'm Mandingo sized but I'm certainly not a pee-wee either and I could often feel how tight her vagina was when I was slamming my penis into her.

She returned back to my house and I immediately asked her what the doctor said. She replied with a slight pout, "He told me that you're too big for me." I busted out laughing!

"That's not funny!" she said.

"I know, I'm sorry babe, but that's kind of rare." I said.

I was thinking about how her conversation with the doctor must have gone. I could have saved her a lot of time by just telling her the truth but I decided that she probably needed to hear it from a doctor. Luckily, she took it all in good stride but unfortunately we weren't able to have sex for the rest of the weekend.

Hanging out with Dana was cool but she wasn't the only girl that I was seeing at the time. I had also recently run into a fine "sista" named Sheila from school who everybody wanted to date. Sheila was tall and beautiful. She had smooth brown skin, thick curves and a sassy attitude. Sheila came across as a spoiled princess who didn't mind putting people in their place. She was an AKA and she always had on some type of pink and green paraphernalia. Sheila had once dated a friend of mine named Waymon while we were in school around the same time I was still seeing Darlene but whenever we would see each other, there always seemed to be a spark.

She was the kind of woman that I had considered making my wife. She was sexy, smart and came from a good family, but there was something about her attitude that just didn't jive with me. Sheila seemed to have a mean streak and she also had a tendency to be bossy. I like an aggressive woman but she had an abrasive demeanor which was hard to deal with sometimes. I would often compare her attitude with Darlene's attitude. Darlene had her moments but overall she was a genuinely nice person, whereas with Sheila I wasn't quite so sure.

I started seeing Sheila more often but Dana was still in the picture. I remember one night shortly after Sheila had left my house to travel back to Greenville; I got a surprise knock on my door. I looked through the peephole to see Dana standing at my doorway; I couldn't believe how close they had come to running into each other. It almost seemed like Dana was waiting for her to leave. I invited her inside feeling a bit awkward about her unannounced visit. She had traveled two and a half hours from Raleigh and simply decided to show up at my house. The look on her face told me that she had fallen in love. She told me that she had to see me. I was tired from my time with Sheila but I didn't want Dana to feel unwelcome either.

We talked for a little while and I could see by the look in her eyes that she wanted to tell me how she felt about me but she held back, probably assuming that her unannounced long distance visit would say *all* that she couldn't say.

This was an awkward confluence of events, I was still sexually attracted to Dana but I had started developing feelings for Sheila. Eventually, I started seeing less of Dana as me and Sheila's relationship started to blossom. A few weeks later, I caught wind that she was seeing Phil Henderson, former Duke basketball player who had recently won a championship with the Blue Devils. I had met Phil a few months earlier and I recall introducing her to him on one occasion and I could tell that they were both smitten with each other. It was kind of odd but I wasn't surprised to hear the news because Dana had an affinity for dating black guys with a "name" or at least looked like they had money. She wasn't a gold digger, she actually seemed unconcerned with money but Dana definitely was drawn to a certain type of black man.

Meanwhile, Sheila and I grew closer. I had never traveled outside of the States and I suggested that we take a cruise to the Bahamas. She was excited about the idea, so I immediately booked a trip for us to fly down to Fort Lauderdale and catch a cruise ship to Freeport. We were both excited in anticipation of our trip. Sheila always had a nice body and I couldn't wait to see her in a sexy bikini on board a big ship.

Once we arrived in Fort Lauderdale we checked into our hotel to rest and prepare for our adventure the following day. It felt great to travel and be away from home. We relaxed and watched TV, had amazing sex and fell asleep shortly afterwards. The whole trip made us feel like grown-ups, we were both 23 years old at the time on an adult escapade to another country.

The next morning we headed over to the Fort Lauderdale port which was quite a sight, packed with gigantic ships preparing to depart into the open seas. As we walked up the steep incline towards the entrance of the boat, we gazed around at the enormity of the ship. Once we reached the top, a friendly guide asked us to stop and take a picture together before entering the boat. The picture came out great; we looked like a happy and healthy couple.

However, once we arrived at our room, we were disappointed in how small our cabin was -- it felt like the size of my closet; it certainly wasn't what we had imagined. That's when I realized that it's always better to pay more for better accommodations when you travel (if you can afford it) which I certainly could at the time.

Never the less, we made the best of our cozy cabin. We settled in quickly and headed out to the pool area where we discovered the infamous Bahama Mama drink. If you've ever been to the Caribbean Islands, you know that they have a "heavy hand" when they pour their drinks. We sat at the bar and each had two Bahama Mamas, complete with tiny umbrellas and lots of rum. Within just a couple of hours of being on board the boat, we were well on our way to being smashed.

A few minutes later, we heard the captain's voice over the loud speaker announcing our departure. Everyone was excited (and drunk) including us and we couldn't wait to venture out into the ocean. The feeling of a cruise ship moving away from the dock is similar to a small earthquake. It's a bit unsettling at first and you have to kind of brace yourself. Sheila and I decided to retreat to our cabin, stumbling and laughing the whole way in anticipation of having great sex in our tiny room. When we arrived back at our room, we started to feel the swaying of the ocean and a sudden queasiness in our stomachs. Neither of us had ever been on a big boat and we both started feeling seasick, not to mention we were both extremely buzzed. I think the ship operators encourage their patrons to drink up before departure to offset the nauseous seasick feeling.

We felt the boat pick up speed as we rocked along with the motion of the ship. Eventually it smoothed out after a few minutes but it killed our desire for sex as we were both borderline puke phase by now. We snuggled on our cozy bed and comforted each other until we both felt sober enough to venture back out for dinner. After showering and changing into our nice casual dinner attire we headed down to the main dining room, where we were treated to a smorgasbord of food, including delicious desserts and seafood.

We sat beside an older couple from New York who thought we were on our honeymoon. Sheila and I thought it was kind of amusing that they would think that but I could tell that she delighted in the idea of being my wife and us being on our honeymoon.

Sheila politely replied, "Nooo we're not married... yet," as she glanced at me with a devilish smile. I just chuckled because I knew exactly what she was implying. Sheila and I definitely enjoyed each other's company but I wasn't convinced that we were on our way down the aisle. As our trip continued, her attitude became more aggressive and abrasive. I recall her being very disappointed that we didn't win a Hula Hoop contest one night aboard the boat. She was a natural as she shook her thick curvaceous booty along with the rhythm of the music, however when it was my time to hula, I wasn't as adept at shaking the hula around my legs. I had difficulty keeping the hoop in motion and had to pick it up a few times and start over. It wasn't a big deal to me because I was buzzed and uninterested in competing with other vacationers, but apparently Sheila was very interested in winning despite the fact we were supposed to be on vacation.

It was that part of her personality that made me question whether or not I could tolerate her sometimes abrasive demeanor. She had an attitude of entitlement and she was very driven to succeed and make people bow to her demands. After spending four days on a boat, overeating and overdrinking and seeing her true personality emerge, I realized that Sheila and I probably would not have a long-term relationship. Her drive was too intense and it drove a wedge between us. By the time that our ship was headed back to Florida, we were almost on nonspeaking terms. I was contemplating leaving her in Fort Lauderdale and making her find a way back home but I decided to "man up" and endure the short flight back home the next day.

Once we arrived back in North Carolina it was pretty clear that our relationship was over. She gathered her things from my house and loaded up her car shortly after we had arrived and began to make her way back home. We didn't speak for a few days until one day she called, sounding very somber on the phone.

"So how are *you* doing?" she said.

"I'm good...What's going on with you?" I replied.

"Well I'm *not* doing so good."

"You're not? What's wrong?"

"Well this morning I found out that I was pregnant."

There are a handful of moments in a man's life that he will never forget and one of them is the first time that a woman tells him that she's pregnant. It was the last thing that I expected to hear from her and I was shocked.

"You're pregnant!?" I replied in disbelief.

"Yep I sure am, how do you feel about *that?*" she said in a sarcastic tone.

"I'm not sure how I feel, are you sure you're pregnant?"

"Of course I am. Do you want me to send you the test strip?"

I started thinking about all the recent times that we had sex without a condom. Like most new relationships, we started out using protection but then we gradually did without it. I felt like a fool for letting a woman be in a position to determine the course of my life. Having sex with her without a condom felt great, but now I was in an unfamiliar situation with a woman who was supposedly pregnant and had the power to decide whether or not she and I would bring a child into the world.

"So what do you wanna do?" I replied.

"I'm not sure yet, maybe we should talk in a couple of days." She suggested.

"Okay that sounds good."

I hung up the phone feeling like I had been punched in the gut. Sheila had told me that she was on the pill and

I was curious as to how she could be pregnant. I started to wonder if she was simply getting back at me for an awful vacation. I knew that she was a vindictive type of a person and pretending to be pregnant in an effort to upset me was certainly something that she was capable of.

When we spoke a couple of days later, I was clearheaded and forthright with her about not wanting to have a child with her. I offered to send her the money for an abortion to which she seemed pleased to hear. I knew that she was planning on pursuing her MBA and that having a child at her age probably wasn't going to happen. I told her to call me in a few days to let me know how much money I needed to send her.

Days went by but I didn't hear back from Sheila. I called and left her a message but I didn't hear back from her. As time went on, I came to the realization that she was never pregnant and she simply wanted to get under my skin because I had the audacity to reject her.

Sheila and I eventually stopped communicating and drifted apart. I didn't see her again until a couple years later, after I had moved to Atlanta and ran into her at a party.

I learned a lot from my acrimonious vacation with Sheila but the main thing that I learned was: *The true test of a relationship is whether you can travel with that person and still return as friends.*

Chapter 9

Money, money, money...

The O'Jays sang about the evils of money and how the love of money can corrupt the soul. People always say that if they became rich, they would never change. That's a lie because you *have* to change. You have to change your outlook on life and the importance that money has in helping you achieve your dreams. My parents both had good paying jobs when we were growing up and we had most of the things that we wanted as kids -- but now that we had a windfall of money, things started to change for the better *and* for the worse.

I remember pulling into our driveway in my Mercedes and musing about how much our lives had changed. Our driveway resembled a *Wheel of Fortune* TV set. There were brand new trucks, jet skis, convertibles and motorcycles. It was evident to all of our neighbors that we had come into a lot of money and along with that money came envy and jealousy.

My youngest brother Jack had recently bought a brand new Camaro and one day while leaving his high school, he found a note on his windshield that read: "We don't like rich niggers." He didn't seem too upset about the situation probably because most of his friends were white, but I was incensed about it because I knew that some of those same people that he considered to be friends were actually closet racists.

My sister and I had lived in a black neighborhood prior to moving out to the "boonies," but my younger brothers grew up in a neighborhood where most of their friends were white. Consequently, they began to see themselves as white and I could tell that they did not have a healthy sense of what it meant to be black. I used to joke that my brothers were the nicest white guys that you could ever meet. All of the women that they dated were white and their circle of friends was also white, but as they grew older, they struggled with their identity as black men in a white world. Both of my brothers had trouble with the law and they both struggled to hold down a good job. This is not unusual for kids who were exposed to a lot of money at a very early age. There have been numerous stories of kids from wealthy families that struggled to fit into society and become productive citizens.

My mother had set up a trust fund for both of them until they reached the age of sixteen. She was required by law to give them access to the money when they turned of age and they didn't waste any time blowing through their portion of the settlement. Both of them bought new sports cars, even a collectible Corvette -- jet skis and fast motorcycles all while in high school!

Their spending and lack of attention to their school work caused a lot of consternation within our family. I've never been really close to my brothers because of our age difference but I could see that they were headed for destruction and there wasn't much I could say because I was also apparently enjoying my windfall as well.

My long-time friends started treating me different, trying to make me feel obligated to give them money or pay for certain things. I was generous but I was no fool either. I would pay for dinner, tickets to Hornets games or buy a round of drinks but that was my limit. I had a friend, who once asked me to finance a motorcycle for him, which I thought was the most ridiculous thing that anybody could ever ask of me. I started hearing whispers that I had changed. In reality, I hadn't changed all that much, it was the people around me and my so-called friends that were changing. I had a good friend from school named Kenny, whose mother swindled me out of $500 to supposedly pay for their younger son's tuition. When I told Kenny about the money, his only response was, "How much did she get?"

After a few months of being unemployed, sleeping with lots of women and burning through my cash, I decided that I needed to get a job or start a business and make some investments with my remaining windfall of about $50,000. I had researched different businesses that would allow me to generate passive income. I had always been impressed with the photo booths that I had seen in the malls around town and I decided that would be a great business for me to invest in.

I found a guy in Raleigh who had a used machine for sale and I hastily made arrangements to travel to Raleigh and pick it up. Prior to purchasing the machine, I had already secured a lease at the Greensboro Mall in the middle of the food court. The mall manager seemed a bit surprised to see a young black guy pitching him on the idea, but I won him over with a solid business plan and a healthy amount of enthusiasm. I had grand visions of owning several photo booths throughout the Southeast and building a residual monthly income that would allow me the freedom to travel and collect my money.

The photo booth did well for the first few weeks but then it started breaking down almost every other day, which became annoying because I was losing money and having to travel 40 minutes to Greensboro to try and fix the machine. I had made a deal with one of the security guards at the mall named Billy, who happened to have one of the worst stuttering problems I've ever heard. We agreed that he would call me whenever my machine broke down. The ironic thing about him was that he didn't stutter very much when he sang. He told me that he was an aspiring singer and let me listen to some of his tracks.

I'm not a fan of making fun of people with handicaps but his phone messages to me were completely hilarious. He sang in a real soulful **R&B** style voice and he would leave messages like, "Hey man your your machine is is is broken..." I always had to contain myself from laughter whenever I had to listen to his messages.

Finally, I contacted a guy based out of South Carolina who owned several machines and had helped me repair my photo booth on a few occasions. I called him up one day and asked him if he was interested in buying my machine. I had grown exasperated with the constant breakdowns and last-minute trips to the mall to fix my booth. He seemed very interested and within a couple of weeks, I had unloaded this pain-in-the- ass machine to him at a decent profit. I initially paid $3500 for the photo booth but I sold it to him for $6000 because I still had a new lease in a very good location in the mall.

The photo booth experiment didn't go very well but it taught me to be resourceful and to seize the opportunity to turn a negative situation into a positive situation.

Chapter 10

Women do cheat!

With my daily cash burn rate still very high, I was fortunate to land a job working with the City of Winston-Salem as an intake counselor for adults and underprivileged students who were seeking employment. The job paid fairly well and helped me to stabilize my cash flow and it also gave me a chance to interact with young students and help mentor them towards their educational and employment goals. There were also plenty of professional women who worked in my office building. It didn't take long for me to start receiving a lot of attention. I would show up in my gleaming white Mercedes looking dapper and wearing finely tailored suits and ties. There were a few really attractive girls who were also recent college grads like me and a few older women who expressed interest in dating. I had my pick of just about every single girl in my building but I was discreet about who I went out with because some of them were friends and I knew that they would talk.

I eventually started seeing three different girls in my building but none of them really knew each other. One of the girls that I started seeing was named Lynn. She was a really smart girl who had just graduated from college. Lynn was statuesque, she was fair skin and tall with a set of the biggest knockers I had seen on a girl her size. Her chest was so big that she seemed self-conscious about her body. Lynn and I quickly hooked up. Within a week of her starting her new job, we had sex at my house several times. Sometimes at lunch we would sneak away to my house for an "afternoon delight." There were a few times when we returned to the office to be greeted by curious looks and whispers. We didn't really care. We were young and horny.

There was also an attractive older lady named Karen who always dressed really nice. She always wore expensive, tight fitting suits to show off her amazing curves. She used to walk by my window and flirt with me almost every day. Karen was about 15 years older than me and she was in great shape and I could tell that she was a freak. One day I received a phone call from her while sitting at my desk, inviting me out to lunch with her. I quickly accepted her offer of lunch which eventually led to drinks over dinner and then a nightcap at my house. Karen was a sexy and experienced older lady who liked to please. She was the first woman that I had been with that not only gave me a great blowjob but also tickled my scrotum with her tongue -- that was a *great* feeling and she really seemed to enjoy doing it.

The other girl that I started seeing was named Lana. She was a beautiful girl with a great body and a flirty attitude. Lana would pretend like she wasn't interested in me. I'm sure she saw the number of girls that were flirting with me and probably wanted to let me know that she was different. Lana also had a boyfriend but she would often stroll by my window and roll her eyes at me. I quickly realized that this was her way of flirting with me. One day I ran into Lana on the street as I was leaving work. She told me that her ride had not shown up yet and asked me if I could give her a ride home. I agreed to give her a ride, thinking that this would be a great opportunity for us to connect. Lana and I had never really had an in-depth conversation and this would be the perfect chance to get to know her. She was the prettiest girl in my building and I was initially disappointed to find out that she had a live-in boyfriend. I didn't think that there was any chance that Lana and I would hook up, but on the ride home things started to change. She was flirting and asking me questions about girls that I had dated in the building. She seemed like a totally different girl. I started getting a really sexy vibe from her. When we arrived at her apartment building, she directed me towards her parking space. I placed my car in park and wished her a goodnight.

She surprisingly said, "Thanks, you wanna come up?"

I couldn't believe that she was inviting me up to her house.

"Isn't your man at home?" I replied.

"No, he's not coming home until later."

I thought seriously about going up to her place but I didn't want to take a chance on her boyfriend coming home sooner.

"Naw I think I'm going home, we can hang out at my house sometime." I said.

She shrugged her shoulders and smiled, "Okay that sounds cool, just let me know."

She exited the car and started making her way up the stairs. As I watched her walk up the stairs, I started having second thoughts about her offer but I decided that it was too risky. On the way home, I thought about how great her sexy body would have looked in the nude. Lana was built like a brick house and she had a gorgeous face to match. I had often fantasized about having sex with her and I was elated to discover that she felt the same way.

A few days later, we made plans for her to come by my house on a Friday night. I was excited about the idea of having sex with Lana on my bed. Prior to her arrival, I took a couple of shots of vodka to calm my nerves.

There's something about alcohol that makes me last a lot longer. I didn't want to have a premature experience with her, so I made sure I was a little buzzed so that I could enjoy our night together. A few moments later, I heard my doorbell ring. I casually walked towards to the door with my heart beat now racing. I had been with a lot of girls but being with Lana seemed special, maybe it was because I never imagined that we would actually hook up. Once she was inside, I offered her a drink but she refused. I was impressed that she didn't drink; it's refreshing when a woman doesn't have some of the same vices as me. I've never really been a big drinker but sometimes it comes in handy in these types of situations.

We relaxed on my couch which quickly led to kissing and caressing. She was surprisingly aggressive as she let her hands explore my body. I grabbed her hand and led her towards my bedroom. My head was now spinning from the alcohol and the anticipation of good sex. Lana reclined on my bed and allowed me to start sliding her clothes off. Once I had her panties off, I started kissing on her curvaceous thighs. I slowly worked my way up to her vagina. I teased her with my tongue as she writhed in ecstasy. I hadn't planned on going down on Lana but I couldn't resist once I saw her beautiful body sprawled out on my bed. I wanted her to remember our first time together -- tonight I would pull out all the stops! I cupped her nice round hips in my hands and pulled her closer to my face. I grabbed her hips even tighter and began to sink my tongue deeper into her. Her body convulsed as she arched her back and screamed out my name. By now, I was rock hard and ready to feel her wetness. I climbed on top of her and tried to position myself inside her but she started pulling me upwards towards her lips. Once I was straddled over her face, she started inhaling my penis which felt awesome. I was ecstatic about how passionate she was; I didn't expect her to be so sexually aggressive.

Her passion made our night together unforgettable. We rolled around on my bed, contorting ourselves into different positions and making love like we had been together many times before. She was incredible! Lana lived up to the old saying, "A lady in the streets but a freak in the sheets." Sometimes when you're in a relationship with someone, the sex becomes routine –- so maybe she was feeling exuberant about being with someone different.

I learned over the years that women *definitely* cheat and it's not always because they're sexually repressed or feeling neglected by their man. Sometimes a woman will simply decide that she wants to have sex with a certain man to fulfill her desires. Especially in this age of female empowerment, women are making more money and heading up single family households. There are more women working in corporate America and leading companies than ever before and along with that comes sexual empowerment. There have a been few studies that suggest that the more money a woman makes, the more likely it is that she will cheat -- especially if she makes more money that her man!

During my grandmother's era, women were dependent upon their husbands to provide for them and to be the primary bread winner in the family. The dependency upon a man to provide for the wife and the family has slowly eroded over the past 50 years, as women have become more educated and more accepted into the working world. I'm sure there were many times when my grandmother wanted to leave my grandfather, but financially she depended upon him as a provider.

As women have become more financially empowered, their sexual behavior has evolved to mimic the attitudes of men. What happened between me and Lana is very common; a flirtatious relationship begins at work despite the woman's "significant other" and culminates into a one night stand. Lana and I never slept together again but we shared an unforgettable and intimate night together.

Chapter 11

Tina

Back in the early 90's, my buddies and I would get dressed up and drive to Greensboro on Saturday night for a weekly singles event at the Hilton Hotel. It was a great venue for a large gathering of young professionals. The cavernous conference room would be transformed into a club-like atmosphere with a DJ blasting the latest beats and of course there was a plethora of fine, sexy ladies strutting around in their tight dresses and high heels. One night while hanging out at the hotel, I ran into a sexy pecan brown girl wearing a skin tight dress as I was leaving the men's room. We immediately locked eyes as if we were both struck by a bolt of lightning. She approached me and said, "Hey I like your suit." "Thanks you're looking *very* nice yourself." I replied. She told me her name was Tina and we chatted for a bit, while I occasionally caught myself staring at her breast. I discovered that she also lived in Winston-Salem. Tina was a different type of girl; she seemed like the kind of black girl that didn't date black men very often.

Her mannerisms and her proper speech gave me the impression that she preferred white guys, but there was obviously something about *me* that she liked.

She had smooth brown skin, a full chest and a slender yet curvy frame. Tina was a fun girl; we danced and had a few drinks as the night went on. While we were dancing, I couldn't take my eyes off her chest which looked like her breast were about to pop out of her tight fitting dress. She had a bubbly personality and a killer body to match. I knew that I had a good chance of taking her home, so I shouted over the loud music, "Hey you want me to take you home!?" She smiled and said, "I came with my girlfriends but yea, you can take me home."

We started leaving the dance floor as she began to search for her girlfriends. I followed closely behind until she located her posse. I stood a few feet away as she informed her friends that she was leaving with me and I could see a couple of her friends giving me the look of approval.

Once we arrived at my car, she was very impressed. I opened up the door for her as she slid into the comfortable interior.

As we began to make our way home, she suddenly asked me, "Are you rich?"

I busted out laughing!

"Am I rich? That's a funny question."

"No I'm serious, you look like somebody who's rich and famous."

"Wow, that's a nice compliment. No I'm not rich *or* famous but maybe I will be one day, who knows?"

She seductively smiled at me and caressed my face while I was driving.

"Maybe we should go to my place?" I said.

"To *your* place?"

"Yea we can go there and hang out for a little while."

"Okay but you have to promise me that we're not going to have sex, okay?"

I laughed and said, "Sure if that's what you want."

When we arrived at my house and started making our way towards my door, she repeated, "No sex right?" "Right no sex." I said with a wink. Once we were inside, we immediately started kissing and fondling each other. I started kissing on her neck and squeezing her firm breast. "Oooh that's my spot baby." she moaned. I continued to kiss on her neck and work her tight dress up over her hips. She started groping my penis and reaching for my zipper. I quickly grabbed her hand and led her to my bedroom. We were both feeling the heat from our passion.

We reclined onto my bed as I continued to undress her. Once we were nude, she climbed on top of me and grabbed my erect penis and carefully guided it inside of her. She let out a loud moan as she began gyrating and bouncing on my manhood. I relaxed and put my hands behind my head, staring up at her big round bouncing boobs. Tina was loud and she started screaming like she had been possessed by a spirit. "Oh yea! Oh yea! Come on baby!" she shouted.

I could feel her body to start to quiver. She was working my stick like a cowgirl as she continued to bounce on top of me. I could feel her getting closer to orgasm so I started pulling her in closer and thrusting myself into her from the bottom position. She started shaking and screaming as she pressed her hands against my chest. Suddenly we both came to a euphoric orgasm. Tina collapsed onto the bed. I could see her chest heaving from the intense encounter. We both laid in silence for a few minutes and then I playfully said to her, "No sex right?" She chuckled a bit and said, "Yea right no sex."

Tina and I were very compatible. She was always fun to be with and she always wanted to have sex. She also told me that she hadn't dated a black guy in a long time which didn't really surprise me. Tina liked to dress up in cowboy boots and cowboy hats and hang out at the popular white bars in town. Her attitude was kind of refreshing; she was very care free and spontaneous. Neither of us had ever been to Vegas, so I surprised her and booked a trip for us to "Sin City."

I had learned my lessons about traveling with women on vacation from my awful experience with Sheila in the Bahamas. Tina was cool, I knew that no matter what happened, she wasn't going to flip out on me and throw a tantrum.

A few days later, we were off on our adventure to Las Vegas. It was very exciting because I had never traveled west before and I was anxious to see the city that I had only seen in movies. After our four hour flight, we landed at the McCarron Airport and as we entered the arrival area we could hear the clinging and ringing sound of slot machines. We were both amazed that they had slot machines in the airport. There were passengers waiting to depart, playing slot machines right in the middle of the terminal. It was one of those, "You're not in Kansas anymore" moments.

We quickly gathered our bags from the luggage carousel and hitched a ride with a taxi to the Bally's Hotel. Along the way, we stared in amazement at the tall hotel buildings and blinking signs promoting each hotel's marquee act. I noticed that Dolly Parton was premiering at a few different hotels, which was quite surprising for me. I had expected Vegas to be an urban and sleek city that offered a variety of entertainment but it seemed like everybody had on cowboy hats and Dolly Parton was the main attraction all over town.

When we arrived at our hotel, we quickly unpacked and changed into our formal attire. I put on a grey tweed blazer and black dress pants, while Tina had on a black tight fitting evening gown. Our only perception of Vegas casino attire at the time was what we had seen in the movies. I recalled seeing old movies starring Elvis Presley in a Las Vegas casino and how, he and everyone else were always so dapper. We assumed that patrons were required to wear formal wear in the casino area; however, when we arrived downstairs, we quickly discovered that most people had on jean shorts and t-shirts.

We both felt a bit overdressed but it didn't matter, it actually made our visit a bit more romantic. We looked like we had money and we couldn't wait to try our hand at gambling. At the time, I wasn't experienced in playing any of the card games so I saddled up to a slot machine which seemed pretty simple to play. Tina sat a nearby slot machine and quickly started feeding it with coins.

We were both excited as we watched the colorful wheel adorned with cherries, lemons, etc. spin around and tease us with near wins. After pumping the machines with money for a few minutes, a scantily clad waitress approached us and asked if we wanted to order drinks. I said, "Sure!" and started reaching into my pockets for money. The waitress said, "Oh you don't have to pay for the drinks sweetie, they're complimentary." Tina and I both looked at each other in amazement.

"Free drinks huh?" I said to the waitress.

"That's right, but of course we always appreciate tips." She said with a friendly smile.

"Well in that case, bring us a couple of rum and cokes sweetie." I said in fake country accent.

Tina and the waitress were cracking up. I was having a good time while mimicking our cocktail waitress. She hurried away to get our drinks as Tina and I returned our attention back to our slot machines. I continued to pump dollar bills into my machine; I was determined to win some money on my first day in Vegas.

After a few near wins, I gave the machine another spin and watched as the first wheel landed on a cherry, then the next one landed on a cherry as well. I started getting excited in anticipation of the third wheel landing on a cherry for a big win! The wheel spun around and then....boom! Jackpot! I stared in amazement at the three bright red cherries and suddenly the siren on top of the machine started going off. It was an amazing feeling. I looked at the graphics on top of the machine to see how much I was going to win and it read: $5,000. Tina was amazed; she started shouting, "Baby you won! Baby you won!" The floor supervisor quickly came over as a small crowd started to gather around me.

"Hey looks like you're a lucky guy today." He said with a smile.

"Did I win the jackpot!?" I replied.

"Not quite, you see that sign on the bill acceptor that says one dollar or three dollars?"

"Yep."

"Well in order to win the $5,000 you have to play three dollar spins."

The small crowd let out a small sigh. Tina and I were a little disappointed but still excited.

"Well what did I win?" I said anxiously.

"Looks like you won $1000." he said while resetting the machine.

Tina and I looked at each other and shrugged.

"Hey that's pretty good babe, we've only been here for a few hours and you've already won $1000."

The waitress returned with our drinks to see that I had won.

"Hey congratulations!" she said handing us our drinks.

"Thank you!" I replied. I gave her a generous tip as a few bystanders congratulated me on my win.

Winning money is an intoxicating feeling. I started feeling like a real winner, someone destined to go home with my pockets full – and that's how Vegas will get you!

Most people who win money in a casino on their first day, usually go home broke. I was a casino virgin and the excitement and admiration that I was feeling was simply electric.

After I cashed in my winnings, Tina and I had a celebratory drink at the bar. We both started getting hungry so we went and had dinner at the seafood buffet in the hotel. We had our choice of fresh fish, scallops, shrimp, mussels and lobster. I was in heaven at this point; I piled lots of food on my plate and stuffed myself until I couldn't eat anymore. Tina was enjoying her food as well, but she wasn't being a pig like me.

After our meal, we decided to walk around the hotel and look for different slot machines. Tina was feeling a bit jaded that she hadn't won any money yet, so we found a new set of slots in the hotel and quickly sat down to try our luck again -- accompanied by more free drinks, of course.

As the evening grew closer, we were both feeling a bit jet lagged from our travels and all the excitement from our first day. We decided to go up to the room and relax. We were both pretty buzzed from our drinks and I was still stuffed from my earlier feast at the buffet. When I arrived at the room, I tried to relax on the bed and chill out for a while but my stomach started to hurt and I started feeling very dizzy. Tina started rubbing my stomach and making fun of me for eating so much. I appreciated her affection but it didn't prevent me from feeling even worse.

After a few minutes of lying on the bed, I suddenly jumped up and ran to the bathroom. I closed the door and immediately threw up in the commode. I also started having a diarrhea attack at the same time! I felt awful and my body felt like it was trying hard to get rid of *all* the food and drinks that I had that day. For about an hour, I vacillated between throwing up in the sink and sitting on the commode. It was horrific! Tina would occasionally check on me from the door, but I tried to pretend like I was okay but it was obvious that I was not.

A few minutes later, I emerged from the bathroom feeling like I had been in the worst fight of my life. I staggered to the bed where Tina tried comforting me. She rubbed my stomach and said, "How's that seafood treating you?" I couldn't even muster up a laugh. My stomach was still tied in knots. She did her best to nurse me back to health and I was happy that she was there for me. I later realized that I probably ate some contaminated food but I couldn't figure why Tina wasn't sick -- maybe she had an iron cast stomach or just got lucky that she didn't share my plate.

The next morning I felt a lot better so we decided to go check out the city. We went to Caesars Palace which had been recently renovated. As we walked down the long ornate corridor towards the main entrance, we walked through the aquarium where we saw dolphins and other exotic sea life. We stopped to take pictures like the other visitors and then proceeded towards the animal sanctuary where we were amazed to see a pair of beautiful white Bengal tigers.

They were lounging around in their habitat and ignoring the numerous patrons stopping and taking pictures. It was awesome to see the rare white tigers but I felt sorry for them being trapped in a faux environment. I think that if you want to see rare exotic animals, you should take a safari trip and see them in their natural habitat -- but this was Vegas and people paid a lot of money to travel there to see the unexpected.

The rest of our trip was great as we explored the city and occasionally played a few more slot machines. Tina and I enjoyed our four day trip but after eating all we could eat and drinking our fill, we were more than ready to go home.

Over the next few weeks, we continued to see each other but I wasn't in love with her. I could tell that she was developing feelings for me but I didn't see Tina as wife material. She wasn't college educated and had no desire to further her education. She was a "good time" girl who was fun to hang out with but I couldn't see her being the mother of our children or being my ideal wife. We eventually drifted apart and the last I heard about Tina was that she was a stripper. I'm sure she did very well in that profession with her friendly personality and her voluptuous breast.

One of the other habits that I had developed, other than having sex with numerous beautiful women, was a passion for reading. During my college days, reading felt more perfunctory, but now that I was an adult; I started reading for pleasure. I would often visit bookstores and spend hours browsing through various books and magazines. I developed an appreciation for autobiographies, some of my favorites were about Michael Jordan, Mike Tyson, Donald Trump, Nelson Mandela, Bill Clinton, Martin Luther King Jr., Arthur Ashe and Malcolm X just to name a few.

Reading allowed me to expand my horizons and gain more knowledge and insight into the world. I would also spend hours catching up on old classics like *Moby Dick*, *The Adventures of Huckleberry Finn*, and *To Kill a Mockingbird*. One of the benefits of developing a love for reading was a significant improvement in my vocabulary. I became curious about the etymology of certain words and would often spend time simply reading the dictionary and educating myself on various words and their meaning.

The other benefit that I discovered was a major improvement in my writing skills. In college, I had developed an appreciation for writing but now I was inspired to write about subjects that were of personal interest. I've always had a creative imagination and a love for movies so I decided to write my first screenplay. I researched books about proper screenplay format like the well-known book by Syd Field, *Screenplay: The Foundations of Screenwriting.*

I started with an outline of ideas for my plot. I had decided to write a story about a young, up-and-coming attorney, whose fiancé had been suspiciously murdered and as a result; he became a prime suspect and suddenly found himself in the middle of a murder mystery. It was entitled, *Person of Interest*, (no relation to the TV show) and it was a suspense thriller with a very surprising ending (his jaded ex-girlfriend did it.)

It took me about six months to complete the manuscript. My neighbor had given me a laptop which looked like the first of its kind back then. It was bulky and only ran basic DOS but that was all I needed was a word processor to save my work. In college, I had to use a typewriter like most students but now with a laptop computer; I didn't have to worry about loading paper and using white-out.

Finishing my first screenplay was a great feeling, I had meticulously dedicated myself to writing every day and I was proud that I had finished. It was about 115 pages long and well formatted but it was lacking basic structural techniques, however, I did receive positive feedback on the dialogue, storyline and overall character development.

Writing my first screenplay gave me the confidence that I could start with an idea and see it through to completion. Many nascent writers abandon their projects well before they've even begun to develop their storyline. I developed a habit of completing my manuscripts regardless of how difficult or exasperated I would become. Writing is a very cathartic process. Even now as I'm writing, I feel a sense of accomplishment in my efforts. It's also helped me to think more objectively about the trials and tribulations that I've experienced in my lifetime.

I had often visited Atlanta to party and hang out with my friends that had moved there, so I decided that it was time for me to move to a bigger city. The small town life just wasn't ideal for an ambitious mover and shaker who had big plans in the works. Prior to preparing my move, I received a phone call out-of-the blue from Darlene, my college sweetheart. I was really surprised to hear from her. She told me that she missed me and wanted to come visit me soon. I told her that I missed her as well and that I couldn't wait to see her. I started thinking that this was a good sign, a possible reconciliation and perhaps a fresh start for us. About a week later, she arrived at my house, making the five hour drive down from Maryland. Our initial encounter was a bit awkward. We had not seen each other in almost two years and it was clear that we both had changed. Darlene seemed a bit more "earthy," she had changed her diet and insisted on eating mainly raw vegetables while she was with me.

I had also started eating better as well; I had completely given up on pork. Back then it was in vogue for many black people to say that they didn't eat pork. I think it had something to do with changing mentalities and trying to live in accordance with a biblical diet. I gave up pork initially because I didn't like the idea of eating a pig. I would gradually throughout my life give up *all* meat and only until recently reincorporated seafood into my diet, which I will discuss later in this book.

Darlene and I tried to rekindle our love but so much time had passed that it was obvious that we weren't going to be together. I was hoping that things would be the same and that maybe we would get married. We had been through so much it just seemed natural that we should be together; however, that was not our fate. Darlene and I parted ways after spending a few days together. She returned to Maryland to complete her MBA and I prepared for my move to "Hotlanta."

Chapter 12

ATL

It didn't take me long to get settled in Atlanta. I had a few friends from college who had moved there and I quickly found a cozy one bedroom near Decatur. My remaining settlement stash had dwindled to about $10,000 due to excess spending and poor money management. I was determined to scale back on my lifestyle to accommodate my new financial reality.

I found a job as a Contract Specialist working with the City of Atlanta. The department that I worked for was part of the mayor's job training partnership with the federal government. The city received an annual grant from the government to provide job training and placement assistance for low income applicants. My job involved reviewing RFPs to determine which vendors would be selected to provide job training and I would also make regular visits to their facilities to ensure that they were compliant. It didn't take long to realize that *all* of the vendors had a connection to Mayor Bill Campbell who was later convicted and sentenced to prison for embezzlement and fraud.

Mayor Bill Campbell was a protégé of the late Atlanta Mayor Maynard Jackson. Jackson was the first black mayor of Atlanta and he was very instrumental in renovating the Atlanta Hartsfield Airport during the early 90's. Jackson made sure that a handful of African-American contractors and vendors were selected for the multi-million dollar renovation; however, there were constant accusations that he had accepted kickbacks in exchange for their participation.

Mayor Campbell had recently assumed his position as mayor around the time that I started my position with the city and it seemed as though he had picked up right where Maynard had left off. Cronyism was just a fact of life within the Atlanta city government. All of the directors were close friends of the mayor and they constantly reminded their constituents of their connection. It was quite evident that there were two types of people who worked for the city; those who *knew* the mayor and those who didn't. I was always well dressed and affable, so people assumed that I was part of the mayor's inner circle. People would often ask me if I had intentions on running for political office but at the time I had no plans to be a politician; *especially* after seeing first-hand how politics and government truly function.

Atlanta has traditionally been a city with a plethora of single attractive ladies. The local colleges like the all-female Spelman College typically attracted young ladies to the city from various parts of the country. One of my favorite events was Spelman homecoming which brought a slew of fine, educated "sistas" back to the city.

The most notorious event that Atlanta was known for during that time was Freaknik. Freaknik was a weekend festival during the summer that brought people from all over the east coast as far as New York. There were concerts, car shows and lots of scantily clad women walking around looking for attention. Whenever Freaknik was in town, it completely took over the city. From downtown to Piedmont Park, there were people everywhere looking for some fun. Fly exotic cars with big rims and custom paint jobs would snake their way down Peachtree Street with girls hanging out the rooftop, flashing their breast.

Guys would be on the prowl, looking for a freak to take pictures with and possibly take home. I recall seeing a guy flirting with a girl in the passenger seat of the car behind him. She was daring him to come and lick her vagina. Suddenly he jumped out of his car and approached the girl who immediately spread her legs for him while sitting in her seat as he dropped to his knees and began going down on her. I was in shock! I couldn't believe what I was seeing -- at that moment I realized why they called it Freaknik.

I had been to Atlanta during Freaknik a couple of years prior to moving to there, so I wasn't that interested in just hanging out and looking for girls; I was interested in making money. I had designed my own T-shirts with a catchy logo on the front and the back and I was hustling the whole weekend, selling my shirts all over the city. I was doing really well with my sales until I noticed a group of rowdy kids gathering near an athletic shoe store in the Atlanta Underground. The business had closed early and the windows were protected by a heavy gate but that didn't stop a group of thugs from somehow breaking the lock on the gate and bum rushing into the store. Once a few bystanders saw that the gate was open, they rushed into the store by the dozens. I saw guys and girls emerging from the store with an arm full of sneakers and clothes. Within just a few minutes, the whole scene became a riot. Police were doing their best to stop the looting but they were outnumbered by the young revelers intent on cleaning out the shoe store. Meanwhile, I was standing a few feet away with a backpack full of T-shirts to sell while watching these hooligans walk away with free loot –- which meant that they obviously weren't interested in spending money on *my* merchandise.

Living in a bigger city gave me the opportunity to meet women from different backgrounds. A lot of professionals were moving to Atlanta during the mid-1990's and it was quickly becoming a hot spot for young African-Americans. The cost of living was very affordable and the weather was much milder compared to the frigid winters that a lot of east coasters were accustomed to. Atlanta was becoming known as a party city and fortunately I had a few good friends who were well connected and always seemed to get me on the guest list at the best parties.

During that time, there was a nightclub called 112 that was the most popular spot in the city. There would always be extremely long lines to get inside all night long. It wasn't unusual for people to wait for hours to get access to the club, unless you were VIP or knew someone who worked at the local hip hop radio station. My buddy Clancy had recently gotten a job with HOT 97 as a sales rep and he would often get me in free, which was great because I hated to wait in lines, especially for a nightclub. The club was so popular that the late Biggie Smalls had a verse in one of his songs, shouting out the club by rapping, "Club 112 where the players dwell..."

I never had a problem meeting women at the club and would occasionally get lucky and take home a pretty girl. I remember meeting a tall, fair skin and svelte looking girl named Leigh one night while waiting for my car. She was unlike any other girl I had ever seen. She was hanging out with her friends and we instantly hit it off. Her top was loosely fitted and as I was talking to her, I could almost see her entire breast. Leigh seemed oblivious to her exposed cleavage and continued chatting away with me until my Mercedes arrived from valet. We exchanged numbers and agreed to meet up soon.

The whole ride home I kept thinking about her. I was excited about going out with her and wondered what it would be like to have sex with her. She was built like a model with legs that seemed to stretch for miles and she had the perfect nose adorned between her beautiful high cheek bones.

A few days later we met up for lunch, which was the beginning of a short but sweet romance between us. Leigh told me that she had recently graduated from the Air Force, which was hard to believe based on how she looked. She told me that she was doing some modeling on the side while working on completing her degree. When she arrived she was wearing another loose fitting silk blouse with her bra showing slightly through the material. I had been accustomed to dating Southern women who were sexy but dressed a bit more conservative than Leigh. She had her own unique style which took some getting used to at first.

We started spending a lot of time together, she was often at my house since she still lived with her parents. It was great having her lovely face around my apartment; she was a really laid back girl who was okay with just chilling around the house sometimes. We were an attractive couple and we each had a strong sex drive. Leigh and I spent a lot of time enjoying each other. We were both young and horny all the time (at least that's what I thought). One day she confessed to me that she didn't think that she could truly satisfy me. Her confession caught me by surprise, I knew there were times when it seemed like I was always wanting more but now she was confirming that it wasn't always mutual.

I realized that she was not as sexually experienced as I was. I tried to be less demanding and forceful in bed but it was her beauty and her sex appeal that kept me horny all night. Leigh and I continued to see each other for a few weeks but there was something about her style that sort of bothered me. She wore nice clothes but she didn't always wear them with class. I recall an occasion when my mom and my sister had come to Atlanta to visit with me and we all went out to dinner together. We were having dinner and Leigh excused herself to go to the restroom. When Leigh was safe enough away from the table; my mom said to me and my sister, "That girl's bra is showing right through her shirt, that's not very ladylike."

Moms always know best and she was exactly right about my girlfriend's attire. I think a lot of women assume that men like to see women with their bras and thongs hanging out of their clothes, but a truly classy woman doesn't have to show off all of her goods. A woman who carries herself with grace and class is so much sexier than a woman who lets it all hang out. It also depends on the man's perspective as well, if he's accustom to dating women who dress provocatively then that's his prerogative but I prefer a woman who has effortless class.

It's also important to date women who have good manners because if she becomes your wife, she will be the standard bearer for your kids (especially girls) when it comes to proper etiquette.

Leigh and I dated for a few more weeks and we eventually drifted apart. She was a sweet girl but she was a bit rough around the edges. I've learned over the years that you can't remake people into the image that you prefer for them. If you can't accept them for who they are, including their flaws, then it's probably not going to work out.

My first celebrity date was in Atlanta. One day while having lunch at the now defunct Spaghetti Factory on Ponce de Leon Avenue, I ran into a familiar face. Her name was Barbara Weathers and I recognized her immediately. She was the former lead singer of the R&B band Atlantic Starr. Their biggest hit was a song called, *Secret Lovers* which is now a classic that's still played frequently on a lot of urban radio stations.

She was entering the restaurant with some friends as I was leaving and we instantly locked eyes.

"Hey, how are you?" I said.

"I'm good, I'm Barbara." she said with a twinkle in her eye.

"Yea I know who you are." I replied with a slight bit of laughter.

"I'm Barrington, nice to meet you."

We shook hands and I could see her friends getting restless in the background.

"Why don't we exchange numbers and maybe go out to lunch sometime?" I said.

She said okay and we quickly jotted down our numbers. I left the restaurant feeling ten feet tall. I had just gotten the phone number of a beautiful lady that I had admired for a long time. I remembered seeing her videos on BET and listening to her music during my high school days.

I waited a couple of days to call her up, I didn't want to seem too eager and blow my cool. When she answered the phone, I was hoping that she would remember me. Fortunately, she did recall our meeting and quickly told me that she was glad to hear from me. We had a brief chat and at the conclusion, we agreed to meet for lunch the next day.

The following day we met at a café in Midtown. When she arrived, she looked even more stunning than the day we met. I knew that she had recently had some problems with drug abuse but she seemed to have a natural glow and a strong inner self confidence.

We talked over a light lunch about our backgrounds. She was from the Greensboro area near where I had grown up. I didn't bother to ask her questions about her career or about her struggles -- I didn't want her to feel like I was just annoying fan. We just talked about life, politics, church and life in Atlanta. She told me that she had recently started attending Charles Stanley's church in downtown Atlanta, primarily because she was dismayed with a few of the black churches that she had attended. I was hoping that our lunch would lead to a second date but there was no spark between us. We talked on the phone a few more times afterwards but that was the beginning and the end of my short flirtation with Barbara.

My date with her gave me the confidence that I could meet just about any woman and be considered a serious suitor, regardless of her fame or fortune. A lot of men would have been hesitant to approach her for a date but I saw her as my equal and I think my confidence was a huge attraction for her.

One of the most indelible moments of my life was the night of the Atlanta bombings during the Olympics in 1996. Some friends and I were inside the makeshift House of Blues near the newly created Olympic Park in downtown watching James Brown perform. I had never seen him perform and I couldn't stop from laughing throughout his show because I kept thinking about how accurately Eddie Murphy had spoofed him on SNL. I couldn't understand a lot of what James was saying and it seemed like for a moment, it was actually Eddie Murphy on stage performing. It was still great to see a legend on stage and he still had a lot of energy for his age. Michael Jordan, Scottie Pippen and a few other NBA players were hanging out near the stage that night and James suddenly invited Michael on stage to perform with him. The crowd was delighted as they began to chant, "Michael! Michael!" Jordan waived his hand in the air, dismissing the idea of going on stage. James replied, "Dats alright, dats alright...we still love ya' Michael...so I guess dis means, *I'm* the greatest on dis here stage tonight."

Once the concert was over, we walked over to the VIP area where the ball players were sitting to hopefully catch a glimpse of Jordan. As we walked up, I saw an exotic looking Puerto Rican girl approach him. She casually took a seat on his lap and started rubbing his bald head and probably whispering the most vile and salacious thoughts that she could imagine in his ear. He was smiling and nodding his head in agreement with everything that she was saying. I assumed that this was normal for Jordan. He was a mega star at the top of his game -- both on and off the court, apparently.

When we walked outside, the atmosphere was quite different. There was smoke everywhere and I saw injured people being carried away from the park. It looked like we had stepped into the middle of a war zone. People were frantic and screaming as they rushed away from the scene. I stopped a lady as she was passing by and asked her what happened. She replied, "A bomb just went off!" I couldn't believe what I had just heard. Just a few minutes ago, I was inside the House of Blues enjoying a concert and now I was in the midst of total chaos. We quickly left the area and by the time I arrived at home, news of the bombing was on every station.

I was saddened to hear that a young lady who was close to the outdoor stage had been killed by the blast. I started thinking about how lucky I was that I wasn't near the bomb. The previous night, I had gone down to the Olympic Park to see some bands perform and I was thankful that I not returned on that fateful night.

The bomber, Eric Rudolph was eventually captured a few years later while hiding out in the remote woods of North Carolina. I'm sure that his arrest was gratifying for all of the victims of the bombing; however, it did leave a stain on the memory of an overall successful Olympic games for the city.

After living in Atlanta for about four years, I started thinking about moving to a bigger city. I had never lived outside of the South and I was seriously considering moving to LA to pursue my dreams of becoming a screenwriter. I didn't know anyone who lived in LA at the time until one night while watching a movie at the theater entitled, *Above the Rim* and I instantly recognized an old friend from high school named Tyrone, who had a small role in the movie. The film starred the late Tupac Shakur as a hustler, trying to persuade a young hoop star played by Duane Martin to attend a college that Tupac had been secretly compensated by to convince the hoopster to attend. Tyrone played one of Duane's friends in the movie and he even had a few speaking parts. I was really surprised to see him acting on the big screen and I took that as a sign that I should contact him and possibly move to LA to pursue *my* dreams.

I reached out to his cousins who were still in North Carolina and gave them my number. A few days later, I received a call from Tyrone who told me that he was living in LA and encouraged me to come out for a visit. During our conversation, he informed me that he was good friends with actor Kadeem Hardison, who was currently starring on the ground breaking African-American TV show entitled, *A Different World*. I was very impressed that he had such great connections in Hollywood and I quickly made arrangements to fly out to LA.

At the time, I had started seeing Sheila again. We had run into each other a few months prior at a rooftop bar in downtown. We were instantly drawn to each other. She was still attractive and I still had feelings for her so we started spending more time together. However, Sheila was not happy about the idea of me visiting LA. She assumed that I was going there to party and meet other girls and eventually leave her.

On the day of my departure, Sheila reluctantly took me to the airport and agreed to pick me up upon my return. I was thrilled to make my first visit to LA; I had already made up my mind that I was going to relocate there if everything went well. My four hour flight seemed to fly by, I read a book and watched a couple of movies and then it was time to depart.

Tyrone lived in the San Fernando Valley and instead of picking me up, he instructed me to take the bus from the airport to the Valley. I quickly found the bus terminal near the airport, paid my fare and watched as they loaded my bags in the luggage compartment.

On the ride to the Valley, I was blown away by the number of cars on the freeway. The sun was shining and the weather was beautiful and I saw people driving with their top down in the middle of the day as if they didn't have a care in the world. LA was unlike any place I had ever been. I saw Ferraris, Lamborghinis and fast motorcycles darting in and out of traffic. It was rare to see a really expensive car in Atlanta during those days, but in LA -- they were everywhere!

When I arrived inside the terminal, I found a vending machine and decided to get myself a snack. I couldn't believe how much more expensive the prices were compared to other places. A bag of peanuts was almost twice the price that I was accustomed to paying. I knew then that in order to live in LA, you had to have some hustle because nothing was cheap (not even the peanuts).

My friend Tyrone showed up a few minutes later. We "bro-hugged" and then he helped me load my bags into his late model hatchback. On the way to his apartment, he showed me different areas of the Valley that were known for good restaurants and bars. It seemed like every street was lined with palm trees, which reminded me of all the movies I had seen over the years in Hollywood.

Once we got to his house, he helped me roll my bags into his decent size apartment. It wasn't a studio but it wasn't much bigger either, just enough space for a young actor to reside. He showed me the kitchen and the couch, which is where I would be sleeping. I noticed that he had several scripts lying around his apartment. I was intrigued and quickly inquired about his life as an actor. He told me that he was auditioning for a few commercials and he also had some recurring roles on a couple of TV shows. Tyrone was from New York and he was a natural born hustler. I could see that he was serious about making it as an actor. Acting was not something that I had seriously considered, I wanted to write -- but several people had encouraged me to pursue acting, which I thought was flattering.

Within a few days, I had met a lot of his actor friends who I recognized from various TV shows. He had introduced me to quite a few people, including the sexy

Mari Morrow who had just starred in a movie called, *How to Be a Player* with Bill Bellamy. Mari was very sexy, she was driving a brand new Range Rover when I met her and she was definitely flirting. She winked at me a couple of times during our conversation and asked how long I was visiting. Tyrone quickly told her that I was leaving but that I might be moving out there soon. I learned later that he was supposedly seeing her on the side. I wasn't sure what to believe, it didn't really matter because I was leaving anyway in a few days.

The next day we met up with Kadeem Hardison and his crew to play some pick-up basketball in a gym near the Valley. I was intrigued about what type of person he would be; I had never really hung out with a true celebrity. During that time, he was very well known as "Dwayne Wayne" of the top TV shows in the country, which aired immediately after *The Cosby Show*.

He introduced himself, telling me that he heard I was coming out to visit. We all started stretching and preparing to play some ball and when the game started, everything changed. Kadeem and his boys were on the opposite team and Tyrone and I played together. I've always been a pretty good basketball player and I quickly started hitting shot after shot. I was being more aggressive than normal because I wanted to show him and his crew that I had some skills.

After a few more shots, I could see Kadeem start to pick up his game. He wasn't a great ball player but for a celebrity he had a decent game. He decided that he wanted to check me since I was hitting most of the shots; that was a great compliment and a great way to introduce myself to his crew. Kadeem started playing tight defense on me but I still managed to continue my hot shooting. He just shook his head and shouted to Tyrone, "Hey man, you didn't tell me this dude could ball!"

Once the game was over, we were all huffing and sweating on the sidelines. Kadeem asked me if I was planning on moving to LA, which indicated to me that I had made an impression on him with my aggressiveness and basketball skills. I told him I was thinking about moving there but I wasn't sure yet. Tyrone chirped in and said, "Yea he's moving here...you know you like this LA life." I chuckled because it was true. I felt like I belonged in their crew and that maybe my dreams of becoming a Hollywood screenwriter would come true. It seemed like the weather was always perfect and people were happy about pursuing their dreams.

Later on that day, we all met up at Kadeem's house which was located way up near Agoura Hills Canyon. The first time we made the trip up to his house, it felt like we were lost. He lived in a remote area atop the canyon which was only accessible by a single lane dirt road. It seemed like an odd place for a black man to live. His house was built like a bungalow set on a cliff and there were three different sections of his property that were all detached. Tyrone gave me a tour of his house and at the end, he showed me Kadeem's cars. He had a silver Ferrari truck that I had never seen before in my life; I didn't even know that they made trucks. He also had a green Ferrari coupe parked next to it that just looked super-fast even when it was parked. There was also a black Volvo sedan that was parked in the driveway.

The house was immaculate, the canyon air was clean and the cars were stunning but I kept wondering why he lived in such a remote area. Tyrone replied, "Fame. Lotta people were knocking on his door when he lived the city...had to get away." I shrugged my shoulders and said, "Makes sense," as we walked towards my favorite part of the property -- the man cave. Kadeem had built a large hang out area near the entrance of his property. It reminded me of a big tree house but inside he had a gigantic TV in the wall, along with pinball machines and comfy couches. He had his various acting awards and photos displayed in a cabinet that ran along the length of the TV cabinet. When I walked in, I immediately recognized Darryl Bell, his co-star and good friend. He was hanging out with some other actors that looked familiar. As I met each of them, I discovered that they all had a connection to the *A Different World* TV show. One of them was named Mike Ralph, his sister is a famous actress named Sheryl Lee Ralph. I also met Matt Robinson, whose sister is Holly Robinson-Peete.

Matt was not an actor but he was one of the coolest guys that I would meet in Hollywood. I found out later that Matt and Holly's mom was a long time Hollywood talent manager. I also discovered that Kadeem's mom, Bethann Hardison owned a well-known New York modeling agency. One of the other conspicuous faces I saw was Christopher Williams, the R&B singer and actor from the movie, *New Jack City*. He was chilling on the couch while playing Kadeem in an intense game of Madden on the big screen.

I was little overwhelmed at first, it felt like I had been invited to an exclusive celebrity party, but there was no party, just a bunch of cool black celebrities and power players hanging out. I was even more impressed with Tyrone and his Hollywood connections after meeting all of his friends. I relaxed and waited my turn to play Madden when all of a sudden I smelled some good ganja in the air. It had been a while since I had smoked, but I wasn't about to punk out in the midst of this celebrity cipher. Tyrone had brought some strong ganja with him. He took a big pull and then passed it to me. I gladly accepted and inhaled a massive amount of smoke into my lungs.

I started feeling the effects of the bud right away. California weed has always been more potent than most other places. I was having second thoughts about how much I had inhaled but it was too late, I was well on my way to being stoned. Suddenly, a beautiful vision appeared in the doorway. It was Chante' Moore, the lovely R&B singer and Kadeem's secret wife who was apparently pregnant and glowing like an angel. For a moment, I thought I was dreaming because when she opened the door there was a halo of sunlight surrounding her and it seemed like she was floating in mid-air.

I had always had a crush on Chante' and I wasn't expecting to see her looking so majestic and breathtaking. Everyone paused and welcomed her into the room. Tyrone gave her a hug and then quickly introduced us. She smiled and nodded as she slightly wobbled into the room and received hugs and kisses from the crew. I looked at Tyrone, smiled and shook my head. I couldn't believe I had just met the incredible Chante' Moore. She was at the top of her career around that time as a singer and she looked great even in her pregnancy.

I was completely stoned at this point but I was enjoying myself as I began playing Tyrone in a game of Madden. I've always been pretty good at video games, especially Madden. I had played the game so much, I already knew my audibles on offense and was able to slice and dice apart his defense. Kadeem was watching our game as if it were a real NFL matchup. He was a big gamer and he spent a lot of time playing video games since he wasn't currently filming or working on a TV show.

Each time I would score, Kadeem would seem more impressed. He also started teasing Tyrone in the process, "Hey man, you gone let your boy come out here and embarrass you like that?" he said. Tyrone wasn't concerned; he was high and just laughed it off. We hadn't hung out since our high school days and he was probably surprised at my skills in video games.

I quickly realized that within his crew, there was a pecking order and that order was determined first of all by how well Kadeem knew you and secondly, how well you played video games. If you had skills on the "sticks" as we would say, you garnered a lot of respect within the circle.

We played games for a few more hours while I listened to them tell funny stories about their Hollywood adventures. It was clear that Kadeem was the alpha male in his group and everyone seemed to cater to his ego; he had the most money and the most fame, something that each of his buddies were striving for.

A couple of days later, my LA adventure had come to an end. Tyrone gave me a ride to the bus terminal where I boarded my bus en route to the LAX airport. Along the way, I contemplated how differently my life would be if I were to move to LA. I was grateful that Tyrone had been a great host and I was really impressed that he had such great connections in Hollywood.

However, when I returned to Atlanta there was a completely different vibe waiting for me. Sheila had agreed to pick me up at the airport but she was nowhere to be found. I tried calling her but she wouldn't answer her phone. Finally, I decided to catch a cab to her place which was quite a distance from the airport. Throughout the entire cab ride I was furious as I saw the meter ticking higher and higher. I knew that she was ignoring me on purpose. Sheila had convinced herself that I was in LA cheating on her and that I was planning on leaving her. I had feelings for her and I had considered getting married to her but there was always something about her personality that prevented me from fully embracing her as my potential wife.

When we arrived at her house, I had to pay the cab driver approximately $70.00 which I definitely wasn't happy about. He also knew that I was steaming mad about being left at the airport. He was an African guy who told me to take it easy and not to be too upset with my girlfriend. I gathered my luggage and began walking towards her apartment. I rang the bell a couple of times and after a few minutes; she wistfully came to the door. I looked at her with disgust; I knew that she was trying to hurt me by leaving me stranded. I barged into her house, I didn't say one word to her -- I simply started gathering some of my clothes that I had left at her place and once I was done, I quickly left, slamming the door as I departed.

Chapter 13

Go West Young Man

About a week later, she called me to apologize but I was in no mood for apologies. I had already made up my mind that our relationship was over and that I was *definitely* moving to LA. I told her that I understood her feelings but on the night of my return, I needed her as a friend *not* just a girlfriend and she completely let me down. When we hung up the phone, I knew that our three year on-again-off-again romance was officially over.

I started preparing for my move by selling most of my furniture and belongings. My funds were running low at the time so I stayed with my good friend Clancy for a couple of weeks while saving up money for my cross country drive. I had sold my precious Mercedes a couple of months earlier to raise some capital and I financed a sporty brand new Honda that I was quickly falling behind on in payments.

I had blown through most of the settlement money and I didn't really have a lot to show for it. I had purchased a rental property with almost no money down before leaving Winston-Salem but the cash flow wasn't enough to meet my expenses and my middling pay from the city just didn't seem to keep me afloat. I had gotten carried away with credit cards while in college like a lot of students did back then and now it was coming back to haunt me.

All of my circumstances seemed to indicate that it was time for a new beginning. As my departure date neared for my cross country drive from Atlanta to LA, my buddy Clancy informed me at the last minute, that he had purchased a return ticket for himself. I was happy that he was willing to make the journey because I had mentally prepared to go it alone.

We calculated our route and discussed how much the overall trip would cost us, including gas, lodging and food. However, once we hit the road, we only stopped for gas and food. For nearly three days, we blazed a hot trail across the country. We would take turns driving while the other slept. Whenever we would get to the point of exhaustion, we simply agreed to keep pushing instead of pulling over to rest at a hotel.

The longest part of the trip was Texas, it seemed like it took us a whole day just to drive through that state. There were long open roads scattered with road kill and occasional tumbleweeds that darted across the highway. I remember we stopped in Texas at an old rundown looking gas station with a diner on the side. When we went inside it looked like everybody in there was from a different era. Many of them had on overalls and they were moving slow and talking even slower. Clancy and I paid for our snacks and headed back to our car feeling like we had just been through a time warp; their pace of life was obviously quite different from where we had come from.

After a couple of days of watching the sun rise and fall over the thousands of miles of highway, we were elated to see a sign that read: Los Angeles 150 miles. Our journey was nearing an end and we couldn't wait to see LA. We were exhausted but as we began to approach the city, we became more energized. I stopped to call Tyrone and let him know that we were close. The last few miles felt like the last leg of a long distance marathon. When we finally pulled into Tyrone's driveway it felt like we should have received a trophy for perseverance and endurance. Tyrone couldn't believe how fast we made it to LA from the other side of the country. It was a grueling trip that I never wanted to repeat again but a few years later, I would find myself driving across the country once again en route to North Carolina.

Tyrone invited us inside and offered us a beer as a reward for our successful trip. Within a few hours, we both passed out on his floor, completely exhausted from our travels. The next morning we were rejuvenated and anxious to explore the city. Clancy had a friend from Atlanta who was living in LA, so we dropped him off at

her house in Hollywood. She was an aspiring actress who
was very attractive and I assumed that we wouldn't see
him for a couple of days.

Tyrone and I drove around the city for a bit and
then we jetted off to Paramount Studios where they were
filming a new TV show entitled *Claude's Crib* starring
Claude Brooks.   Tyrone had some friends who were
actors on the show and he also wanted to introduce me
to some of the writers on the set. When we pulled onto
the lot, I was amazed. I had never been on a studio lot
before but I tried not to show my excitement at the time.
We parked and then made our way into one of the large
studio lots where we entered through a long hallway
towards the actual TV set. As we walked up, I could
see cameras and crew members milling about.   There
was also an audience full of people seated in stadium-
like bleachers. However, *we* were on the floor where the
actors and the crew members were located and it felt like
I was truly in Hollywood. Tyrone introduced me to a few
people, including a tall guy who was a main character
on the show, he went by the name Chicago and he was
apparently a good friend of Shaq's because he had on a
diamond studded TWISM chain.

As I looked around, I saw someone who looked
familiar sitting in the audience. It was Clancy sitting
beside his pretty actor friend!   It was one of those
moments that you never forget. The odds of us running
into each other on a TV set in LA so soon after arriving

in LA was phenomenal; we gave each other the thumbs up as a sign of mutual admiration. I could tell that he was impressed with how quickly I had found myself on a TV set since my arrival.

Tyrone had a friend who was the costume designer for the TV show and he led me towards the back where her office was located. When we walked in, I immediately recognized Shari Headley, who played Eddie Murphy's love interest in *Coming to America*. She was the one that he eventually married in the end. Shari was looking good but I hadn't seen her in any new movie roles since the success of the movie. We all hung out for a few minutes, the three of them chatted away as I mostly sat and listened. I couldn't help but occasionally stare at Shari; she looked like the kind of girl that I would marry. I knew that she had recently gone through a divorce from Christopher Martin who was known as "Play" from the dynamic old school rap duo Kid n' Play. When we walked out of the office, I casually asked Shari if she wanted to have lunch sometime. She looked at me and said, "Thanks for the offer but I don't do lunch." Her response was quite surprising; I thought to myself, "Who doesn't eat lunch?" I was expecting her to simply say, "Thanks but no thanks." "Maybe Hollywood actresses don't eat lunch, maybe they're too busy?" I pondered. Then I realized that she probably wasn't interested in dating someone who couldn't help her career, especially someone who had just driven across the country in a

Honda. I wasn't upset, I was just curious to see what her response would be. I was proud of myself for asking -- at least I had the moxie to ask a beautiful actress out on a date.

The following day we had a basketball game in a gym in the Valley. It was a celebrity basketball league composed of actors, writers, crew members and ringers like myself. Tyrone had signed me up to play on his team which was representing the TV show, *Living Single* starring Queen Latifah. When we arrived, I was introduced to my new team and presented with a fresh looking jersey with "Living Single" emblazoned on the front.

We were playing against Martin Lawrence and his team from his hit TV show, *Martin*. Martin was nothing like I had imagined him to be. He was very stoic and stone faced. He wasn't the comedic personality that everyone was accustomed to seeing on TV. Martin had on his game face but he also seemed very medicated. I knew that he had an episode a few months earlier, where he ran into the middle of traffic with a gun in his hand and started shouting at people in their cars, which probably explains why he looked so medicated. .

The gym was packed with familiar looking faces from various TV shows including the guy who played "Tommy" on his show. There were also quite a few very attractive ladies there as well. Once the game started, it was obvious that Martin was intent on winning. He was hustling all over the court and every time he would score, the crowd went crazy. Martin wasn't very tall and he didn't have a great basketball game but he was definitely competitive. I eventually came off the bench and entered the game for the first time. I was a little bit nervous but that quickly dissipated as I began to get into the flow of the game. I didn't take a lot of shots initially, I was trying to play team ball. I was focused on playing defense and I was able to change the game in our favor by causing a couple of quick turnovers that resulted in easy layups.

The game was pretty close throughout the contest. It was late in the second half and we were down by three points with just a few seconds to go. Everyone was standing as Tyrone dribbled the ball at the top of the key while I was positioned a couple of feet behind the three point line. He put his head down and tried to penetrate through the lane but he was immediately cut off and then delivered a crisp pass directly to me. Without hesitation, I elevated and released my jump shot with perfect rotation and watched it sail through the basket -- all net! Everyone went wild! The game was tied but Martin's team didn't waste any time inbounding the ball and they were able to rush down court and score an easy layup. There was still a couple of seconds left, so we called a timeout and tried to come up with a winning game plan. The plan was for me to roll off of a pick set by our big man and then pop out for an open jump shot on the baseline. When we returned to the court, everyone took their places as we attempted to inbound the ball. Once the referee handed the ball to my teammate, it was clear that Martin's team was not going to allow me to get the ball. I was frantically trying to get open but there was no clear inbound lane, so my teammate lofted the ball to our big man who threw up a wild shot that bricked off the backboard. The horn sounded and the game was over, Martin's team had defeated us in a very close matchup. They stormed the court to celebrate their victory. After the game was over, we all shook hands in the middle of the court. I ran into Martin who slapped my hand and said, "Good shot boy." "Thanks man." I coolly replied.

I wasn't too upset about the loss. After all, my LA adventures had gotten off to a great start. I had asked a beautiful actress out on a date and hit a game tying three point shot in a celebrity basketball game, all within 48 hours of arriving in the city.

When we went outside the weather was incredible. There were people hanging outside in the parking lot. As I gazed through the parking lot, there were several expensive sports cars and I'm sure one of them belonged to Martin. My impression of what black people were like in LA was completely off. I had only seen videos of Snoop and Dr. Dre and they always seemed to be barbequing and cruising around in low riders, so I assumed that's what black people did in LA. It wasn't like that at all, most of the people I met were from the East Coast and they had come out to LA to pursue their dreams just like me.

There were a couple of cute girls that approached us who happened to know Tyrone. He gave them a hug and then he introduced us. "This is my boy B. Rose and his buddy Clancy -- B. just moved out here to be a writer." It was a great introduction; I loved hearing those words because it sounded more like a self- fulfilling prophecy than just a dream. One of the girls was instantly attracted to me. She was brown skin with braids and she had a very nice shape. "So where's your low rider? Aren't y'all having a barbeque today?" I said. She was cracking up laughing, "You're funny...and cute too."

Our conversation was interrupted by the sound of motorcycles revving their engines as they pulled into the parking lot. There were three girls each wearing colorful helmets that matched their racing bikes. When they flipped up their visors, I could see that the leader was Tichina Arnold who played "Pam" on the Martin show. She was laughing and talking to some of the guys from Martin's team. I heard her say, "Oh y'all won? That's wassup!"

I didn't expect to see her looking so macho and riding motorcycles. It was certainly quite a sight to see three attractive black ladies riding together like they were in a bike club.

I exchanged phone numbers with my new friend and then we headed out towards the car. Clancy seemed a bit in awe of how things were progressing. We joked on the way back about how different LA life was compared to Atlanta. I told him he should consider moving to LA but he was adamant about remaining in "A-town." A couple of days later I dropped him off at the airport and thanked him for making the drive with me.

As my first week in LA went by, I started getting adjusted to my new life. I was sleeping on Tyrone's couch and I was living out of my suitcases until I decided on my next move. He was planning on moving to a different apartment and he seemed upset that I wasn't very interested in being his roommate. After Clancy left town, his attitude started to change towards me. I recall there was a time when I returned to his house and asked if there were any messages for me. He angrily replied, "No! No messages for you." I was baffled by his response and I knew that I couldn't live with him so I wound up sleeping on another friend's couch named Eric. Eric was an actor who had been in a few Spike Lee movies and ironically he and I had a better rapport than Tyrone and myself at the time.

One of the first things that I noticed about their lifestyle as actors was that none of them were working. They didn't have regular jobs and I discovered that many of them lived off of unemployment checks until their next gig came along. Apparently, all they had to do was prove that they had recently been on a paid project and that would qualify them for a few weeks of unemployment checks. I couldn't imagine myself living like that, it just seemed too precarious. I was accustomed to working and getting regular paychecks. I admired them for their sacrifices but there was no guarantee that they would make it big as actors, so I decided to go get a job. Within a few days, I had successfully secured a position with a big healthcare company in the Valley as a claims reviewer. I recall one morning while leaving for work in my nice dress clothes, Eric asked me where I was going. I replied, "To work!" He had a puzzled look on his face as I left. I guess he thought I was just another wannabe actor who would spend my time playing video games and smoking until I landed a gig.

My plan was to work a regular job and work on my writing during my off hours, in hopes of selling a screenplay or landing a job on a TV show. I had no idea what the future was for me but I knew that I had to have some regular income. Things were going well for me on my new job and they even offered me a promotion to be a technical trainer after only being there for a few weeks. My job as a trainer involved standing in front of a classroom full of employees and training them on the newly implemented paperless software that was supposed to reduce overall costs.

Sometimes trainers can be a bit monotonous and boring but I made sure that my training sessions were lively and entertaining. I recall one day, I asked the trainees to introduce themselves and tell me something interesting about themselves. There was one lady who stated that she worked in Accounting and that she was a "Cancerian" which sounded kind of odd. I quickly replied, "Well I'm a Libra, so does that make me a librarian?" The classroom erupted with laughter!

That kind of humor always made the class a bit more enjoyable and it also gave me the confidence to stand in front of a crowd and deliver funny material, which eventually led to my desire to do stand-up comedy. I was never known as a class clown or a "cut up" but I was always good at coming up with punchlines.

My classes became so popular that people would come up to me afterwards and tell me how much they enjoyed "the show." After a while, the company began sending me to their regional office in Sacramento to conduct training there as well. I was happy with my job but I was still determined to become a successful writer. I was still working on new scripts and specs whenever I had free time.

I was making good money but I was still behind on some of my bills from my time in Atlanta, especially my car payment on my Honda. I was paranoid that I would walk out to my car and discover that it had been repossessed almost every day. One day after returning from the grocery store, I parked my car on the street, instead of in the garage where I normally parked. I dashed inside with my groceries and returned to the street about 20 minutes later. As I was walking towards where my car was parked, I felt a sense of panic because I didn't see my car. I continued walking down the sidewalk in hopes that I had forgotten where I parked. My car was *nowhere* to be found. I was in a complete state of panic. I walked back inside the apartment and convinced myself that the *next* time that I walked outside, my car would be where I left it.

I retraced my steps back to the street and the reality that my car was actually gone began to sink in. I wasn't sure what to do, I knew that I had not paid my car insurance in a while so if it *was* stolen; I would be on the hook for the remaining balance on a new car. My gut feeling was that it was stolen. The area that I was living in at the time was North Hollywood and it had a reputation for stolen cars. I rushed inside to call my insurance company to verify if I had still had coverage. I waited anxiously while the customer service rep put me on hold to research my policy. Finally, she came back and said, "Mr. Rose, you're in luck, your policy expires tonight at 12 midnight." I couldn't believe how fortunate I was! It was a moment that I will never forget. I felt as if a higher power had intervened on my behalf in my time of despair. I was supremely grateful because I knew that having my car stolen was probably the best thing that could have happened to me. Even though I was behind on payments, the insurance company still had to pay me fair value for the stolen vehicle. Not only did they have to pay me, they also had to pay for a rental car until I received my check. A couple of weeks later the insurance company told me that they found my car. They said that it was in downtown LA and it had been completely stripped down. Apparently, there was a ring of car thieves who used a tow truck to quickly jack up specific cars that were in high demand for parts and obviously Hondas were high on the list.

I went down to the location where my car was located and when I saw my car, I was in shock. They had completely stripped out the seats, the dashboard and almost everything else of value in the car. I had a sentimental attachment to the car because it brought me safely all the way from Atlanta to LA. I looked through the car to find some pictures that I left in the glove box but they had taken those as well.

The stolen car episode gave me reassurance that I was destined to be in LA. I had an unshakeable confidence that God was watching out for me. I used the insurance money to buy an older model Nissan that leaked oil but it was mostly reliable for my needs. I had come a long way from my days as a fly guy who drove a new Mercedes and lived in a fancy apartment. I was now sleeping on a friend's dirty couch and driving a "bucket." The one thing that kept me motivated was my job and my writing. I could have left the couch behind sooner but I was sacrificing and saving my money to get a better place.

I eventually saved up enough money to get my first apartment in LA. It was a really nice two bedroom condo in Sherman Oaks, it was spacious with a large patio and a fireplace. One of the guys in our crew became my roommate. His name was Bill and his brother-in-law was Ernest Dickerson, who directed *Juice* starring Tupac and Omar Epps. Ernest had also directed a movie called *Bulletproof* starring an up-and-coming comedic actor named Adam Sandler along with funnyman Damon Wayans. Bill had developed a close relationship with Adam and his buddies. One day he asked me if I wanted to go up to Adam's house and play basketball. My response was, "Hell yea!"

So we headed up to Adam's house in my car, I was excited about meeting him and playing basketball with his crew. He lived in the exclusive neighborhood of Bel Air where we had to drive up several steep roads to get to his house. Once we arrived, I was surprised at how conservative his house looked. It reminded me of the Brady Bunch house, but much bigger with ivy covering much of the front. In the driveway, I saw a black Cadillac and two other American made cars. I was expecting to see a bunch of exotic sports cars, but I later learned that Adam didn't drive those types of cars. We parked in the driveway and I followed Bill around the side of the house towards the back area which was completely different from the entrance. As we walked into the backyard, I could see a large tennis court at the bottom of a slope with basketball rims on each end. There was also a Jacuzzi and a pool that overlooked a spectacular view of a tree lined ravine. It was an enormous backyard and I could see a few of his friends already on the court and warming up to play.

We walked down towards the court and Bill quickly introduced me to Adam's friends. Their names were Dante, Laughlin, Nick and Johnnie. If you've seen a lot of Sandler's movies, these were the same guys that appeared in almost all his films. I would later discover that each of them were not only friends with Adam but they also worked for him at his film company, Happy Madison. They all seemed like cool guys and we joked around while shooting baskets and waiting on Adam to come down. Finally, I saw Adam walk onto the court wearing his basketball gear.

He approached Bill and jovially said in his iconic and gruff voice, "Billlly! My man, good to see you."

He then made a beeline towards me and before he said anything, I jokingly said, "Happy Madison wassup!?"

He laughed and quickly shook my hand. "Glad you could make it, you're a friend of Billy's huh?" he said. "Yea Bill is my boy." I replied. "Good good, we're gonna have some fun out here tonight." He said picking up a basketball and firing it towards the rim.

We all started getting loose and running up and down the court shooting baskets in preparation for our game. After everyone had worked up a sweat, we picked teams. Bill and I were on separate teams and Adam was on my team. Once the game started, it was clear that they played hard. Everyone was hustling and playing defense. I was kind of surprised at the intensity of our backyard pick-up game. Adam made a couple of layups and I hit a few early jumpers as I started to get into a rhythm. Bill was guarding me and he was hitting a few shots as well.

Their team had driven down court and missed a layup. I snatched the ball out of the air and started dribbling down court when one of the guys suddenly tried to steal the ball. I quickly dribbled the ball behind my back, took a few more steps and drained a long three point shot. Suddenly, I heard a voice shout from outside the gate, "Nice shot!" I turned around and was surprised to see Dustin Hoffman and his son standing at the top of the hill. "Thanks!" I shouted. He nodded in approval.

"Not bad huh?" Adam yelled to him. Dustin replied with a thumbs-up.

As the game continued, I started getting more aggressive. Adam was passing me the ball and looking for me to score. I got into a zone and hit three consecutive pull up jumpers. Bill was getting flustered and things started to get chippy. We were trash talking each other as we went down the court. Our team eventually won the game and afterwards Adam jokingly said, "I see Billy and Barrington going at it, they might need Uncle Adam to give'em both the old one-two." He started imitating a boxer and punching the air as we all cracked up laughing.

It was classic Sandler, there were very few times over the next few months that he wasn't "Happy Madison." He was always in character and he seemed to be a genuinely nice person, although there were a couple of times while in his studio at Sony when he was *all* business as he reviewed the footage for one of his upcoming films. There was no smiling or goofing off, he seemed like a different person when it was business time. I guess that's how someone can build up a fortune worth over $300 million and still be considered a nice guy.

After a couple of games of basketball that night, we all retreated to the pool and Jacuzzi area. It seemed like that was their typical thing to do after they played. Adam was swimming around in the pool and I was sitting in the Jacuzzi with a couple of his buddies. Someone had brought out some cigars and I started to feel like Tony Montana from Scarface, so I did my imitation of him while puffing on a stogie. "Joo know what a hasa is Frank? Dat's a pig dat don't fly straight." They were laughing at my impromptu impression. My comedic side usually comes out when I'm around silly people. Adam was smoking a cigar and doing silly impressions of other people and somehow the subject of Magic Johnson's new talk show came up. I chimed in and said that he would be the first talk show host to use subtitles throughout his show -- laughter ensued! I'm a fan of Magic but during that time he wasn't very articulate and he didn't seem to have a talk show type of personality, with quick wit and clever punchlines.

As we were sitting in the Jacuzzi, I was surprised when one of the guys fired up a small pipe and passed it around. I took a hit and it almost immediately sent my head into outer space. I should have known that celebrities didn't smoke regular weed. Everyone took a hit except Adam; he was hanging on the side of the pool enjoying his cigar. Of all the times that I would eventually hang out with him and his crew, I don't recall seeing him smoke, although I was told that he does occasionally partake.

Later on we went inside to chill out, everyone was hanging out in his kitchen talking about wrestling (the fake kind). Adam was a big fan of wrestling and we started talking about our favorites like Wahoo McDaniels, Tony Atlas, Ricky Steamboat and Rowdy Rod Piper. His assistant Laughlin was showing me around the house and we eventually wound up in the music room just off the main living room. They had a makeshift stage set up in the room, complete with drums, guitars and a microphone. Adam and Dante followed us into the room and began preparing like they were about to play a song. Adam grabbed his guitar and Dante jumped on the drums and I decided to grab the microphone.

Adam started strumming and Dante was tapping on
the drums, attempting to create a harmonious vibe with
Adam's guitar playing. Once the sound started coming
together, I abruptly started singing. It was a strange
feeling because I had never sang into a microphone and
what came out sounded *really* good. I wouldn't say that I
have a phenomenal voice but I can certainly hold a note.
Bill jumped up and ran into the room to see who was
singing and he was surprised to see me belting out a song
on the microphone. I was singing the words to a poem
that I had written a while back. It was kind of a dark
poem and even though my voice sounded good, Adam
started to clown me.

He started mocking me by singing, "Barrington that
was the most depressing song I've ever heard, ever ever
heard." I started laughing as he and Dante continued
their playing. Their lives seemed so content, I couldn't
help but admire how privileged they were to indulge
themselves in whatever made them happy -- whether it
was music, film and even sports.

During that time, Adam had an annual July 4th
party at his house and he invited us to come by and invite
a few friends. On the day of the party, Bill and I showed
up along with a friend named Cordova who had recently
moved to LA from New York. Cordova has always been a
character, his personality was bigger than life and he was
always doing something to keep people laughing. The
funny thing about Cordova was that he looked like Eddie

Murphy with dreadlocks and he was just as funny as Eddie. When we arrived there were a few people already there, including a lot of A-list celebrities. The backyard had been transformed into an outdoor party atmosphere. They had several tables with white linen tablecloths and white folding chairs to match.

As we were walking in, I immediately noticed Brad Pitt -- he was hanging out by a tall fence with some friends. He looked like he had a lot on his mind and just a few minutes later, I saw him trying to climb up the fence! It was bizarre to see him looking so distant and trying to scale the fence. Later on, I heard that he had just broken up with Gwyneth Paltrow and perhaps he was just letting off some steam.

There were lots of people roaming around the grounds and everyone seemed to have a drink in their hands. We ran into Adam's buddies – Dante, Laughlin, Nick and Johnnie when we approached the house. They were all glad to see us and welcomed us to the party. I went into the kitchen to find a drink and I saw a guy named Joshi who was a really cool white guy with dreadlocks. I had seen him at the house a couple of times before and as we walked in, he was meticulously molding cookie dough to prepare for the oven. There was another guy in the kitchen that I also recognized; he was an aspiring wrestler who looked like Stone Cold Steve Austin. Joshi offered me one of his "special" cookies and I politely refused. The wrestler on the other hand was eating them by the handful. I just shook my head because I knew that his night was not going to end well. About an hour later, I ran into him outside and his eyes were blood shot red and he was barely coherent.

After I grabbed my drink, I wandered into the living room area to see who was there. I immediately saw David Spade who was with two beautiful blondes and I also saw Stephen Dorff, who I initially thought was John Cougar Mellencamp. I grabbed a seat on the couch to chill out and enjoy the party when I noticed Henry Winkler walking around and introducing himself to some of the guests. I couldn't believe that he was there -- I had always been a fan of "The Fonz." He walked over and introduced himself to me by saying, "Hi I'm Henry Winkler." I stood up, shook his hand and replied, "Man I know who you are, you're my idol." "Well thank you very much, nice to meet you." I was in awe that I had met "The Fonz." Of all the celebrities I met that day, he was by far my favorite. Adam walked in a few minutes later and started teasing David Spade about the way he was dancing with his two blondes. He and David seemed to be really good friends, probably from their days together on SNL.

Adam shook my hand and told me that he was glad I could make it. I've never really been awestruck by celebrities but this party was packed with so many famous faces it was difficult not to feel as though it were a dream. I started to reminisce about my long, grueling cross country road trip and how it all seemed to be worth the adventure so far.

A few minutes later, I stood up and wandered outside to see Cordova sitting at a table and having a very animated discussion with Jim Carrey. Jim was laughing hard at Cordova's antics which was a complete twist of irony because Jim Carrey was usually the guy making everyone laugh. I took a seat beside them and enjoyed their back and forth comedic banter. Seated across from us was Drew Barrymore and some of her girlfriends, they were also enjoying the impromptu comedy sketch that was taking place between Jim and Cordova.

Cordova was one of those guys that had all the talent and potential in the world to become a major star but he never honed his act and took his career seriously. Hollywood is filled with those types of people -- "Arrested development" is the term that's used to describe them. But as a comedian friend once told me, "Funny people are not always comedians, it takes work to be a comic."

A while later, a girl that I been dating from work named Jasmine arrived at the party. I had called her from Adam's house and told her to come over. Jasmine was an Armenian girl who always dressed very nice. A lot of the women at work were envious of her finely tailored outfits. Jasmine was a bit short with dark hair and a tight curvaceous body. Physically we weren't the ideal couple but we enjoyed each other's company. When she arrived, she was in complete awe. She couldn't believe how many A-list celebrities she saw when she walked in. I knew that inviting her to the party would make a great impression on her.

I walked her into the kitchen to get a drink where we ran into David Spade. She was a big fan of his and immediately asked him if he would take a picture with her. He didn't seem too happy about taking pictures but he reluctantly took a photo with her. After that, she was over the moon! We chilled outside by the pool as it became dark. She was asking me how I knew Adam, "So this is the life you're living when you're not pretending to be a trainer."

We spent a few more minutes talking when suddenly a guy at the party decided to strip down and jump into the pool naked. He made a big splash which made Jasmine jump. "Did you see that guy!?" she shouted. We both laughed about how crazy the whole party seemed.

After about an hour, the party had thinned out and Jasmine and I decided to leave together. We drove towards Malibu and parked along the cliffs overlooking the ocean. She was still star struck from our evening together as we started making out. Jasmine decided that she wanted to thank me in a special way. She started going down on me in the car which felt awesome as I gazed out the window at the waves crashing against the rocks down below. It was an unforgettable night with a great ending.

Hanging out with Adam Sandler
at Longest Yard wrap party.

Playing hoops with Woody Harrelson
at Sports Club LA.

My first (and only) date with Teri Polo
(Meet the Fockers).

Hanging with Tichina Arnold at NBA
All-Star game in LA.

*Steve Kroft after filming episode of
CBS 60 Minutes.*

Pete Rose on set of Between Brothers TV show.

Chapter 14

LA Hustle

My job at the healthcare company came to an abrupt end. They were having layoffs and my division was one of the first to feel the effects. Suddenly, I was without a job and anxious to find new employment. I decided to drive to a job fair in Orange County which was about an hour and a half from the Valley. Once I arrived, there were several different companies with booths set up inside the arena. I stopped and talked to several people and apparently someone from a staffing agency received my resume and decided to call me the next day. They invited me to meet with the hiring managers in their local branch in the Valley.

When I showed up for the interview, I was surprised to meet with a young African-American guy who was about my age named Lawrence. We had a great interview during which he explained to me what it meant to be a recruiter. Afterwards, he introduced me to the rest of his team which also consisted of two other African-American guys who were very tall; their names were Lutrell and

Ahlee. The other members of the team were, a well-dressed Hispanic guy named Christian and a really cool guy named Carlos Friedman. Carlos was funny because he had monopolized all of the internet porn companies in the Valley as his clients. They seemed like a cool bunch of guys that were eager to make money and I felt like it would be a great place to work.

A couple of weeks later, I showed up for my new job with the agency. They showed me to my desk which was right in the middle of the bullpen, where I could hear recruiters all around me on the phone pitching their respective candidates on our job openings. I was initially hired to recruit for a couple of senior account manager's job openings but within a couple of months they were recruiting for me. This was during the days of the Y2K hysteria, when a lot of companies were struggling to hire enough programmers to rewrite their legacy systems to prevent a meltdown of their entire operating systems. It was also the beginning of the dot com boom of the early 2000's when almost anybody with a good idea and enough financing could start up an online company, go public and get filthy rich. It was the era of easy money that gave birth to companies like Google, Yahoo, Doubleclick, Askjeeves and a host of others. I had managed to monopolize almost all of the dot com companies that were operating in LA. I was very aggressive about approaching them and selling them on why they should work with me. Within just a couple of months, I had senior recruiters within our company calling me on a daily basis, eager to know how I was generating so many new accounts. It was actually quite simple, I read the newspapers and business magazines daily to find out who had received financing and then I would call, congratulate them and set up a subsequent visit to discuss how I could help them achieve their staffing goals.

The other strategy that I used to my advantage was a constant monitoring our internal database. Every time a new candidate was entered into the database, I would review their qualifications within minutes of their disposition and before my coworkers could call me to pitch their candidate; I would already be in the process of scheduling an interview for their candidate. This super aggressive strategy endeared me to a lot of nascent recruiters but it also created some envy and derision from some of the senior recruiters. They couldn't understand how I was able to get up to speed so quickly and become a top producing recruiter in just a few months.

My second month as a recruiter I generated $80,000 in business for the agency and I was selected as the recruiter with the highest percentage gain from the previous month. As a reward, I was selected to attend our annual top achievers retreat in Orlando, FL as a rookie. My first year in the business I brought in $400,000 in recruiting fees and made $140,000 for myself which was the most I had ever made in my career. It felt great to be making money and along with being the alpha male in my group, came lots of attention from a few female recruiters. After hours, a lot of recruiters in our office would go across the street and have drinks and dinner at the local restaurant. Drinks would be flowing and it wasn't unusual to see coworkers sneaking out together at the end of the night.

There were four attractive girls that worked in my division and within a few weeks, I had slept with all of them. Two of them were beautiful Asian girls who were close friends, then there was a thick, light skinned freak named Adele and the other girl was half black, half Asian and 100 percent sexy. Her name was Ivana. Ivana had a great ass and she would always wear the tightest dress pants to work. She didn't dress very classy but she always looked sexy. Prior to Ivana's arrival, I had an on-going sexual relationship with the two Asian girls and an occasional hook up session with Adele. No one in the office knew about my secret office romances. One day I walked into my office and looked around to see all of the girls sitting together in a cubicle. The fact that I had slept with all of them hit me like a lightning bolt. During that time, I clearly wasn't exercising any type of moral constraint when it came to the women in my office. I was the lion who was spreading his seed all over the jungle. They were attracted to me because I was making a lot of money and they needed my help. I recall one weekend while working in the office on a Saturday, one of the Asian girls surprisingly showed up for work wearing black, tight fitting yoga pants. Her desk was located right next to mine and we were the only people in the office that day. She had a really nice body with thick legs, nice round bottom and a firm chest. I was standing up talking on the phone and I glanced over my cubicle to see that she had propped her legs up on her desk pointed directly towards me and I could see the full outline of her bulging vagina as she smiled at me with a look that could kill. I knew exactly what she wanted.

Once I finished up my sales call, I casually sauntered over to her desk and started rubbing on her legs. She had such great legs, she wasn't built like a typical Asian girl, she was shapely and busty. I continued rubbing on her legs and her ass but I was hesitant to go too far, out of fear that someone would walk in on us. After a few minutes of fondling each other, we suddenly heard a door slam in the front office. My heart started racing! I was fully erect and on the verge of having sex with her right there in the office.

I scrambled back to my desk as she quickly gathered herself. A few moments later, one of the guys who worked in the Accounting division walked in looking for a bag he'd left behind from the previous day. We tried to act nonchalant as the coworker approached our area. "Working on Saturday huh?" he said. We both smiled, nodded and pretended to be busy. A couple of minutes later the intruder was gone. "Close call huh?" I said. "Very!" she replied.

Later on she invited me to her friend's house who happened to be our mutual coworker. She was house sitting for the other Asian girl that I was sleeping with but she had no idea about our secret affair. Until that point, we had only had car sex. Sometimes after work, we would go to her car and have awkward sex in the front seat of her coupe. She told me that she was separating from her husband and that they had not had sex in quite a while. When we arrived at our friend's apartment, she showed me around while I pretended like I had never been there before. In fact, I had been there *several* times before.

As we lay in her bed, I couldn't help but think about how ironic it was to have slept with both of them in the same bed without their knowledge. Finally, I couldn't contain myself – so I told her about me and the other coworker. She was shocked but she wasn't upset, considering that she wasn't officially divorced from her husband yet.

Ivana and I started seeing each other almost immediately after she started with the agency. We both had the same type of personality; she was aggressive and eager to make her mark so we were naturally attracted to each other. We started spending a lot of time together outside of work and it became obvious to almost everyone in our office that we were dating. After a while, I started having serious feelings for her but I wasn't sure if the feeling was mutual. Ivana was immature and I started getting the feeling that she was playing me. She started making up excuses about why she couldn't come over to my house. As a result, our relationship at work and at home began to deteriorate. I felt like she was using me to help her career and that our relationship was really just a farce.

One day, I was asking her to come over to my house but she kept saying that the drive was too far. I knew that she had started spending time with our other coworker Adele who lived two blocks from my house and that they were becoming very close. I knew that Adele was bisexual and that she had a crush on a couple of girls in the office. I gave up on convincing Ivana to come over but my spider senses told me to drive by Adele's house to see if Ivana's car was there. As I pulled into the driveway, I saw Ivana standing in the parking lot talking to Adele. She was wearing Daisy Dukes and holding a cheap, yellow, plastic flower in her hand. All of my questions were answered at that moment. I slowly pulled up to them and rolled down my window and casually said to her, "Too far to drive huh?" She and Adele were surprised to see me and they knew that I had busted up their secret romance. It was heartbreaking to lose a girl to another girl. It was difficult to fathom the idea that she preferred to be with her instead of with me.

The next few weeks at work were really difficult. I had decided to ignore Ivana and pressure her to leave the company. I had a scorched earth policy towards her and anyone who dared to help her. Most of her success was because I had gone overboard to help her make money but that came to a screeching halt. I no longer returned her emails or phone calls or any request she had for assistance. Our other coworkers could feel the tension between us and it made the work environment very awkward.

I was so intent on forcing her to leave that I became consumed with the idea and it started to affect my overall state of mind. I had become a monster. I was no longer a pleasant person to be around at work. I had also started feeling slighted about the amount of money I was making for the agency compared to my salary. The combination of my scorned feelings towards Ivana and my angry disposition towards my company made me a pariah in the office. People started complaining to management that I was being an asshole and that I was difficult to work with. I didn't really care what they thought because we were all working in a dog-eat-dog environment and I knew that management wasn't going to reprimand me because I was their star recruiter.

Eventually Ivana left the company, but by that time a lot of my friends were also leaving. Recruiting is just like any other sales job; there's always a high turnover and new faces all the time. The good times that we had together as a team were over. A few of my fellow coworkers had left to start up their own agencies which was something that I also began to consider.

I was still generating a lot of money for the company and for myself so I decided to go buy me a new car. I went to the local dealership in Beverly Hills and picked out a black BMW 5 series with sweet factory rims. It was definitely an upgrade from my current ride and it felt like a reward for all of my hard work.

As the neophyte recruiters came on board, management was encouraging me to take a leadership role within the company but I wasn't interested in management, I just wanted to make money. I didn't love recruiting; it was simply a means to an end for me. I had a Machiavellian type approach to my career and I decided that I would use the money I was making to help me pursue my Hollywood dreams.

After hours, I was still hanging out with Adam Sandler and Kadeem Hardison. My close connections with them made me even more determined to achieve my goals. I hadn't driven all the way to LA to become a recruiter, I wanted to be a writer or maybe even a director. My life was a dichotomy between the fast paced world of sales and the dreams of Hollywood. I assumed that my persistence and determination would eventually open up a few doors for me to pursue my dreams. Everything around me was pointing towards success; I was making great money and mingling with A-list celebrities at night.

Kadeem had recently started filming a new TV show called *Between Brothers* starring himself, Dondre

Whitfield, along with the off-the-wall comedic actor Tommy Davidson. Now that I was part of the crew, I would often hang out on set and mingle with some of the pretty actresses and hob knob with special guests like Pete Rose, Barry Bonds and Sally Richardson. I definitely gained an appreciation for the film making process, it was the first time that I had unlimited access to the making of a TV show. The energy was always exciting; everyone seemed to be pumped up and in good spirits. There was usually a live audience and occasionally Tommy Davidson would entertain them with his crazy antics. Sometimes there were long nights when filming would go on into the late evening. You could see some of the actors and the crew getting fatigued but Tommy Davidson *never* seemed to get tired. He was always up and energetic. In between shots, he would be cracking jokes with the crew and making fun of the crowd. He once told my ex roommate that he looked like a dirty Q-tip. We all just busted out in hysterical laughter. He didn't mind calling people out and no one was off limits. His energy definitely made the long nights a lot more tolerable.

Even though I wasn't getting paid to stand around and observe, I felt like I was getting a valuable education in how things work in Hollywood. I was hoping that Kadeem's new show would be a success and that I could eventually get a job as a writer and maybe do a little acting. Unfortunately, the show was canceled by the studio and only lasted a few episodes. However, the experience of being on set for those few episodes was transformative. After the show was canceled, I was even more determined and focused on my writing. I had also recently met a few writers who were working on hit TV shows.

One of the people that I met was a really cool white guy named Matt who was a writer on Queen Latifah's show *Living Single*. A couple of the writers from the show were also on my celebrity league basketball team. One day Matt invited me over to check out the show while they were filming. He was impressed with the fact that I had written a couple of full length screenplays, which I thought was odd because I assumed that most TV writers were also diligently working on their screenplays when they weren't taping.

When I arrived on set, he quickly introduced me to some of the writers. One of the first people that I met was the showrunner. She was a cute and friendly white girl that I instantly clicked with. Matt also introduced me to a black girl named Linda, she was modestly attractive with an oversized chest and an ill-fitting bra that could barely contain her overflowing breasts. Her look wasn't very classy and I was somewhat surprised at how sexual she appeared to be while working on set.

I was also surprised to discover that she was the only black girl writing on a show that featured four African-American women. Yvette Lee Bowser was the show creator and she was the first African-American woman to develop her own prime-time series. I'm sure she was involved in the writing process but there were only a couple of black writers on the show and the rest were white males like Matt.

During those days, I discovered that black writers were only recently given the opportunity to write for TV shows. There were a few black writers prior to the success of shows like *Living Single, Martin, Moesha,* and *The Cosby Show* in the late 90's -- but it was this era in black television that would give a black woman an opportunity to create her own TV show and open up doors for African-American writers. I was very surprised to see so many white faces behind the scenes of a hugely successful black TV show. It was hard to fathom how a white male could relate to the everyday life of an urban professional black woman, but it didn't matter because they were white and they were selected to lead the creative writing process. However, it was *very* rare to see a black writer on a successful white TV show like *Friends* or *Seinfeld.*

Matt took me down to the set where I saw Queen Latifah, Kim Coles, Kim Fields and the lovely Erika Alexander congregating during a break in filming. He didn't introduce me to them because I don't think he knew them very well but I could see them whispering and gazing over in my direction. I was flattered to be receiving attention from them as they were probably trying to figure out if I was an actor or maybe a new writer.

Once the taping started up again, Matt took me back upstairs to the writer's room. When we walked into the cozy office space overlooking the TV set, the cute showrunner welcomed me and said, "Come on in, you havin' fun?" "Yea this is great...so this is the war room huh?" I replied. "Yes! That's exactly what this is." She said with a chuckle. The other writers in the room seemed to agree that "war room" was an appropriate description. My casual demeanor and timely comments helped to impress their team and I started to feel as though I were on an observational interview. Getting a job as a writer in Hollywood is really more about making the right connections and leveraging those contacts; that's something that I had not been able to do since I was working full time as a recruiter.

Even though I had written a few screenplays, I began to realize that in order for me to land a job on a TV show, I had to start meeting the right people. Most of the writers that I met were not really avid writers and many of them had never written a screenplay. It seemed like they were passive writers who had connections with the producer, the director or another writer on the show. Until this point, I had assumed that getting a job as a writer was predicated on the quality of my work but I soon realized that Hollywood was a town built on connections. I also noticed that the most successful people were the ones who were willing to do *anything* to make it. I admire people who decide to take a chance in life and pursue their dreams but I've never been the type to do *anything* to succeed. I also didn't like the fact that my viability as a writer would be determined by having the right Hollywood connections.

I was making close to 200K per year in my recruiting job and I wasn't anxious to give up my income for a fledgling chance at becoming a TV writer. After all the sacrifices I had made to get to LA and become a writer, I started to question whether or not the journey was worthwhile.

Chapter 15

Hollywood Burn

I decided to keep working as a recruiter and focus on my writing, in hopes of selling one of my scripts. Based on the research I had done, a really good script could be sold for around $250,000 or much more depending on the writer's track record.

Shortly after my arrival in LA, I had written a short film called *Perfect Cuts.* It was named after my favorite barbershop in my hometown of Winston-Salem. I had given the script to a couple of trusted friends who were writers and their feedback was phenomenal. They all had very positive comments and congratulated me on writing such a compelling short story. Around that time, I had also met a young music producer who I will call "Kojo." I knew that he and his dad were well connected in the music industry and that they were managing some of the biggest names in R&B at the time.

During that period, I didn't have a literary agent. I had been trying for a number of years to retain an agent, but in Hollywood getting an agent is a game of Catch 22. The number one rule in signing with a literary agent in LA is: *You must have a referral from a current representative of the* agency; that person could be another writer, director or an actor but if you don't have those contacts they will not read your script. I had A-list contacts in LA but none of them knew me well enough to introduce me to their agent.

During my time in LA, I was briefly signed to the Irv Schechter Agency through my connection with director Ernest Dickerson. Ernest was renting a really nice home in Hancock Park from one of the senior agents and he decided to "back pocket" me as a way of keeping good faith with Ernest. A "back pocket" arrangement basically means that I was able to use theiragency cover pages with their logo emblazoned on top for my script submissions to the movie studios -- without agency representation it would be very difficult to get the big studios to read my material.

I had copyrighted my script and gave it to Kojo in hopes that he liked it enough to consider producing a feature length movie based on my characters. A few weeks went by and I ran into Kojo at the gym and asked him what he thought about my script. "Aww man I really liked it, I'm going to talk to my dad and see if we can do a project together." He replied. I was elated that he was interested in working with me to produce my screenplay. I started feeling as though I would finally get my big break. However, over the next few months, I rarely heard from Kojo and whenever I saw him at the gym, he never wanted to discuss the project. I decided that it was just a tease so I continued on with my work and my writing. About a year later, while watching TV, I saw a trailer for a new movie called *Barbershop* that looked very familiar. I noticed some of the scenes from the movie were similar to my storyline. My immediate reaction was that they had stolen my short script and produced a feature length movie. I hastily researched the internet to determine who was associated with the film. I discovered that the movie was produced by Ice Cube's film company and that one of Kojo's artists was on the soundtrack. After researching the name of the director, Tim Story, I discovered that he had directed a couple of music videos for Kojo.

At that moment, I was in disbelief. I decided to call up Kojo and ask him some questions about his involvement with the film. The following is my best recollection of our conversation:

"Hey Kojo this is Barrington, I wanted to ask you some questions about this new *Barbershop* movie."

"Questions!? Questions!? I got some mother fuckin' questions for you!"

"What!?" I replied.

"Yea I got some questions, like can I fuck yo' wife?"

"What are you talking about fool?" I said.

"I made my money the right way and cats always tryin' to claim that somehow they got somethin' to do with it."

"Look man, I don't care about any of that nonsense. I just want to know what's up with my script and this movie."

Suddenly, I heard his dad in the background asking what was wrong. I heard him say, "This nigga callin' me about this *Barbershop* shit."

At that moment, I knew for certain that he had stolen my script. Why would someone who's innocent react so violently? He was probably shocked that I caught him off guard and had the audacity to question him.

When we hung up the phone, I was in a state of shock. Not only had I realized that my script had been stolen but I was also extremely disrespected by someone who I once admired. Kojo had always been lighthearted and easy going whenever I talked to him and I knew that he had graduated from a top university, however, during our heated phone call -- he was sounding like a bully and a gangster.

I called up a couple of my writer friends and told them about my conversation with Kojo. They had already seen the trailer and immediately informed me that they thought it was based on my script. I felt instantly validated and I began to consider my legal options but I noticed that although Kojo's artist was on the soundtrack, his name was nowhere to be found on the film.

I knew it would be difficult to sue him directly without being able to prove his involvement. In legal terms, I needed conclusive evidence or a "smoking gun" to tie him to the film. As the weeks went by, I came to the realization that I couldn't sue him or the studio because I didn't have enough incontrovertible evidence to present a strong case of copyright infringement -- not to mention -- the studio had an army of lawyers on their side. Furthermore, without conclusive evidence tying Kojo or his dad to the film; the studio could simply claim that they had no connection to them. Hollywood is a town built upon lies and I knew that it would be near impossible to expose the real truth about how they discovered my script.

The other problem with a potential copyright lawsuit was that the movie was not completely based upon my storyline. After anxiously waiting to see the movie in the theaters, I walked out feeling like they had borrowed certain characters and scenes from my script but had purposely rewritten them to avoid a possible lawsuit from me. One of the scenes involved a young lady who was dating one of the barbers. She came up to the shop and started destroying his car which was parked outside because she thought he was cheating on her. In my script, a young lady comes to the shop and gets into a big argument with him because she had just found out she's pregnant.

The wise older barber played by Cedric the Entertainer was also based on my character. There was a scene in B*arbershop 2: Back in Business*, where he convinces an angry young man to not burn down their *barbershop*. In my script, there's a scene at the end where the old wise barber convinces an angry young man to put down his gun.

The first Barbershop movie generated over $77 million at the box office. The sequel generated over $65 million and spawned a spinoff movie for Queen Latifah called *Beauty Shop* and a subsequent TV show. The total worldwide revenue for the franchise was over $243 million as of 2005. As the original writer and creator of the storyline, I have yet to receive one single dime for my creative efforts.

Many people have asked me why I chose not to sue. It's difficult to explain to them the legal hurdles that I would have had to endure. In order to win a copyright lawsuit against a major movie studio, you have to not only be able to prove that certain elements were copied but also endure a long legal battle against an army of attorneys determined to defeat your claim – even though they know their client is at fault. I've often wondered if not suing was the best decision but I realized a couple of years later that I would need all of my amateur legal skills and prowess to defeat another giant disruption in my life – which is something I will discuss later in this book.

I recently discovered while writing this chapter of my book, that Kojo and his father were under federal investigation for fraud and false tax filings relating to several artists that were on their record label.

I had also written a script entitled *Mafia Misfits* around that same time and I recall submitting it to a few different production companies. About a year later, I just happened to be watching the animated movie *Shark Tale* which was produced by Dreamworks when I noticed a familiar storyline. While watching this movie, I suddenly realized that the premise of the movie was almost *exactly* like my storyline in *Mafia Misfits*. My story was based on a shady character named Frankie who was a New York street hustler who everybody called "Frankie the Con." He suddenly discovers that his biological father is a notorious well-known gangster who wants him to be part of his "family business" before he passes away.

So Frankie is reluctantly brought into the "family business" by his father's henchmen. His first assignment was to meet with the Godfather of their rival family who suddenly dies from a heart attack during his visit. People start to assume that Frankie intentionally killed the rival Godfather and he quickly transforms from "Frankie the Con" to "Franco the Don."

Shark Tale is based on a very similar storyline about a care free shark who suddenly finds himself the center of attention after allegedly killing a well-known gangster shark which was played by Robert DeNiro. The main character of the animated movie transforms from being a lovable loser to being a respected gangster. See any similarities? So did I, but there was one major problem with pursuing a copyright lawsuit; I had never sent my script to Dreamworks. To further compound my situation, I had no idea who could have presented my script to their studio.

As an unrepresented writer, I had submitted my work to a few different production companies and only received a couple of responses, including one from Danny DeVito's company and a well-known company called Working Title Films. Each of them seemed mildly interested in the script because of its unique storyline but it never materialized into a meeting.

So once again I was faced with the dilemma of having my script stolen and being unable to demonstrate how the studio procured my manuscript. I had fallen victim to one of Hollywood's dirtiest little secrets – scripts are stolen *all* the time. Studio executives and production companies will often conspire to pilfer the work of an unestablished writer and dare them to pursue legal action, while they make out like bandits, generating millions of dollars from stolen ideas.

One of the most famous examples of a stolen screenplay was the script for the hit movie *Coming to America*, which was originally written by well-known writer Art Buchwald. Buchwald had presented his script to Jeffrey Katzenburg who was with Paramount studios and had received an option contract for the studio to turn his script into a feature length movie.

About a year later, Paramount had begun to shoot a movie based upon the same premise that Buchwald had created for his script. Buchwald sued and eventually accepted a settlement from the studio. The difference between me and Buchwald is that he was an established writer with documented proof of meetings and contracts with the studio. I, on the other hand was simply a writer trying to break into the industry by utilizing any means necessary to get my material read by the studios.

It's a common conundrum that many new writers face when trying to get their material read; I had no agent and no proof of how the studios received my material. I had taken my scripts to several literary agencies but they all rejected me because I didn't have an "agency referral." Despite having A-list connections, I was still just an outsider looking for a way in. The ironic thing about signing with an agent was that they usually didn't sign a writer unless there was already some interest in your work from a studio. I had assumed that literary agents signed writers based upon their potential but I soon discovered that signing with an agent was really more of a perfunctory process once the studio had indicated interest in your project. In my case, the studios were obviously interested in my projects, but they weren't interested in having me involved -- or sharing in the profits.

Chapter 16

What Happens in Vegas

I was disheartened by my Hollywood experiences and I decided to stop writing for a while and focus on my recruiting career *and* on having some fun. I had met a girl named Lysette at the grocery store who was about my age and had recently broken up with her boyfriend. We went out on a couple of dates and we seemed to get along fairly well. My birthday was approaching soon, so I decided to book a trip for the two of us to Las Vegas. On our short flight from LA to Vegas, we had a couple of drinks on the plane and Lysette started to get frisky. She was rubbing on my penis during the flight and telling me how she couldn't wait to get the hotel room. I had to calm myself down before deplaning, there's nothing more awkward than getting off a plane with a boner.

We checked into the beautiful and recently built Venetian hotel right on the Vegas Strip. It was a sprawling oasis of fountains and marble and statues. When we checked into our room, we were instantly impressed with how spacious and luxurious everything seemed to be. Once we began to settle in and make plans for the evening, I decided that since it was my birthday -- we should do something risque'.

Lysette had told me about how she and her ex (who was now in prison) would have threesomes with other women.

So I boldly asked her, "Hey you know it's my birthday, right?"

"Uh huh." She seductively replied.

"I was thinking that maybe we could uh...have a threesome?"

"A threesome!?" She said with disbelief.

"Yea you know – me, you and another girl."

Lysette's attitude completely changed.

"Why would you want to have a threesome? I'm not good enough for you?"

"No that's not it, it's just you know, my birthday..."

She had become almost irate and then she simply started staring out the window. A few minutes later, she went into the bathroom and surprisingly emerged completely naked. She sauntered across the room in her birthday suit displaying the biggest, hairiest vagina bush I had ever seen. It looked like she had Buckwheat trapped between her legs and all I could see was this massive amount of pubic hair coming towards me.

Lysette and I had sex once before our trip but I didn't recall her being so hairy. She confidently walked over towards me and said, "I want you to eat me." I was thinking to myself, "I will never be *that* hungry." The whole mood of the trip had completely changed. I started to question why I decided to travel with her to Vegas on my birthday. Lysette was modestly attractive but she was no stunner and now she was demanding that I "eat her." I was no longer in the mood for sex and I simply told her that we should go downstairs and have dinner. She was not happy about my rejection and she began to withdraw even more. Feeling like my birthday weekend was about to be ruined, I decided to go downstairs and do some gambling. She wasn't interested in joining me so I left her behind to stew.

Once I went downstairs, I played a few hands of blackjack for about an hour and then returned to my room to discover that she was gone. Lysette had ordered up a bunch of room service and apparently had caught a flight back to LA. I was dumbfounded; I couldn't believe that she was so ghetto. I was also a bit relieved that I didn't have to spend my entire weekend with her either.

Suddenly, I found myself alone in Vegas on my birthday. So I decided to seize the moment and make it a great weekend – with or without a date. I went back downstairs and played blackjack for a few hours and won about $500. Things started to change for the better and as the evening approached, I decided that I would go to a nightclub and enjoy myself. The club was filled with drunk, horny people looking to hook up with someone, but I didn't see any girls that I was excited about meeting; so I went back up to my room around 2am in the morning and called it a night. Once I was sound asleep, I felt a slight rumbling of my bed. It was enough to startle me out of my sleep but I tried to lie back down and continue my rest.

A few minutes later, I felt another really strong rumble and it was strong enough to shake my bed. At this point, I was still semi-conscious and trying to figure out what was happening. I knew that I was in Vegas and not LA, which meant that it couldn't be an earthquake. A few seconds later, the whole building started to feel like it was going to collapse. The Venetian is a massive structure but this unexpected earthquake was shaking it so violently that it felt like a tiny doll house. I quickly jumped out of bed and looked in the hallway to see people running and screaming for their lives!

I didn't know what else to do, so I joined them! I was running as fast as I could to reach the elevator which seemed like it was a mile away. By the time I reached the corridor, the shaking was so bad – I started to succumb to the thought that I might die in the hotel under a pile of rubble. I was on the 33rd floor and I knew there was no way I would make it to the ground floor. So I grabbed onto a large column near the elevator and prayed for the best. While I was gripping the column, it was swaying back and forth while I held on with all my might and then -- suddenly it stopped. Everyone was in a state of panic, there were dozens of people walking around looking dazed and confused. People were screaming, "Get me outta this damn hotel!" I was in shock as well, I seriously thought that I was about to die.

I slowly made my way back to my room only to discover that I had locked myself out. I also realized that I was only wearing a T-shirt and my underwear. Feeling disoriented and lucky to be alive, I walked back towards the elevator and waited along with several other guests who were startled and talking a mile-a-minute.

I noticed that most of them had on bathrobes but I was unfortunately stuck in my briefs. Luckily they weren't "tighty-whiteys," they were the athletic briefs that I like to wear but still they were underwear. So once I reached the casino level, I could see how panicked everyone was. I quickly made my way down the long corridors of the casino towards the front desk where I politely asked them to let me into my room.

One of the security guards escorted me back to my room as I once again trekked back through the casino in my underwear. When I finally got back into my room, I was just happy to be alive. I was wide awake like everyone else at this point, so I decided to take my mind off my near death experience by going back downstairs and playing some blackjack.

When I sat down at the table, everyone started commiserating about our awful earthquake experience while trying to concentrate on winning a few dollars. It was definitely an unforgettable birthday weekend and I can safely say that I'm one of the few people to ever walk through a casino in their underwear.

Chapter 17

Hollywood Hookup

While hanging out at a hip hop club in Beverly Hills one night, I noticed a girl who I recognized from the movies. Her name was AJ Johnson and she had starred in the *House Party* movies with Martin Lawrence and Tisha Campbell. I was hanging out by the DJ booth and she was standing a few feet away with her girlfriends. I got my nerve up to go over and say something to her and when I approached her, I sarcastically said, "Hey aren't you Thelma from Good Times?" She looked at me with a look of disbelief. I wasn't sure how she was going to respond but then she started laughing and said, "Thelma? Good Times? You are a trip, what's your name?" "I'm Barrington, nice to meet you." "I'm AJ." she replied in her distinctly sexy and raspy voice. From that moment on we hit it off; we spent the rest of the evening talking and vibing to the music. Around the end of the night, we exchanged phone numbers and agreed to go out on a date soon. My friends that were with me, were very impressed. They could see that I had no apprehension when it came

to meeting famous women. A confident man can meet
any woman he wants as long as he believes that he's
worthy and attractive enough.

Of the few famous women that I've dated, my initial
introduction exuded confidence and reassured them
that I wasn't just another guy looking for an autograph
-- I wanted their phone number. AJ and I became good
friends, she would often come by my house whenever we
had parties and we would occasionally go out to lunch.
There was always a few people who would recognize her
and ask to take pictures when we were out, which made
me feel even more confident about myself.

One of the benefits of dating a celebrity is that you
get invited to all the best parties. One night, AJ and I
went to a Christmas party in Beverly Hills where there
were several celebrities, including Chante' Moore and a
few other notable faces. When we arrived, I could feel the
eyes upon us, trying to figure out who I was and if I was a
celebrity. She introduced me to a few of her male friends
who worked in the industry and I was surprised at how
"catty" they were. A couple of them rolled their eyes at
me after shaking my hand. They were so phony and the
could hardly withhold their contempt for me that I was
with AJ. I thought it was funny, so I squeezed her tight to
show them that I was a "boss" and that she was definitely
going home with me.

Throughout the night, I couldn't help but notice Chante' staring at me. I wasn't sure if she recognized me from hanging out at Kadeem's house but she was definitely flirting --there's something about being with a female celebrity that instantly enhances a man's overall attraction. Of all the times I had seen Chante', she never once flirted with me, but on this night she made it clear that she was interested.

AJ and I made our way towards the restroom and while I was waiting for AJ to return, I saw Chante' walking up the stairs. I wasn't sure if I should talk to her because we had never really had a conversation. I thought about asking for her number but I thought it would be too tacky and too risky to get caught exchanging numbers. I knew that she was no longer married to Kadeem and he and I were not exactly best friends. So we both smiled at each other as she walked by and sure enough -- just about that time, AJ emerged from the bathroom and quickly gave Chante' a hug. I watched from a few feet away, thanking myself for not being a fool.

That night I realized that Hollywood was an insular playground where celebrities comingled and sometimes flirted with each other in a very discreet manner.

AJ and I had started dating around the time that she began filming the iconic movie Baby Boy, starring Tyrese Gibson and Ving Rhames. She was so excited to be a part of the movie because it had been a while since she had a prominent role. She would often invite me on set to watch the filming but I always refused. I knew that she had once dated the director John Singleton and I didn't want to be paraded around like a show dog to make anyone jealous. From the times that I had spent on set, I knew that egos can get out of control. I also didn't want to see her flirting with her co-stars and schmoozing with the other actors like Snoop Dogg and Ving Rhames.

My reluctance to visit her on set eventually became the downfall of our relationship. We had only been seeing each other for a couple of months and we had enjoyed our time together but we weren't in love. AJ was like a lot of actresses that I met, they were focused on their career and it seemed like everything else was secondary. I had always thought that it would be cool to be in a long term relationship with an actress but I started realizing that I preferred someone who wasn't "Hollywood." The constant demands and unwanted attention an actress receives can wreak havoc on a relationship. The last time I saw AJ was one year ago at a restaurant in the Valley, and she nonchalantly acknowledged me and hastily continued on to her table with her girlfriends.

Chapter 18

Mallory

I had joined an exclusive gym near Westwood called Sports Club LA. It was a high end gym complete with two restaurants, a spa, a salon and a clothing store. There were always exotic cars parked outside and lots of celebrity members. I figured it would be a good way to network with business people and meet beautiful women. Basketball was also a main attraction; it wasn't unusual to be on the same team with Sandler, Woody Harrelson or Nelly.

Along with exotic cars and famous celebrities came lots of beautiful women. Many of them had breast enhancements and other forms of plastic surgery but most of them still looked attractive. Although, it was always funny to see a hot chick feverishly working out on a treadmill while wearing full make up and flashing her diamond Rolex.

Some of the members that I would see on a regular basis were Michael Bay, Jamie Foxx, David Blaine,

Carmen Electra and Woody Harrelson. As a regular guest, I would sometimes be invited to various celebrity events at their homes. I recall going to a pool party at Jamie Foxx's immaculate house near Calabasas. His house was enormous, complete with an Olympic size swimming pool and a fleet of horses in a nearby pasture. I gained a new level of respect for him because his immediate family was living with him, including his disabled sister.

While playing basketball one day, I noticed a beautiful blonde working out on a Stairmaster that overlooked the basketball court. While I was playing, I would occasionally catch a glimpse of her smiling at me. Once the game was over, I headed upstairs to pretend like I was stretching but I was actually trying to get a better look at her. She had an amazing body, she certainly wasn't skinny and her shape reminded me of Britney Spears, curvy and athletic.

I casually walked up and introduced myself to her while she was still working out. She was all smiles as if she had been waiting for me to approach her. She told me her name was Mallory and we chatted for a few minutes while she continued climbing away on the Stairmaster.

"You were pretty good out there." She said with a flirtatious smile.

"Ahh, just gettin' some cardio that's all." I replied with a wink.

We talked for a few minutes and then I asked for her phone number. I could see other members walking by and attempting to eavesdrop on our conversation. Mallory was a stunner and she was the type of girl that guys were excited to see at the gym.

She slowly ended her workout and climbed down from the machine to officially shake my hand. She was taller than I expected, I'm 6 feet tall and she was almost looking me square in the eyes. Her presence was a bit intimidating at first; she was wearing colorful tight fitting workout gear, a pink diamond watch and matching earrings. Mallory looked like the kind of girl that a rich white guy would have by his side while cruising around in his convertible Ferrari.

At first glance, most people would not assume that we were an ideal couple but I soon learned that Mallory preferred dating black guys -- that was both a bonus and a burden. When some of the other black guys in the gym started seeing us together, I got the impression that they thought they could replace me. I recall having lunch with Mallory in the gym restaurant when this tall guy with dreadlocks who claimed to be a rapper, boldly walked up and started talking to her as if I wasn't there. He was asking random questions in an effort to see if he could get her phone number. After a few moments, she stopped him in mid-sentence and said, "Do you mind? I'm trying to have lunch with my boyfriend." He quickly glanced at me with a look of defeat as I shook my head at him in disgust. He shuffled away and returned to his group of friends that were watching from a distance. They were laughing at him for being such a fool.

I was impressed with the way she handled him. I hadn't known Mallory for very long and I wasn't in a position to jump up and confront this guy. She was an extremely attractive girl and I just assumed that dealing with annoying guys was a daily regimen for her.

As we continued to see each other over the next few weeks, I discovered that Mallory was one of the most sexually aggressive women that I had ever been with. She had tried getting into Playboy magazine but they didn't like her because she wasn't as skinny as the other girls. She had also been a model in Thailand for a few years and had recently done some soft porn movies in the Valley. Soft porn movies are the kind of flicks where they simulate sex but they're not actually having sex. Mallory told me that she had been offered a lot of money to do "real" porn but she wasn't interested because she had a young son.

Sex with her was amazing! There wasn't *anything* that she wouldn't do to please me. We both had the same sexual energy and we almost never went to bed without having sex -- although, I never had sex with her without a condom because I recalled one night while we were in bed, she confidently said, "I'm definitely going to have a black baby." From that moment on, I made sure that

I *always* had a condom with me. Mallory was sexy and attractive but I couldn't see myself raising a child with her. She was the ultimate arm candy but not my idea of the perfect wife.

When she wasn't doing soft porn movies or working out at the gym, she would spend her weekends in Vegas working as a stripper. She would come back with stacks of bills from her weekend trips stuffed into her $10,000 designer purse. I had never met a woman like Mallory before -- she was a hustler, a stripper, a porno star and a certified freak.

After seeing each other for about four months, she started to develop feelings for me. I wasn't in love with her but I was enjoying the attention that she brought to my life. I remember going to a Halloween party up in the Hollywood Hills with her and a few of my friends. Most of my friends had not met her until that night and they couldn't believe that I was able to snag a girl like her. I've never considered myself a guy with drop dead gorgeous looks; however the difference between me and the other guys was my swagger. I never felt like a woman was too beautiful or too rich or too famous for me; that attitude allowed me to date women that were supposedly out of my class.

While hanging out at the party, a frisky brunette girl "accidently" brushed up against me and grabbed my penis while I was standing in the kitchen. It was quite surprising; I think she was turned on by the sight of me with my beautiful date. There were also a few times when Mallory and I had gone out to nightclubs and women would approach us and hint that they wanted to go home with us. It was so bizarre because if I had been alone, I probably would not have gotten that type of attention. However, bringing an attractive girl to the club somehow increased my overall attractiveness and made a few curious women envious enough to offer themselves up for a threesome.

Mallory had told me that she had been with women before and it didn't seem like a big deal for her. I, on the other hand was not accustomed to this type of attention. She seemed to take pleasure in seeing other women approach me. We had talked about a threesome but we never hooked it up, I think I was hesitant about bringing another girl into our bed because I knew that Mallory was aggressive and I didn't want to see her sexually ravaging another girl.

After a few more weeks, the novelty of being with her began to wear off. I wasn't in love but she had started to get attached. It was difficult to forego our great sexual relationship but I knew that I had to move on in hopes of finding true love. Mallory would often leave me messages, letting me know that she still cared. Somehow she was convinced that we would eventually be together but it was time for me to move on.

Chapter 19

Ah Paris!

A few weeks later, while hanging out in a nightclub I met a sweet and sexy girl named Gabrielle. I spotted her from across the room while she was dancing with her girlfriends. She was wearing a green dress that accentuated her shapely body. I walked over to the edge of the dance floor to get a closer look at her. She looked up and instantly caught my eye. Gabrielle started dancing and glancing at me as if she wanted me to come closer. So I smoothly made my way onto the floor and started dancing with her as if I had known her for a lifetime.

We didn't really talk a lot while we were dancing but our eyes were saying plenty. She turned around and started teasing me with her big round "J. Lo" booty and I was in heaven. Gabrielle had a killer body and the face of an angel. There was something sweet and innocent about her demeanor even though she was teasing me on the dance floor.

After a couple of dances, we walked over to the bar area where it was a bit more quiet. As I was talking to her and looking into her eyes, I started thinking that maybe I had found my future wife. I had always been leery about meeting women in a nightclub because it usually didn't work out but there was something about Gabrielle that was different.

She gave me her phone number and I called her a day later and left a message. She didn't return my call until a few days later which made me think that maybe she wasn't as smitten as I was about our encounter. When we finally spoke on the phone, she apologized and told me that she was out of town visiting her sister. Gabrielle had a soft yet raspy voice that sounded like she was Caucasian on the phone. She had a proper way of speaking that didn't sound phony or contrived.

We talked for a while about our backgrounds and I was surprised to learn that she was a police officer. I had imagined that maybe she was a nurse or a teacher but I would have never guessed that she was a cop. Gabrielle also told me that she had a young daughter. She seemed reluctant to tell me out of fear that I may no longer be interested. My idea of who she was prior to talking to her on the phone had completely changed -- I certainly wasn't expecting her to be a cop with a kid. I started asking questions about what school she attended and she gave me the name of her high school which let me know that she had not attended college. None of these revelations were adding up to my expectations of Gabrielle. However, I was still interested in dating her because she seemed to have a "good heart." She was also very attractive and ten years younger than I was at the time. I had just turned 35 and I was ready to settle down and have a family. I convinced myself that whatever traits that she may lack could be overcome over time -- which was a mistake. I've always believed that you should accept a person as they are without expectations of their potential but I ignored my own advice with Gabrielle.

We went on our first date a few days later at a trendy new restaurant in Koreatown. While we were having dinner, a sweet older lady walked up to our table and said, "You two look so handsome together." We were both appreciative of her compliment. "How long you have been together?" she said. We both replied in sync, "This is our first date." The older lady gushed and replied, "Oh my, well I wish you both the best." As she walked away, Gabrielle and I looked at each other in amazement; it was as if the old lady's comments were some type of positive omen. Later on, I jokingly told her that I paid the lady to come over to our table. Gabrielle just laughed and rolled her eyes, "You're so crazy."

Gabrielle and I dated for almost a year. Our relationship was filled with adventure, excitement and acrimony. I had recently left the agency that I was working for and started my own executive search company from my house. Working for myself allowed me the freedom to set my own hours and also keep more of the money that I was generating as a recruiter. Flush with cash and a strong sense of adventure, I would take Gabrielle on spontaneous trips to Vegas to see shows like Cirque Du Soleil's "O" and Blue Man Group (a bit overrated if I may say so). Once during a trip to Vegas, I got on a hot roll at the blackjack table in the opulent Venetian hotel.

I was sitting at a $10 table and over the course of a couple of hours, I had won $2500. Gabrielle was sitting beside me the whole time as a small crowd started to gather around us. I think people were amazed to see how I was able to turn a $10 bet into $2500 in just a few hours. I've always been a pretty good blackjack player because I understand the science of how to turn the cards in my favor. Many novice blackjack players simply rely on "the book" as a guide to how they should play the game. The only problem with always going by "the book" is -- it doesn't account for the old lady who just loves to split her pocket queens. There are so many variables to consider when you're playing blackjack; however, I had devised a way of staggering my bets to account for the inevitable bad hands that I would be dealt. My theory was simple, bet the minimum for a few hands until I felt the cards changing in my favor. Once I started to see more face cards on the table, I would bet anywhere from $100 to $200 per hand and the payoff would be phenomenal -- and on this night my strategy was working like a charm! Once

I started to build up a stack of chips, I took command of the table as other players were frequently asking me for advice on how to bet. I always try to play "third base" when I'm at a table because I have the advantage of seeing the card flow throughout the entire game which allows me to make an educated guess about the dealer's hand. I got into a rhythm and started busting the dealer on almost 70 percent of the hands. Everyone at the table was making money and the dealer couldn't believe how well I was doing. She bluntly asked me while shuffling the cards, "How are you able to do this?" That was a great compliment coming from a dealer because I'm sure they've seen it all.

Gabrielle was also impressed as my chip stack started to grow. Each time I would win a big hand; the small crowd would applaud and congratulate me. It felt great to be there with Gabrielle and winning money. She was also looking very sexy in her cocktail dresses and high heels the whole weekend. After a few hours, I began to get tired and decided to cash out. I stood up and pushed my stack of chips towards the dealer for her to count. She quickly counted up the colorful chips and exchanged them for $100 black chips. Once I had my loot, I tossed her a $100 chip and asked for a fifty piece in return and told her to keep the change. She was very appreciative and wished me good luck. One thing that I've learned about playing card games at a casino: *Always take care of the dealers and they will take care of you.*

Gabrielle and I walked away feeling like winners. We hurried over to the cashier to collect my money and then we decided to do some shopping. We walked around the extravagant hotel shops that sold everything from Louis Vitton luggage to high priced diamonds. Gabrielle and I decided to drop by a jewelry store to check out their diamonds. She quickly honed in on a brilliant diamond engagement ring. It was a sparkling, oval shaped diamond that was about four karats. The ring was priced at $60,000 and the salesperson asked if she wanted to try it on. I quickly replied, "$60,000? Naw, I think we're good. I don't test drive cars I can't afford." We both chuckled about the price as we continued to peruse the store.

I had really deep feelings for Gabrielle but I wasn't completely convinced that she would be my wife. There were little things that I just couldn't ignore -- like the way she chewed her food. Whenever we were having a meal, she would "smack" her food as she ate with her mouth slightly opened like a cow grazing on grass. It sounded awful and not very classy. I finally got up the nerve to confront her about her lack of etiquette and she was devastated. "Wow, I can't even enjoy my food. You want some woman that eats with her pinky in the air, huh?"

A few days later, after picking her mother up from the golf course I heard a familiar sound in the backseat as her mother delightfully chewed on a bag of red grapes. With each grape that she popped in her mouth, there was a "smack" and then another. I gazed at her in my rearview mirror and suddenly realized that *she* was the reason Gabrielle had this awful habit. The fruit doesn't fall far from the tree as they say.

There are certain things that people can change about themselves but relearning how to eat is very difficult, especially when no one has ever taught them differently. She had her flaws and I had mine as well so we continued to see each other over the next few months.

Initially, I didn't spend a lot of time with her and her daughter but we gradually began to spend more time together as a family unit. Her daughter was seven years old. She was beautiful, smart and very outspoken. One of the things that I admired about Gabrielle was that she was a great mother. She really cared about her daughter's well-being and invested time in her school work and other activities. I recall once giving Gabrielle a $500 gift card to Niketown in hopes that she would go purchase some nice tennis outfits for our infrequent tennis outings. She bought one outfit and spent the rest of the money on her daughter.

I soon realized that Gabrielle would never be the woman that I wanted her to be but I continued to date her because we had developed such a bond. I loved the fact that she liked to read. She would often read my scripts and give me constructive feedback. Gabrielle always had a book with her and she spent her quiet hours reading mostly mystery and romance novels.

One day I surprised Gabrielle and told her that I had purchased two tickets for us to travel to Paris. She was initially a bit shocked and then she became overjoyed at the thought of traveling to France. I could tell that she was also a bit apprehensive about leaving her daughter behind for a whole week. We had traveled to Vegas a few times and I could always sense how eager she was to get back to her kid. I thought the trip would be good for both us since we had never been to Paris, so Gabrielle made arrangements for her daughter to stay with her mom and dad during our trip.

A couple of weeks later, we were off to the land of fine wine, fine art and historical museums. During our thirteen hour flight from LA to Paris we had a lot of time to relax, watch movies and play games. About three hours into our flight, Gabrielle started to get frisky. She had placed a blanket over our laps and started massaging my penis. Eventually, she undid my zipper and began stroking my exposed penis under the blanket. It felt awesome (and risky). Most of the other passengers were sleeping so we weren't too concerned about being caught. After a few minutes of stroking, she looked at me and whispered, "You want me to give you a blowjob?" I nodded my approval. Gabrielle discreetly laid her head down on my lap to appear as if she were sleeping. She slowly started pleasing me without making overt head movements. She continued teasing me with her mouth as I tried to pretend that I was asleep as well. The feeling of getting a "BJ" while flying was incredible. Gabrielle was using her tongue and slowly massaging my penis with her lips as I tried to maintain my calm. Once I was done, she raised her head and kissed me on the cheek and softly said, "I love you." "I love you too babe." I replied. It was one of the most erotic yet loving moments that I had ever experienced. We had started the "I love you," phase of our relationship prior to our trip and this was her way of thanking me for taking her to Paris. After our secret fellatio session, we were officially members of "The Mile High Club."

Once we arrived in Paris, we gathered our luggage and jumped into a cab. The cab was a newer model Mercedes sedan which was very common in Paris. As the driver took us towards the hotel, I tried to practice the few French words that I knew by saying things like, "beaucoup traffic" whenever we were stuck in traffic. He smiled and replied, "Oui monsieur beaucoup traffic." Gabrielle on the other hand was unwilling to attempt to speak one single word of French while we were there. She seemed deathly afraid of embarrassing herself. I've always believed that when you travel overseas, you have to make an effort to expose yourself to the language and the culture in order to fully appreciate a different way of life.

Her reluctance to fully immerse herself in the culture and enjoy the city became a growing source of contention between us. She clearly didn't share my passion for discovery and her attitude began to weigh heavily upon our trip. At one point, I thought about leaving her in the hotel and exploring the city by myself but I decided to try and make the best of the situation.

There were a few sweet moments, including the night we spent listening to live music and drinking Pinot Noir at a swanky jazz club. We also dined alfresco one night at the hotel restaurant until about 10pm while the sun slowly set during our dinner. This was during the time of year in Paris when the days were long and the sunsets were usually late into the evening.

One of the not-so-sweet moments was during an afternoon stroll through the fashion district. I decided to drop into a jewelry store on the corner to possibly purchase my first Rolex watch. I was hoping that the favorable exchange rate would allow me to purchase a Rolex at a discount. Gabrielle and I were both well-dressed and well-mannered but when we walked into the store, all of the salespeople started to hastily put away their merchandise. They all had a look of fear as if we were about to commit a robbery. Their unexpected behavior was a bit unsettling but we both smiled and proceeded to peruse the store. Once they realized that we were friendly Americans, everything returned to normal. I had not expected to be treated so rudely while I was shopping for an expensive watch but I soon realized that racism wasn't just confined to America. I quickly glanced at a few watches and decided that I was not interested in spending my money in a store that treated black customers as if they were criminals.

Gabrielle and I continued our stroll in disbelief of the way we had been treated. We didn't let it put a damper on our mood, but it was certainly an eye opener. Over the next couple of days, Gabrielle started to loosen up and we tried to visit as many sites as we could -- including the Champs Elysees, Church of Notre Dame and the Louvre museum. We took lots of pictures that we couldn't wait to share with our friends and family. We also brought back lots of souvenir gifts as well; however, Gabrielle would later inform me about two weeks after our return that she had brought back a "special" gift.

She came by my house one night and somberly told me that she was pregnant.

"You're what!?" I said.

"I'm pregnant, I just took the test this morning."

"How could you be pregnant? I thought you were on the pill?"

"I was. I must've forgot to take them before we left."

I started pacing the room to call myself down and then I started to wonder if Gabrielle had gotten pregnant on purpose. Over the past few months, I had spoiled her with gifts, lavish trips and entertaining shows and I suspected that she was expecting a proposal during our

Paris trip. However, the only thing that I had proposed was that we take a vacation. I think her mom and her sisters had implanted this idea that I was going to propose to her, which explained why she was so difficult to deal with on our trip. Gabrielle was waiting for me to ask for her hand in marriage and the intentional pregnancy was supposed to be a way of sealing the deal.

I had thought about getting married to Gabrielle but once I realized that she was planning on having my child whether we were married or not, it completely changed our relationship. I couldn't believe that she was willing to have two kids by two different men, neither of which she would be married to. I knew that her daughter's father had come from an affluent family and I started to suspect that her high school pregnancy was a way of marrying into his family. She had a very contentious relationship with his mother which was probably because she suspected the same.

All of my hopes and aspirations of what Gabrielle and I could have become were dashed. I began to see her as an opportunist who was content to have babies in hopes of being provided for. She wasn't really interested in furthering her education and making a better life for herself, she was only interested in taking the easy way out.

I convinced her to have an abortion because I didn't want to raise a child with her in such a dysfunctional relationship. I've never wanted to be anybody's "baby daddy," I think that kids deserve to be raised in a loving atmosphere between two adults who genuinely love each other. It doesn't always work out that way but I believe that the intent is what's most important.

After Gabrielle had the abortion, our relationship completely changed. She seemed devastated that her slick plan didn't work out and it led to a lot of arguments. We would get into loud, argumentative shouting matches almost every other day. We would always make up but it was becoming clear that there was no future for us together. · I still loved her but I was no longer *in* love with her. Gabrielle had begun to act irrationally and immature. I decided that I needed to move on and regain my sense of peace. I moved out of the house I was renting and found a loft style apartment near Culver City and I had no plans of inviting Gabrielle to come with me. I was raised against "shacking up" and I've faithfully avowed by this principle during my bachelorhood. I'm not against living with a woman but only if we're in the process of getting married. Those values are not very common these days, as many young couples regularly share a place together. I think it devalues the relationship when you live together without the intention of marriage. As they say, "Why buy the cow when you can get the milk for free?"

A few weeks after breaking up with Gabrielle, I walked out to my shiny BMW that had recently been waxed to discover messy food tossed all over the hood and the roof. I knew straight away that it was her and her mischievousness. She was immature and out of control, so I decided to call up her police captain at her job and file a complaint. I lived in a gated community with cameras near the entrance that recorded every car that entered the property. I asked her captain to review the footage to determine if and when she had arrived. A couple of days later, I received a call from him verifying that her car was recorded entering the property around the time that my car had been vandalized. He also surprisingly told me that this was not the first time that someone had filed a complaint against her for vandalism. I was shocked! It was probably another bad break up and this was obviously her M.O. whenever she felt scorned. He told me that he would have a conversation with her about the incident and I'm sure she got the message that I wasn't going to tolerate her antics. I understood her pain but I didn't appreciate her childish behavior.

Chapter 20

Stand Up for Your Rights

I was free from my stressful relationship with Gabrielle but the economy had started to slow down dramatically which severely affected my staffing business. The dot com boom was now a bust. The party was over. All of the high flying internet stocks that were going up 300 percent in the first six months were now worth pennies. The stock market had lost almost half its value in just a couple of months. Companies were being shuttered and very few businesses were actively hiring. I was quickly burning through my savings and needed to find a job as soon as possible.

A friend of mine named Eric who once worked in recruiting with me had found a job with a vocational school in Long Beach called Brooks College. He passed my resume along to the admissions manager who hired me shortly after my first interview. I was grateful to have a job but it was far from the glitz and glamor of working in a high rise building in Century City and making boat loads of cash. My primary responsibility was to recruit prospective students into the school's various programs such as Graphic Design, Network Engineering and Fashion Design. Most of the students were black and came from low income households and according to the school's standards they easily qualified for admissions as long as they had a high school diploma (and $50 for the admissions fee).

I knew that certain things about the school's admissions policy and their job placement rates were a bit sketchy but I would later learn just how deceptive the school was in hoodwinking these unsuspecting kids into exorbitant school loans without the possibility of employment.

The school was also very lax about screening applicants for on-campus housing. I recall once during an orientation for new students, a young white kid arrived from out of town with his parents only to discover that his roommate was a 40 year old black man who dressed like a pimp.

Most of the staff members at the school were African-American; however, *all* of the managers and directors were white. No one ever raised an issue about this apartheid-like system until I was in a position to be promoted to a manager. I had been with the school for a few months and as one of the top recruiters, I was naturally a shoe-in for a promotion (so I thought). The school had recently hired a new Director of Admissions named JoAnn and it was obvious that she had no intentions of giving me a promotion. I waited a couple of weeks until after she started to approach her in regards to a promotion. When I met with her in her office, she was very defensive about considering me for a management position. Shortly after our meeting, she began to chastise my work and my performance. I knew that she was trying to discredit me in hopes that I would quit or simply acquiesce my demands.

After a few more weeks of harassment by her, I decided to quit and file a discrimination lawsuit against the school and their parent company. Before I resigned, I met with the local EEOC office and informed them of the school's history of discrimination. The EEOC accepted my case and immediately sent a letter to the school requesting EEOC documents regarding their hiring and promotion practices. Upon my last day at the school, there was a buzz building about a potential discrimination lawsuit and they quickly tried to mitigate their blatant lack of promotions for African-Americans. Shortly after my departure, they promoted two long term employees who had never received a raise or an evaluation. They also hired an African-American guy from another school as a manager to give the impression that they were not averse to hiring black supervisors; however, none of their tactics could erase their history of discrimination. Once the EEOC received the requested documents, it was obvious that within their twenty year history, they had *never* hired or promoted an African-American into a management position at the school prior to my complaint.

I knew that I had a strong case but working with the EEOC was quite challenging. There were several blatant omissions in their investigation and I had to continually guide them in their research. Once the investigation was complete, they sent me a letter indicating that they were ruling in my favor. The EEOC also sent a letter to the school detailing the numerous interviews they had conducted and why they were being held liable for discrimination.

Brooks College quickly dismissed the findings and offered me $20,000 to drop my claim. I scoffed at the offer because I knew that it was just a starting point for a much bigger payout. Once I received my letter from the EEOC, I tried to find an attorney that I could trust to vehemently represent my case. Unfortunately, I kept meeting attorneys who seemed like they were only interested in a quick settlement and a quick buck for themselves. So I decided to represent myself (pro se) until I found a worthy attorney. When I arrived for my initial hearing in the packed federal courtroom, the judge was surprised to see that I was representing myself. He didn't waste time letting me know that he didn't approve of pro se plaintiffs.

"Mr. Rose do you know what Abraham Lincoln said about a man who represents himself?" he said.

"Ignorance of the law is no excuse for violating the law?" I quickly replied.

He seemed shocked at my reply and a brief silence came over the courtroom.

"No! Abraham Lincoln said that a man who represents himself has a *fool* for a client."

"Well your honor, I'm certainly no fool and I'm quite capable of representing myself."

He seemed flustered with my unwavering position. The opposing attorney was a young, recent law grad and she seemed equally surprised at my temerity.

"Mr. Rose what are your damages?" he anxiously replied.

I could sense that he wanted to make quick work of my case and send me away with a pittance of a settlement.

"Your honor, I haven't had the opportunity to properly estimate my damages but I will provide those to opposing counsel once I have them."

The judge agreed with the terms and proceeded to delineate a schedule of hearings and deadlines that I would have to abide by as a pro se plaintiff. After receiving the schedule, I left the courtroom and hastily went home to research all of the legal terms associated with pursuing my case. I started spending a lot of time at the Loyola School of Law library in downtown LA, researching cases that were similar to my complaint.

After a few weeks of research and writing, I became even more confident that I could be a capable litigator. I discovered several areas of the school's case that were controvertible and I began to lay out a strategy, highlighting inconsistencies in their statements to the EEOC.

Even though I was an amateur attorney, I was confident enough to depose specific witnesses from the defense. One of the first people that I deposed was my former manager JoAnn. I had studied and read up on proper deposition protocol and technique. When JoAnn arrived she was accompanied by one of the senior partners from a large firm called Morgan, Lewis and Bockius. She seemed a bit nervous at the prospect of being interrogated by a former employee. Once the deposition began, I started asking her questions about her role in denying me an opportunity to be promoted. With each question, the surly older lawyer would interject, "Asked and answered! Defendant has already answered plaintiff's question." He became such a disruption that I asked the court reporter to stop her typing and then I launched into a vociferous exchange with the attorney.

"You have become such a disruption at these proceedings with your constant interjections, would you mind refraining so that we can proceed with the deposition?"

"Well 'counselor' I'm simply stating my objections for the record that's all."

"Yes, but you're objecting to every question and it's apparently a deliberate attempt to derail this deposition. If you continue with these interjections, I will stop the deposition and ask the judge to issue sanctions for misconduct."

The old surly counselor seemed surprised at my admonishment and retreated in his attempt to disrupt my deposition. When I returned to my interrogation of my former manager, I began to hone in on inconsistencies that she had made in her statements to the EEOC. She had indicated that I was not qualified for the position because my coworkers complained that I was a bully. In response, I was able to produce several affidavits from my former coworkers, stating that I was very qualified for the role. She also stated that she had never given me any managerial responsibilities prior to my departure. In response, I produced an email that she sent me, indicating that I would be responsible for certain managerial duties in lieu of a manager.

Throughout the deposition, I was able to contradict her testimony and hold her accountable for blatant inconsistencies. Once the grueling interrogation was over, I was elated that I had been able to hold court with a veteran attorney and conduct an effective deposition.

I ran into the senior partner a few months later in the elevator at his firm and he strongly encouraged me to attend law school. In a lighthearted manner, I told him that once I won my case against his firm, I would consider it.

The case was a true David versus Goliath scenario. I had never gone to law school and I was battling a well-established law firm with endless resources and I knew that all of my briefings and filings had to be succinct and legally acceptable.

My strategy was very similar to some of the principles taught in the book *The Art of War.* In the book, it discusses specific tactics to keep your enemy guessing and how to utilize the element of surprise when engaged in conflict. One of my effective strategies was the filing of unexpected motions, requesting additional files regarding the case. I suspected that Brooks College and their law firm were secretly collaborating to withhold certain documents that were essential to my case. They probably assumed that since I was a novice litigator, I wouldn't have the sagacity and knowledge of how to request those documents. They were wrong. My strategy worked effectively by keeping them on their toes and causing the school to run up their legal fees in the process.

One day while I was doing some research, I received a call from a producer at *CBS 60 Minutes* named Jennifer MacDonald. She indicated that they were doing an undercover investigation into the school and asked if I was interested in appearing on TV to discuss my experiences working with the school. I couldn't believe what I was hearing and gladly accepted her offer. Jennifer's call was a "game changer" because I knew that I could leverage the attention that I would receive from the show to bolster my discrimination case.

A couple of weeks later, myself and two of my former coworkers met with Jennifer and her boss who happened to be the same producer that orchestrated the infamous Food Lion undercover investigation in 1997. We talked over dinner at the glitzy hotel restaurant, Asia de Cuba located in the Mondrian Hotel. They told us that they had been investigating the school and its parent company for a few weeks and that they had footage of admissions representatives blatantly lying to students about the admissions standards and the job placement rate. We were astounded but Jennifer assured us that there would be no ambush style questions during our on-air interview with veteran reporter Steve Kroft.

A few weeks later we were instructed to meet with the producers at the Four Seasons Hotel in Beverly Hills for our taping. When we walked into the hotel suite, it looked like a makeshift TV studio; there were lights and cameras everywhere. Jennifer and her crew greeted us and tried to make us feel comfortable. As we prepped for our taping, my former coworker Jason decided that he wanted to wear sunglasses during the interview to conceal his identity. I thought it was ridiculous but they allowed it. ·

We sat nervously under the bright lights, waiting for the interview to begin. A few minutes later, Steve Kroft arrived and immediately took control of the room. He shook our hands and took his seat in front of us. After Jennifer helped him attach his microphone to his lapel, he started asking us questions right away about our experience working at the school. We talked about our roles as admissions representatives and how we suspected that the school was being less than honest with the students.

I had previously told the producers that I was concerned that so many of the students who were being duped were African-American and at one point during the interview, Steve turned to me and asked my opinion on how Brooks College's deception was affecting minority students. In response, I launched into a passionate monologue about how the school's deceptive practices were adversely affecting minority students who could least afford to pay off exorbitant loans incurred while in school. I was certain that part of my dialogue would be in the final cut, but when I saw it on TV; they didn't include one single sound bite from my lengthy reply.

After the interview was over, we chatted for a bit in the hotel suite and took pictures with Steve. Later on, we went downstairs to the hotel lobby to have refreshments and mingle. I had googled Steve prior to our meeting and he was impressed that I knew he attended Columbia. As we sat in the lobby, we spotted several celebrities milling about the room. Benny Medina, who was J. Lo and Will Smith's manager, was sitting directly behind us and he seemed interested in overhearing our conversation. It was certainly an unforgettable night, filled with nervous tension and the relief that it was finally over.

After the episode aired on TV, I ramped up my attack against the school. I was an agitator and a force to be reckoned with. At one point, I had professionally printed signs made up that read: Brooks College Practices Discrimination. I stood outside their campus for a week, talking to every passerby warning them about enrolling in the school. I became such a menace; they called the cops on me. When the cops arrived, I explained my position to them. They listened and empathized with me about the school's deceptive practices and eventually they left me alone to continue my protest against the school. I had made my point and they soon realized that I wasn't going to be an easy litigant to get rid of.

I knew that they were preparing a summary judgment in an attempt to have the judge dismiss my lawsuit. I was also preparing a summary adjudication motion which would have granted me a legal victory based upon the overwhelming evidence in the case. It took a lot of long sleepless nights and days to complete the paperwork, but I was able to present a strong case for judgment in my favor.

On the day of the summary judgment hearing, I arrived once again into the packed courtroom. The room was buzzing with anticipation of the judge's arrival. There were several attorneys sitting around and talking with their clients. When the defense attorneys for Brooks College arrived, they arrogantly handed me a booklet detailing their strategy for defeating my motion. I flipped through their booklet and quickly tossed it aside to continue preparing for my presentation.

When the judge finally arrived, the court bailiff asked everyone to stand. I noticed a group of young legal interns filling in the rows beside the judge's lectern and they *all* seemed fixated on me. Once the judge was seated, he quickly called my name to approach the podium. The defense attorneys gathered on their side of courtroom as well. The judge seemed perturbed to see me again and immediately began rendering his decision. I was shocked as I listened to him articulate why he was granting summary judgment for the defense. I had submitted dozens of affidavits, deposition testimony and EEOC documents to bolster my case but I soon realized that he was just a cantankerous (and probably racist) judge who had no regard for my case. He wanted his young interns to see me ridiculed in front of the entire courtroom. After listening to him talk for a few minutes, I tried to interrupt his delivery.

"Your honor may I have word with regard to my case?"

"Not now Mr. Rose! You will have a chance to speak when I am done!" he angrily spouted.

I was stunned at his demeanor but I continued to listen and prepare myself for a rebuttal. I glanced over at the defense table and they were smiling and gloating about the judge's decision.

When I finally had a chance to speak, I mustered up every bit of courage that I had and began to vigorously defend my lawsuit.

"Your honor, I've submitted numerous documents supporting my complaint for discrimination, including numerous affidavits and deposition testimony. However, as I've listened to you render your decision; it appears that *none* of those documents were given any consideration."

Everyone in the courtroom seemed surprised to see me adamantly defend my suit. I knew that my case was strong and I was determined to fight for my rights. After a few more minutes of deliberation with the judge, he eventually decided to withhold his judgment. I was elated!

I glanced over at the defense table and they were flabbergasted. When we left the courtroom, I politely handed them back their playbook for defeating me and confidently strolled out of the courtroom.

However, I discovered a few weeks later that the judge had not rescinded his decision but had simply put it on hold in hopes that we could work out a settlement. I was asking for $500,000 in damages, including back pay, punitive damages and future payments. They offered me $20,000 once again, which infuriated me and fueled my desire to continue my suit. Once the judge realized that the case was not settled, he simply granted them summary judgment a few weeks later. I was devastated and at a loss for words. I had poured several months of research, writing and preparation into my case and with the stroke of his pen, the judge dismissed my case.

After a few days of feeling sorry for myself, I decided to continue my fight in the appellate court. I knew that the chances of prevailing in a federal appeals court were very slim; it's almost unheard of for a pro se plaintiff to win on appeal. Nonetheless, I submitted my voluminous appeal documents on the very last day that they were due and waited for a reply.

After almost a year and a half with no reply, I assumed that the appellate court had simply decided not to review my case. However, one day while checking my mailbox I noticed a letter from the court. My heart started to beat faster! I had all but given up on winning my case but as I began to read the letter, I became excited. The letter stated that they had reversed the district judge's decision and remanded the case back to his court for further deliberation, which essentially meant that it was time to discuss a settlement or continue on to trial.

I will never forget that day. I immediately contacted their attorneys who had already received the notice. The lead attorney was stunned; she couldn't believe that a pro se plaintiff had defeated her summary judgment. I knew that they didn't want to go to trial, so I made them a settlement offer of $120,000 to dismiss the case. A couple of days later, I received a phone call from the attorney indicating that Brooks College had agreed to the settlement. I was elated to finally resolve the case and receive a generous settlement after three long years of representing myself in a very emotional lawsuit.

A few years later the school was closed down and I also discovered that the parent company had hired an African-American CEO shortly after my lawsuit was settled.

Chapter 21

Brazil

After settling my case, I decided that I needed to take a vacation. Brazil was the most obvious destination because I had traveled there once before during Carnaval and it was amazing. I was able to attend the renowned Samba Parade where local Samba schools compete for prizes and prestige. I had seen video footage of the parade on the TV show, *Wild on E!* and it was spectacular. I highly recommend attending the Samba Parade at least once in your lifetime.

In my first trip to Brazil, I didn't know anyone who lived there but this time I had several friends who worked for the airlines and they were constantly visiting Rio. The plane ride from LA to Rio de Janeiro was approximately thirteen hours with a stopover in Miami or Houston. When I arrived in Rio, I took a cab from the airport and met up with my friends who were already enjoying themselves on the beach with drinks and lots of pretty ladies. The Brazilian women were so naturally beautiful it was breathtaking. Many of them had long dark, curly hair and nice round "bundas" like I had never seen before. One of the most interesting things about Rio was that instead of men chasing after beautiful women, the roles had been reversed (especially for American men). I remember walking down the street and seeing an extremely attractive lady passing me by. She gazed at me as if she had seen her favorite celebrity. I couldn't believe how aggressively she was flirting with me. I knew that most of the beautiful and aggressive women were looking for compensation. I had never paid for sex but this seemed like a good time to start.

In Brazil, prostitution is not considered taboo. It's an acceptable way of making a living for a lot of beautiful women. In the hotel that I stayed in, they had a resident hooker who was very shapely, very beautiful and available for the right price. I talked to several women who told me they were teachers, secretaries etc. but they moonlighted as hookers to make extra money. I don't want to give the impression that *all* the women in Rio were for hire because that's not accurate but many of those who hung out on the beach near Copacabana *were* available.

I recall hanging out on the patio of a very popular restaurant called Meia Pataca where a lot of young American black guys would gather. I was approached by one of the most beautiful women I had ever seen in my life. She had smooth olive skin, green eyes and jet black wavy hair. She reminded me of Halle Berry (but prettier) and she was begging me to take her home. The dating dynamic was completely up-side-down. If I had met her in the States, I would have been the aggressor but here she was pleading with me to take her back to my place.

Many of my friends who visited Rio, frequently had girlfriends who lived there. They worked for the airlines, so they could fly in and out for a weekend or for just a few days to see their girl. If you had a connection with a girl, even though she was for hire, many times they would become your girlfriend for the week or the month. All of the women I saw in Rio were attractive but then there were a few who were simply exquisite and those were the ones that American guys feel in love with. I saw many guys fall in love with the beauty of a Brazilian woman. They would marry them and try to take them back to the U.S. and start a family, but it typically didn't work out because the girls were only interested in becoming U.S. citizens and once they received their papers, they would flee back to their families. Brazilians are very family oriented and they value their family relations over just about anything else in their life. The attraction for the Brazilian woman was primarily the opportunity to become a U.S. citizen and allow her family to travel to the U.S. and eventually become citizens as well. The cost of a visa for a Brazilian resident to travel to the U.S. is astronomical. This inflated cost is by design; I realized that the U.S. doesn't want a flood of low income Latin American tourists who might decide to stay in the country. In response, Brazil instituted a visa requirement for all U.S. travelers to their country.

One of the things that I really appreciated about Brazil was how comfortable I felt seeing so many brown faces like mine. Brazil is a country of over 90 million black people and for the first time in my life, I didn't feel like a minority. I also didn't feel the subliminal stress of being a black man in America. Many times as black men, we're automatically profiled and treated like criminals regardless of our disposition, but in Brazil I was just another brown face who happened to be from a different country. During my subsequent visits to Brazil, I met older African-American men who had retired from their government jobs and were living comfortably on their pensions. They spoke fluent Portuguese and they had young attractive wives to care for them. Prior to visiting there, I could have never imagined that an older black man could live so well in a Latin American country. Over the course of the next two years, I would visit Brazil at least six times and each time was very memorable.

During one of my trips to Brazil, I met a pretty young girl who was tall and very friendly. She wasn't aggressive like some of the regular girls, she seemed sweet and innocent. I wasn't completely comfortable with the idea of paying for sex but after a couple of nights together, I no longer had to pay. We spent time together during the day, having lunch, laughing and hanging out by the beach.

She was so beautiful and smart and I would often try to encourage her to pursue other interests besides prostitution. She told me that her family was very poor and that she could not afford a college education. I felt sorry for her but I also knew that she had other options besides prostitution. Initially, I was like a lot of neophytes who visited Rio and fell under the spell of the Brazilian beauty but I soon discovered that many of the girls for hire did so by choice.

Despite our language barriers, we would often spend time together laughing and joking around. I felt a connection with her and briefly thought about bringing her back to the States with me. I saw so much potential in her but I had learned my lesson about "potential" during my relationship with Gabrielle. I no longer saw her as a girl for hire, she was a person and I sincerely wanted to see the best for her. We eventually broke off communication and she probably became a Rio regular, someone who had several men like me who took care of her whenever they were in the country.

One of the most fascinating places in Brazil are the termas, they're like a combination of a spa, a disco and a restaurant. Rio has several well-known termas and upon entrance there's a small fee and they give you a locker key for your belongings. Once you're disrobed, they hand you a white robe and flip flops and escort you upstairs to an area that looks like a disco filled with half naked, beautiful women who are eager to please. The first time

I went to a termas, I was blown away. There were exotic women of all shapes and sizes. I saw beautiful blondes with bodies like Kim Kardashian and brown skin girls with nice round booties from the Amazon. Once you enter the disco area, you begin to feel as though you're a superstar and every girl wants to be with you. They flirt with you and reach under your robe to entice you to take them upstairs to a sex room.

On my first trip, I was feeling really horny and decided to take two girls up to the room. They were both exquisite and sexy. When we reached the room, they provided me with a condom (something I always wore); I quickly secured the condom and began to caress their soft, smooth, voluptuous bodies. After a few minutes, we were all over each other. I took turns exploring different positions with them for at least 30 minutes. It took me a while to climax and the girls were impressed with my stamina. They kept saying, "Muito forte, muito forte baby!" Once I came, it was the most glorious feeling in the world. All of my stress and inhibitions were instantly released. I grabbed my robe and followed them back to the disco area with a big smile on my face.

With my libido fully satisfied, I relaxed on the comfy couches with a few of the girls and sipped on a drink from the bar. After chilling out for a while, I decided to leave. I went back downstairs, got dressed and paid my tab at the front desk.

Sexual Healing, as Marvin Gaye so eloquently sang about is a very gratifying feeling. There's a reason why prostitution is the oldest profession in the history of mankind, sometimes a man just needs to get laid. Many people may disagree with my choices but I don't allow their opinions of my sexual exploits to affect who I am as a person. We're all sexual beings. Conservative minded people will publicly scoff at my disposition but in their private thoughts, I'm certain that they have sexual fantasies just like every other person.

Some of my Rio travel buddies tried to discourage me from writing about my intimate adventures in Brazil out of fear that they would be stigmatized for being sex tourists. I didn't consider myself a sex tourist because I didn't travel to Brazil just to have sex. Brazil is a beautiful country filled with lots of interesting people and fascinating places to visit. During my visits there, I learned a lot about Brazilian history and their culture. They're a very proud people who love their "futbol" and cold beer just like Americans and I look forward to traveling there again in the future.

Chapter 22

Leilani

I had recently signed up for Match.com around the time that online dating had become popular. I had been on a few spontaneous dates through the website, so one night while I was feeling bored—I decided to do a search for attractive women that were currently online. After a few seconds of browsing, I stumbled across a photo of a girl named Leilani. Her profile and her pictures were very interesting so I decided to send her an instant message, asking if she wanted to meet up for a date. It was a bold move but she surprisingly agreed to meet up. After a brief conversation, we decided to meet at a bar near the Santa Monica Pier.

As I drove to the bar, I was hopeful that she looked like her pictures because I had been on a few dates with women who looked *nothing* like their profile. When I arrived, I took a seat at the bar and patiently waited for her to arrive. It was a cool, laid back lounge with red leather couches and a DJ spinning in the corner. A few moments later, she walked in and approached me at the bar.

"Barrington?" She said.

"Hey that's me, glad you made it." I said standing up to give her a hug.

Leilani looked even *better* than her pictures; she had a strong resemblance to the singer, Shakira. She was a bit shorter than most girls I had dated but she was well dressed and very attractive. Leilani also had a sexy accent, sort of like a young Zha Zha Gabor. She told me that she was from Morocco and that her dad was black and that she had lived in France for a while.

We ordered a round of drinks and began talking about our backgrounds. We had an instant connection, she laughed at my impromptu jokes and I listened to her talk about her real estate business and her recent travels. As the drinks began to kick in, we retreated to a back room area for more privacy. I reclined on the sofa as she snuggled in closer. Leilani and I had instant chemistry; it felt as though we had known each other for a long time. She had a cute laugh and a pretty face and as the night lingered on we started caressing and kissing each other.

I was in awe of how fast things were moving but she didn't seem to mind. After a few more minutes, we decided to take a walk and get some fresh air. When we left the bar, we walked about a half block when she suddenly pulled me into a dark stairwell and began undoing my zipper. Within a few seconds, she was going down on me as I tried to maintain my cool. She had amazing technique and she seemed to enjoy giving fellatio. As she was pleasuring me, I started thinking, "Wow, I'm really getting my money's worth from Match.com."

Once she was done, she smiled at me and said, "You want to go to my office and fuck?"

"Sure! Where's your office?"

"Right up the street."

"Sounds good, let's go." I said while fixing my pants.

We continued our stroll up the block and within a few feet she said, "Well we're here."

"You work in this building?"

"Yea I sure do, we can go to my office and have sex while you look out at the ocean."

Her sexually aggressive attitude was enticing but also a bit odd. I wondered how many times she had brought guys up to her office for sex.

Once we got to her real estate office located on the top floor, it was completely dark. She flicked on a couple of lights and told me to sit in a chair located near her desk. Within a few minutes, she was on her knees and pleasuring me with her mouth again. Once I was done, she sat on my lap and rubbed my head.

"Did you like that?" she purred.

"Oh yea, that was nice."

"Hey, I just sold the Liberace mansion in Vegas, you wanna go to Vegas with me this weekend to celebrate?"

"You did what!?"

"I sold the Liberace mansion and I'm going out there for the closing. You should come with me."

"Uh sure, that sounds cool."

A little while later, we gathered ourselves and headed out of the building. I walked her to her car which was a brand new Mercedes convertible. Everything about Leilani was intriguing. She was beautiful, smart and very successful.

The next day, she called and told me that she had bought me a ticket to Las Vegas. I couldn't believe how aggressive she was. I had never been with woman who was so assertive. It was definitely refreshing and I started to sense that she and I had the same type of energy and drive.

A couple of days later we met at the airport and headed out to Vegas. During our short flight, she told me that we were going to be staying in the Liberace mansion for one night and then we could book a hotel for the rest of our stay. I agreed to the arrangement and looked forward to seeing the house.

When we arrived at the airport, one of her close friends picked us up and whisked us away to the mansion. As we drove, her friend badgered us with questions about how we met. Leilani and I explained to her that we had only met three days prior. Her friend couldn't believe that we had only known each other for just a few days.

Once we pulled up to the Liberace mansion, it wasn't very impressive from the outside. It had a faded white exterior with ornate gates that looked like they needed to be replaced. We gathered our bags and proceeded into the house. Leilani had a key to the property and once we were inside, I was amazed at the gaudy interior -- it felt as though we were walking through a museum. There were certain areas that were roped off to protect his memorabilia such as his glittery piano and his elaborate costumes. In the foyer, there was also a large picture of him hanging in the hallway. The inside of the house was enormous -- we walked around in amazement at all of the intricate designs and gold laden fixtures.

When we reached the master bedroom, there was a large, white canopy bed with gold trimming and a spooky-looking replica of Michelangelo's Sistine Chapel painted across the ceiling.

After leaving his master bedroom, we ventured down the hall to his mother's bedroom which was also elaborately decorated but not quite as ostentatious. We decided that we would sleep in the Mom's room instead of Liberace's garish and ghostly bedroom. We slid our luggage into the corner and plopped down on her canopy bed which we soon discovered had a mirrored ceiling. We laughed so hard at the idea of his mom sleeping in such an unusual bed.

"Liberace's mom was a freak huh!?" I said.

Throughout the property, there were several pictures of his mother. I recalled hearing rumors from years ago that he and his mom had a "special" relationship.

After relaxing on the bed for a few minutes, Leilani started to get frisky. We started kissing as she climbed on top of me while I was staring up at the mirrored ceiling at her sexy physique. I started reflecting on how awesome my life was. I had just met Leilani a few days ago on Match.com and here we were about to have sex for the first time in Liberace's mansion.

It didn't take us long to get undressed. We made passionate love for quite a while. Leilani was a very sexual person and she had *lots* of energy. After we were done, we both laid naked, staring up at the mirror in exhaustion.

We had a good night's rest but we were both anxious to leave the property the next day. We called a cab to take us to the MGM Grand Hotel where she had booked a room for us. When we checked into our rooms, we were both relieved to be in a much more comfortable environment.

Leilani and I changed into our evening attire and headed down to the casino area. She looked spectacular, I found myself gazing at her sometimes in amazement that she was my new girlfriend. Leilani had scheduled a meeting with the buyers and the sellers of the home in a hotel conference room. I gave her kiss as I headed towards the blackjack table while she handled her business.

I quickly found a table and within a couple of hours I was up about $600. I was feeling good. I was on a spontaneous adventure with a beautiful girl and I was winning in Vegas. A few minutes later, Leilani found me at the table. She had a big smile on her face and a check in her hand.

"Look what I got." She said with a sassy attitude.

She instantly revealed a check for $350,000! It was her fee for selling the Liberace mansion and we were both elated.

"Baby that's awesome, we have to celebrate." I said.

"Yea let's go!" she replied.

I was still sitting at the table but I didn't want to walk away from my chips in a rush. I decided to play a few more hands but as soon as Leilani arrived, my luck started to change. She was getting antsy and trying to change my betting pattern. She was encouraging me to make abnormal bets and within a few minutes, my $600 was gone. It was the first major red flag that I experienced with her. I started getting the impression that she was reckless with her money -- it wasn't the amount of money that I lost -- it was the principle of the matter. She seemed to be more concerned about spending her check than seeing me win.

"Oh don't worry about it babe, let's go have a drink and see a show!" she said.

We quickly found the box office and she purchased two tickets for Cirque du Soleil's acrobatic themed show called *KA*. As we sat and enjoyed the show, I still couldn't get my mind off of how easily she managed to throw away my money. I was happy for her success but I was concerned about her attitude towards money.

The next day was Saturday and I decided to place a parlay bet on the college and NFL games. I had won $1500 the previous week so I decided to take a chance and put $500 on a nine team parlay with a payout of $225,000. I knew that my chances of winning were slim but I had an auspicious feeling that I could actually win.

I spent most of my Saturday watching the games on the big screens in the MGM Sports Bar while Leilani hung out with her girlfriend. After the morning games were over, I was feeling good because I had won all but one of my bets. Notre Dame was favored by nineteen points to beat UNC but the final score was 45 – 26, it was a "push" which meant that my nine team parlay was now an eight team parlay.

I didn't get a lot of sleep that night because I knew that I still had a chance to win a lot of money the next day on the NFL games. I watched intently as the games began the next morning. I started to get anxious as two more of my games fell in my favor but I was keeping an eye on the Panthers versus Saints game and it didn't look good for me. The Panthers were winning in a blowout and I needed the Saints to score at least one touchdown to cover the spread. I had given up hope that I would win my parlay -- but then the Saints started driving with only a few seconds left when suddenly, Drew Brees threw a quick out-route to Marques Colston who turned up field and scampered for a 60 yard touchdown. I started screaming and shouting, "Yea baby! Yea baby! C'mon!" I was amazed at how lucky I was and I started to get a strong feeling that it was somehow meant for me to win, but I still had one more game to go.

Leilani had returned from her outing with her friend so we watched the last game together in hopes that I would score a big win. The last game was Rams

versus Lions and everything was going well until the final
minutes. I had the Rams favored by six points and they
were losing 34 – 33 with only two minutes to play. The
Rams were driving and moving the ball down the field as
we anxiously cheered them on. Suddenly, Marc Bulger
unleashed a pass to Isaac Bruce for a touchdown. We
started screaming and shouting but the Rams were only
up by five points which meant that I would have lost
unless the Rams went for a two point conversion. The
chances of them going for a two point conversion were
slim because they were up by more than three points and
there was less than a minute to play in the game – but
that's exactly what they did!

Leilani and I stood up and cheered as the Rams lined
up to go for a two point conversion. Bulger rolled back
in the pocket and fired another pretty pass to Bruce who
caught the ball for a successful conversion. The score was
now 41 -34 and I was winning, although the game was
not over. The Lions received the ball on the kickoff and
immediately started driving down the field. There were
only a few seconds left and they had already reached the
Rams' thirty yard line. I was watching and shaking my
head in disbelief at how easy they were. moving the ball
-- it was now fourth down and only a few seconds to go.

The Lion's quarterback John Kitna fired a bullet into
the end zone to his receiver who made a spectacular catch
in the back of the end zone. I was completely deflated.
One of the referees initially signaled a touchdown but

they were conferencing in the end zone to determine if the catch was good. Leilani and I were squeezing each other tight as we waited for the decision. A few moments later, the referee emerged from the huddle waving his hands to indicate that the pass was no good and the game was over.

We started jumping up and down and celebrating the miraculous win! At this point, I was both numb and excited. I didn't know exactly how much I had won so we quickly went over to the sportsbook desk to cash in the winning ticket. The clerk processed the ticket and gleefully said, "Congratulations, you're a lucky man today -- you won $100,000." We were so excited but I kept thinking about why I didn't win the original bet of $225,000. The "push" in the Notre Dame game had cost me $125,000! I don't gamble very often these days but I almost *never* bet on Notre Dame football.

I was grateful for the win and I definitely felt the presence of a great spirit guiding me and encouraging me along the way. The manner in which I won was clearly a sign from my creator that he was involved in my improbable win. There were times when I had given up and almost tossed my ticket into the trash but every time I wanted to give up, something miraculous happened. Nonbelievers will simply say that I was lucky, but I know that something greater than me delivered the victory.

My weekend with Leilani was unforgettable. She had just received a check for $350,000 and I had just won

$100,000. We were both over the moon and our energy together was simply kismet. I started to feel as though we were meant to be together and that she was the one I had been searching for.

After our Vegas trip, Leilani and I started spending a lot of time together. I would often sleep over at her apartment in Santa Monica or she would come by my place near Culver City. We were a happy couple who enjoyed the finer things in life. We dined at exclusive restaurants and took spontaneous trips to Jamaica and Cabo San Lucas. During our trip to Cabo, I surprised her with a candlelit dinner for two on her birthday. We dined on the beach as the courteous resort staff waited on us. After our meal, they escorted us to a wooden canopy bed on the beach adorned with white linen drapes. Once we were inside, they politely closed the drapes and wished us a good evening. As we lay on the bed staring up at the stars, I felt like I was in heaven. Everything was going well in my life, I had a beautiful and smart girlfriend and we both had a burning passion for life.

Leilani turned to me and said, "I love you babe, thanks for a great birthday dinner."

"I love you too, glad I could help make your birthday special." I said as we began to kiss.

There were a lot of things that I loved about Leilani but there were also a lot of red flags. She was uber-aggressive and there were times when I felt as though she was competing with me. She was doing very well in her real estate business but she didn't seem to respect my line of work. I had been a recruiter for nearly 10 years and I was doing very well. I recall a time when I received a placement fee from a client for $10,000 and she responded by saying, "That's nice but I'll be glad when you start making *real* money."

Leilani had a way of making snide remarks that were designed to chip away at my self- esteem and over time her attitude became a bit unsettling. She also lacked a strong spiritual life. Her idea of spirituality was reading tarot cards and trying to decipher the meaning of the card she had chosen.

During that time, I had embarked on a spiritual journey which had completely changed my life. While I was fighting for my rights against my former employer, I had a spiritual awakening. I had started reading about Gandhi and his struggles to win freedom for his beloved people of India. I became fascinated with his lifestyle and I saw similarities in our stories. Gandhi was a strict vegan and he also practiced daily meditation which gave him the strength to defeat a very powerful enemy in a peaceful manner. Everything about his life made sense and I decided to become a vegan, eschewing all forms of meat and dairy. I also began to meditate daily and fast on a regular basis. I once fasted on water for seven days to test my limits. The first few days were a struggle but after the third day, I began to gain an inner peace and a surge of energy. The longer I fasted, the closer I felt to God but on the seventh day while walking in the hallway of a client, I nearly blacked out. The fast was over but I gained a spiritual insight like I've never experienced before. I no longer wanted to drink alcohol or occasionally smoke weed.

I had also discovered a worship center in LA called Agape International Spiritual Center where my soul was reignited. The church was led by Reverend Michael Beckwith and upon my initial visit to the center; I was surprised to see how diverse the church was. There were people of all races and some of them wore business suits and some wore sweat suits. Coming from a Southern Baptist background, this was quite a change but as I sat and listened to Reverend Beckwith's message I started to feel as though he were speaking directly to me.

I was accustomed to the Southern preacher's cadence of delivery but Beckwith spoke like a poet. His delivery sounded like he was performing "spoken word." His message was about acceptance of all beliefs and appreciation for God in all forms of religion. It was a message I needed to hear because I had toiled with the idea of someone like Gandhi who had lived a Christ-like existence but had been told by zealous Christians that despite his good works, Gandhi could not be in God's kingdom. The idea of Gandhi being shunned by God was ridiculous and I knew that their thinking was false.

I enjoyed going to church for the first time in a long time and I tried to encourage Leilani to attend with me but she wasn't interested. Her reluctance to attend church with me was a definite red flag but I respected her decision because she was from Morocco and I wasn't sure what type of spiritual teachings she had been raised with.

Leilani was also a great cook and she would often prepare delicious Moroccan style dishes with spices and jasmine rice. For every fault that I found in her, I also found something to love.

Christmas was approaching and Leilani had made plans to travel to Morocco to visit her family during the holidays. We decided that on her return, we would meet in my hometown in North Carolina so that she could meet my mom and my stepfather. Leilani and I had been dating for over four months and starting to get very serious. We playfully talked about marriage during which she indicated that she definitely wanted to have children.

While she was away, we talked long distance from her country and one day, she surprisingly told me that she was thinking about paying cash for a beach house for her parents in Morocco. I couldn't fathom why she had to pay cash for a vacation house for her parents when she didn't even own a house herself at the time. She tried to explain to me the Muslim banking custom of disallowing interest on a mortgage. I had never heard of such a thing and I encouraged her to wait for before making the purchase. However, a few days later, she called and informed me that she had paid $200,000 cash for the vacation home. I was initially upset but she explained that she had always wanted to buy them a second home. I still couldn't understand her reasoning because she had shown me pictures of her family's home which seemed to be in very good condition. They certainly weren't poor or in dire need of a second home. I decided to just let it go but I began to seriously question her money management skills.

When she arrived in my hometown, I promptly picked her up from the airport -- feeling ecstatic about having her back in my arms again. The distance between us had definitely made our hearts grow fonder for each other. I booked a room for us at the Marriott hotel in downtown Winston-Salem. When we settled into our room, we wasted no time getting undressed and reuniting in our lovemaking.

It was great to have her back and I was very much looking forward to her meeting my parents. The next evening we all met up at a family style restaurant near Hanes Mall. My mom was so excited to meet her because it had been a while since I had brought someone home that I was serious about. We sat and talked over dinner while Leilani and I talked about our adventures together, and my mom reminisced about my younger days growing up in our household.

Leilani was always great with people and she had a quick wit with a bubbly personality. We enjoyed our dinner together and over the next few days, she met quite a few other family members who all assumed that we would be married soon -- but underneath Leilani's outward appearance was a dark and manipulative persona. She could be cold and cunning one moment and sweet as pumpkin pie the next. I started to wonder if she was bipolar. There were certain times when her behavior was completely unexplainable. I remember a time when she was shopping for new furniture and we stumbled across a store in Santa Monica next to our favorite coffeehouse. We walked in and checked out a few pieces and Leilani surprisingly started to negotiate with the young salesman over a living room set that she liked. We were the only customers in the store and the sales guy seemed like he was eager for a sale. Leilani started pressuring him to sell the set at a dramatically reduced price and when the sales guy reluctantly agreed, she simply said, "Oh I'm not interested. Thanks!" She then proceeded to walk out of the store. I was stunned and embarrassed for her. The sales guy was in disbelief as I followed her out of the store trying to figure out what had just happened. I scolded her for being so manipulative with the salesman, especially considering that she wasn't going to actually buy the set.

It was one of many occasions where I questioned her state of mind. Bipolar people are typically brilliant people who have a difficult time balancing their emotions and maintaining a grip on reality. Over the next few months, Leilani was spending her money like it was growing on trees. There were large referral fees to her network of brokers, numerous shopping trips and it seemed like *all* of her close friends had their hand out for a loan. Within six months of receiving her check for $350,000, she had managed to spend nearly *all* of her money. She called me up one day and surprisingly asked me to help her pay her rent. I was in disbelief that she had blown through her cash so fast. I scolded her for being so reckless with her money but she didn't seem too concerned because she always felt that she could simply make more.

Her out-of-control spending was a major red flag and I knew that I couldn't be in a relationship with someone who was so careless. As a consequence, our relationship started to suffer because of her erratic behavior. I still had a large amount of my cash but I was concerned that she was depending on me to help her financially.

Leilani was the kind of person who was either rich or poor. There was no middle ground with her and it began to drive a wedge between us. I knew she had the ability to make more money but the way she spent her hard earned money was very concerning.

She had also become a master manipulator. I had been spending a lot of time at her place and I decided one morning to get up early and go home to work on my business. Leilani had a slight hangover from the night before and she insisted that I stay with her, but I wanted to spend my day focusing on my sales without her by my side. I left her house and by the time I reached home, she had sent me a text message telling me that she was on her way to the hospital. I had a strong feeling that she was just trying to get back at me for leaving her. I decided to be a good boyfriend and make a trip back to Santa Monica to be by her side. I tried calling her several times but she never answered. I frantically checked every hospital in Santa Monica but none of them had her as a patient.

Suddenly, my spider senses told me to go by her house and see if she was there. I pulled up to her apartment but I didn't see her car outside. I decided to go up to her apartment and knock on the door anyway. I knocked several times but there was no answer, I continued pounding on the door and finally after a few minutes she wistfully came to the door and let me in. When I stepped inside, I saw an older looking white guy sitting in the corner near her couch. Leilani had told me that she had been married before and I assumed that this strange guy was her ex-husband. I suspected that she married this older guy to attain her American citizenship but I wasn't overly concerned about that aspect of her life. My main concern at that point was: Why the *hell* is this guy in her apartment? And why is she not at the hospital? I started to become enraged.

"You told me you were at the hospital!" I screamed.

"I didn't know what to do!" She shouted.

"Who the fuck is this guy and why is he in your apartment!?"

"He's my ex-husband! He came to take care of me." She cried.

The older gentleman stood up and said, "Hey listen, you're getting out of control here and I think you need to settle down."

"Settle down!? Settle down!? I think you need to get the hell outta here before I whoop your ass!" I shouted.

Neither of them could believe how I irate I had become. I had spent my whole morning searching for Leilani at the hospital only to find out she had never been admitted and here her ex-husband was sitting in her apartment.

She escorted him to the door as I paced around her living room floor. Once she closed the door we had a loud shouting match. She kept saying that she was sick and didn't know what to do. I didn't believe her and I knew it was all a scheme to pay me back for leaving against her will.

That incident was the beginning of the end of our relationship. I suddenly realized that I was in love with a crazy woman. We didn't talk for a few days but I was still in love with her so I called her up to see how she was doing. We talked for a little while but it was obvious that our relationship was over. I was hoping that we could overcome that incident but there had been too many other situations to consider. We slowly drifted apart over the next few weeks as we both went on with our lives.

Leilani was the kind of girl that should have come with a warning label. We had an incredible relationship and I thoroughly enjoyed our brief time together. She would occasionally stay in touch and the last time I spoke with her, she told me that she had purchased a large home up in the Hollywood Hills. Leilani had suffered some setbacks from the mortgage crisis of late 2007, but she apparently bounced back and I hope she's doing well these days.

Chapter 23

Celebrity Encounters

I've met quite a few celebrities over the years and the following is a description of my encounters with them.

Meeting Obama

In 2008, I set up an organization called Project Hope to assist with President Obama's presidential election. I hired several college kids and a few other people to help me run the operation. Initially, we would sell campaign merchandise and register voters on the strand at Venice Beach, but the business venture was so successful that I decided to build a website selling our specialty campaign gear along with Obama's merchandise. Within a couple of months, I was generating over $30,000 a month in web and retail sales.

I had donated the maximum to his campaign so a good friend of mine who was a famous movie director invited me to a fundraiser at a nightclub in Beverly Hills for Obama. When I arrived, there were dozens of people milling about and waiting to enter the nightclub. I was well dressed in a blue pinstripe suit and a bright orange tie. Once I was inside, I waited around like everyone else for Obama to make his appearance. Finally, after a few minutes, he arrived and immediately took the microphone. I was standing a few feet away as he got the crowd riled up with his campaign chant of, "Fired up and ready to go!" He spoke for a few minutes and afterwards a line began to form in an effort to meet him.

There were women everywhere and they all seemed anxious to meet Obama. He had a rock star-like quality and the women were fawning over him as if he were Justin Timberlake. I had never seen a Presidential candidate receive so much attention from young admiring ladies. When I finally got my chance to meet him, I firmly shook his hand and said, "Wow, you're like a rock star huh?" He replied in his distinct mannerism and said, "Well, I appreciate that but I'm no rock star...pleasure to meet ya'." I tried to take a picture of him but my camera wasn't working so I decided to move on due to the crush of the crowd.

I found an area near the back of the club and ran into my director friend. We laughed and chatted for a while about how crazy the whole scene had become. After about two hours, I was ready to leave. I assumed that Obama was long gone but as I was leaving, I looked to my right and saw him standing in a dimly lit VIP area, holding a cocktail and leaning up against the wall, talking to one of his aides.

I was amazed at his casual demeanor. He seemed like a down-to-earth guy who just happened to be running for President. I was upset that my camera wasn't working because I knew that a picture of him in that moment would have become an iconic photograph.

I still support President Obama. He has his flaws like every President does but I don't believe that he's received enough credit for the good things that he's done for our country. Maybe someday I'll have a chance to meet him again (and get that picture).

Meeting Diana Ross

A good friend of mine named Bryan was currently managing Kanye West's new record label and he invited me to a soiree which was a kickoff for a scholarship program that Kanye's mom was sponsoring. Bryan had become very close to Kanye's mom, Donda West and she seemed very fond of him as a person.

The soiree was held in the atrium of the Creative Artist Agency building in Beverly Hills. When I arrived, there were several celebrities already there including, Kanye, Common and John Legend. I strolled around the atrium checking out the vibe when I noticed Diana Ross standing in the back with her kids nearby. I couldn't believe she was there. I tried to act nonchalant as I inched closer to her area. Suddenly, a giant Teddy bear wearing a gold chain emerged from the bathroom area. She laughed out loud and said, "Who's that!?" I was standing a few feet away and sarcastically replied, "That's Kanye." Kanye had created a mascot for his new album *College Dropout* and apparently this was his way of promoting it.

Diana looked at me and said, "You're kidding right?"

"Naw that's not Kanye, that's his mascot." I replied. We both chuckled at the moment.

"I think we might be related." I said.

"Oh really? And what makes you think that?" she said with a puzzled expression.

"Well we're both beautiful and talented and my grandfather's last name is Ross."

She laughed out loud and said, "Is *that* right? What is your name?"

"I'm Barrington, very nice to meet you." I said shaking her hand.

"Well Barrington where is your grandfather from?"

"He's from North Carolina."

"Get out of here! *My* grandfather is from North Carolina." She replied.

"Is your maiden name Ross?" I inquired.

"Yes that's my maiden name, wow what a coincidence."

"See I told you we were related." I said with a chuckle.

She laughed and invited her kids over to meet me. I was surprised she had so many young looking kids. I could see my buddy Bryan staring from a distance in amazement of my audacity.

Diana introduced me to each of her kids and we chatted for a bit a longer. I wanted to ask for her phone number so we could keep in touch but I figured that might be pushing the limits.

Later on, I ran into her very attractive daughter Tracee Ellis Ross, who I've always had a crush on. I saw Tracee walking through the party and I said, "Hey I just met your mom, she's pretty cool." She smiled and looked at me as if to say, "Who the heck is this guy?" and kept on walking.

The highlight of the evening was an unveiling of a portrait that Kanye had commissioned well-known artist LeRoy Nieman to paint for him. The crowd gathered around in anticipation of the unveiling of the artwork, which was hanging from the rafters high above the crowd. Nieman made a few remarks as everyone sipped on their drinks and listened intently. Finally, he withdrew the veil to reveal a large canvas with a collage of heavenly images. The centerpiece was Kanye, portrayed as an angel with wings and being presented with the gift of music by another angelic being. It was the most self-aggrandizing piece of artwork I had ever seen and I'm sure Kanye had some influence on the finished product. I'm definitely a big fan of Kanye but I think that some of his over-the-top antics are designed to be both controversial and newsworthy.

Meeting Teri Polo (Meet the Fockers)

One day while browsing around my local CB2 store in Santa Monica for some new furnishings for my place, I ran into a familiar face. I was joking around with the sales staff about my need to find a "manly" comforter for my new bed when Teri Polo walked by and apparently overheard our conversation. She smiled at me as she continued to stroll around the store. Her face looked very familiar. I couldn't recall her name but I knew that she was a famous actress.

I pretended to browse around the store in an effort to "accidently" run into her again. I found her in the back of the store looking at comforters.

"So did you find your 'manly' bedspread?" she quipped.

I laughed and said, "No not yet, maybe you can help me?"

"Maybe." She said with a smile.

"Are you an actress?"

"Yea I am, I'm Teri...nice to meet you." She said shaking my hand.

"So you live around here?" I said.

"No, I live down in Manhattan Beach, I was dropping my kids off and I decided to do some shopping." She replied.

We chatted for a little while longer and then she wandered off to peruse the store again. Meanwhile, I selected a comforter and while I was checking out, she walked by and said, "Nice to meet you."

"Nice to meet you as well." I replied.

I was contemplating asking her out on a date but I wasn't completely confident that she was interested in going out with me. Once the clerk handed me my bag, I dashed out of the store and found her standing outside.

"Hey Teri, I'm not sure if you're single but we should hang out sometime, maybe get a coffee?"

She paused for a moment, surprised at my boldness.

"Yes I'm single and yes I'd like to grab a coffee with you sometime." She replied with a flirtatious smile.

We exchanged phone numbers and agreed to meet up soon. Unfortunately, I had to abruptly move back to North Carolina for a few months before I had a chance to go out on a date with her. Over the next four months, we engaged in a romantic and steamy relationship via text message. It was a bizarre relationship because I'm not really big on texting. She had started filming her new TV show called *The Fosters* on ABC Family, where she plays a lesbian cop who's married to an attractive black woman. She would often send me pictures of her on set dressed in her cop uniform.

As the months went by, she would stay in touch almost on a daily basis to let me know that she was anxious to go out on our first date. We often traded sexy pictures and she also encouraged me to google her name so that I could discover her Playboy pictures (something I had already done). I pretended like I had never seen them before and feigned surprise when I replied to her request.

I don't typically watch network TV but I started watching her new show and visualizing us together. I wasn't certain if we had a future together but *she* seemed convinced that we did. I knew she was over 40 and probably didn't want to have any more kids but I never told her about my desire to have kids during our four month "textual" relationship.

When I finally returned to LA a couple of months later, we met up at an ocean-side bar in Manhattan Beach. I arrived a bit early wearing a comfortable linen shirt and slacks. I found a cozy spot in the lounge by the DJ booth and waited for her to arrive. When she finally walked in, I stood up and met her in the middle of the room. There were a few people hanging out and having drinks and I could feel their eyes upon us as we embraced.

We took a seat and ordered some wine. The waitress, who undoubtedly recognized Teri, was all smiles as she took our order. Directly across from us was a group of Indian guys who seemed very interested in our conversation. Teri and I laughed and drank wine as we chatted about our crazy, long distance texting relationship.

I pulled out my camera and took a picture of her, when suddenly one of the Indian guys offered to take a picture of both of us. We agreed and he quickly snapped a picture of us as we smiled for the camera.

"Very nice!" he said in his Indian accent.

"Do you mind if I take a picture with your friend?" he said.

I looked at Teri and she shrugged her shoulders in agreement. The Indian guy anxiously slid over next to her and "cheesed" hard for the photo. He and his friends were very excited to take pictures with her and I could feel a buzz starting to build in our area. I could tell that people knew who she was but I could also sense that they were trying to figure out who the heck I was. I wouldn't have been surprised if TMZ showed up with cameras, trying to get the scoop on who she was dating.

While flipping through her phone, she showed me some pictures from her Instagram account and I immediately noticed a posting that had 40,000 "likes!" It was one of those moments when you realize how different celebrities really are from the rest of us.

It was a great feeling to be on a date with a popular actress and Teri really seemed to enjoy the attention. Everything was going well on our date, until I mentioned that I wanted to have kids. Her attitude completely changed and I could feel her energy start to deflate. She pretended as though it was no big deal but I knew that she wasn't interested in having more kids at her age. We continued our conversation and she told me about her struggles with her past relationships, including some recent drama with her kid's father. I sensed a sadness about her as she talked about her past relationships.

I abruptly asked her, "Are you happy?"

She paused for a moment in reflection, "Yea I guess I'm happy."

After our conversation, we decided to take a walk down to the pier. She clung to me as we walked down the steep incline towards the beach. It was. nightfall and it was also a bit chilly. We hugged and kissed while standing on the pier and gazing out over the ocean. The wine had us both feeling tipsy so we decided to walk back up the hill towards her car. Once we reached her car, she gave me a kiss and a hug as we departed.

The next day I received a text message from her indicating that she was not interested in dating anymore. She indicated that we were incompatible on our future goals. I knew that she was alluding to my desire to have kids and I simply responded by wishing her well.

I've never been the type of guy to take advantage of a woman. I could have easily exploited Teri for my own personal gain but I'm not that type of person. I know many guys who would have lied about their intentions just to gain favor with her, but as they say, "Karma is a bitch."

I'm On a Boat (with Nate Dogg)

My good friend Cordova who was a photographer had received a contract to photograph the rapper, Daz Dillinger's birthday party. Daz was part of the rap group *Tha Dogg Pound* featuring Kurupt and Nate Dogg. Daz's wife had rented a yacht for his birthday and we all met around 10pm one evening at the Ritz Carlton to cast off and celebrate. There were probably about fifty people including Nate Dogg, Kurupt, a bunch of their "homeys" and of course, a *lot* of groupies.. Cordova brought along his date who was a pretty, brown skin porn star that he had recently met in Vegas. She was stunningly beautiful in her Daisy Dukes and tank top.

Once we all boarded the boat, Nate and his boys started rolling up blunts and drinking champagne on the top deck. On the lower level, there was a DJ and a dance floor set up for the guests. When we casted out to sea; the captain warned the DJ about blasting the music because there was a noise ordinance in affect for the marina. Daz convinced the captain to take the boat further out into the harbor so that they could turn up the music. The captain reluctantly agreed and warned the guests that the waters would be choppy much further out.

As the yacht slowly made its way out to sea, the currents started to rock the boat. After a few more minutes, the boat ride became unbearable. The speakers on the dance floor were sliding from one side of the boat to the other. Many of the groupies were hanging over the edge and throwing up into the ocean. It was awful.

The captain came over the loud speaker and announced that he was heading back to the marina. The ride back seemed like it took forever. The worst thing about being on a boat is, you can't leave when you're ready to go – and I was *more* than ready to go. The captain brought the yacht back to the harbor where they tried to commence the party but most of the guests were too seasick to celebrate.

Once we were back at the dock, everyone got off and headed back to the Ritz Carlton for shelter. As everyone was arriving, I noticed that Cordova's pretty date was now holding hands with Nate Dogg. Cordova didn't seem to care, he was a character who didn't have a problem meeting pretty women.

Meeting the Tenison Twins

One day as I was leaving the Galleria Mall, I spotted the Tenison Twins sitting in the valet area, waiting for their car to arrive. The twins, Rosie and Renee were famous for their groundbreaking Playboy spread featuring two African-American models back in 1989. They had also done quite a bit of acting on shows like *Martin* and *The Steve Harvey Show*. I had been a big fan of theirs since the early 90's.

So I casually walked up to them and said, "Well, well, well if isn't the Tenison Twins."

They laughed and said, "Yep that's us."

I think they were a bit surprised that someone knew their names -- it had been a while since they were popular.

"So what's goin' on? You ladies gettin' a little retail therapy in today?"

They chuckled and said, "Yea I guess you can call it that. What's your name?"

"I'm Barrington, I'm a big fan by the way."

"Well that's nice to hear Barrington."

As we were talking, their car arrived in the valet area. They stood up and gathered their bags.

"We should exchange phone numbers." I said.

Rosie looked at Renee and suggested that she give me her number. They were extremely identical twins and it was hard to tell them apart but Renee entered my number into her phone before she hopped into their car.

"I'll give you a call." She said with a wink and a smile.

They both waived as they departed. My heart was melting. I had just met the girls of my dreams and one of them seemed *very* interested in me.

A couple of days later, I received a call from Renee asking me if I was interested in going out on a date. I was excited that she called but I tried to play it cool. We decided to meet later on that night near Venice Beach. I was looking forward to our date and I was also a little bit nervous. Renee was close to 40 years old but she still looked amazing. I picked her up from the house she shared with her sister in Venice Beach. When she walked out the door, she was wearing tight fitting jeans and a sexy top. I was very proud of myself for having the courage to approach her at the mall on the day we met.

We drove a few blocks to a popular sushi restaurant called Chaya Venice. We took a seat at the bar and I could feel the eyes upon us, trying to determine if we were celebrities. Renee was looking especially radiant and I couldn't help but notice a few of the women at the bar checking her out. When she got up to go to the restroom, an attractive lady sitting next to us -- looked at me and seductively winked her eye.

Renee and I enjoyed our sushi and our night together. After dinner, we strolled down the boulevard where she took me to her retail store located a few blocks away. Later on, she invited me to her house to chill out and have some champagne. Her house was really nice and spacious. We chilled out on the couch for a while, talking and sipping champagne. I had a really good feeling about her and I was hoping that our night together would lead to wild and passionate sex -- but that was not how our night ended. When she walked me to the car, we kissed for a short while and then I hopped in my car and took off feeling a champion. I had just kissed the girl of my dreams and I was floating on cloud nine.

Renee and I went out on another date a few days later. We met for pizza at a local spot and afterwards we took another stroll. I listened while she talked to a guy on the phone about an upcoming party at the Playboy Mansion. I had never been there and I was hoping that she would invite me but when she hung up the phone, she made no mention of inviting me to the party. I was very disappointed. I had taken her out on two dates and she didn't have the courtesy to ask me if I wanted to go. I didn't want to seem like a groupie and ask her to take me, so I just dropped it.

After our last date, I didn't bother to call her back. I didn't see any future for us. I got the impression that she was accustom to dating white guys and that I was probably not her ideal man.

Mystery Lady

I can't reveal too much about this mystery lady, out of respect for her current relationship. We met at an Obama fundraiser and when I saw her, I knew right away that she was a famous actress. We flirted from across the room and eventually met up and exchanged phone numbers. When we met, she told me that she was separated from her husband and currently going through a divorce. Later on, I discovered that was not true.

On our first date, we met at a restaurant in Torrance which was far from where we both lived. We talked over dinner and I listened to her stories about various Hollywood people. After dinner, we went to her car and started kissing and groping each other. After a few minutes of intense foreplay, we decided to jump into backseat of her SUV, where we had hot, sweaty sex. It was so spontaneous and I was flattered that she was so eager to have sex with me.

A few days later, she invited me to an event that her friend was hosting but she surprisingly encouraged me to bring a date. I thought it was a strange request, but she explained that her "significant other" would be there. So I invited a girl that I had recently met online who was stunningly beautiful. When we showed up to the event, we were supposed to be seated in a VIP area near the stage, but when the mystery lady saw me with this tall and gorgeous date, our seats were suddenly moved to the back of the room. I couldn't believe how petty she was behaving; it was obvious that she was jealous of my date. Instead of being pushed to the back of the room, I decided to leave with my date and find a place that we could both chill out, without all the drama.

I never spoke to the mystery lady again after that incident. We had our moment and that was good enough for me.

Chapter 24

Stand-Up Comedy

As you can probably tell by now, I'm a guy who likes to have fun and make people laugh -- so I decided to give stand-up comedy a try. I had built up my courage to perform and entertain during my days as a technical trainer. I really liked the way people laughed during my training sessions and it made me feel really good to be able to captivate a crowd.

I decided to sign up for a comedy class at a local community college. When I tell people that I took a comedy class, their first response is usually one of puzzlement. Most people think that comedians are just naturally gifted and don't need to take classes to hone their skills, but that's far from the truth.

My first day of class was filled with wannabe comedians from all walks of life. There were older guys and young girls, all anxiously awaiting instruction on how to be a better comedian. The instructor was a guy named Barry who had been doing stand-up comedy for years and had also written jokes for Jay Leno at one point in his career.

He started the class by explaining what it meant to be a comedian. We watched videos of famous comics perform and afterwards, he discussed essential elements such as writing good punchlines and utilizing the element of surprise in our humor. As part of our homework assignment, we had to prepare a five minute stand-up routine for our next class. I was excited about doing my routine because I felt confident in my writing and my delivery.

The next week, I waited patiently as some of my classmates lumbered through their not-so-funny routines. Once my name was called, I confidently walked up to the microphone and launched into my routine. I talked about my struggles to become a Hollywood screenwriter with lines such as, "I came to LA to become a writer and so far, things are going well; I've written at least 100 letters to my parents, asking for more money." The class started cracking up at my self-deprecating humor. I would always joke that there's a fine line between self-deprecating humor and self-*defecating* humor.

My five minute routine received a very positive reaction. There were a few jokes that fell flat but that's why I took the class, so that I could receive instant feedback on my material. Once I started going to open mic sessions at comedy clubs around town, I saw a lot of aspiring comics who could have benefited from a comedy class. Sitting through an open mic comedy session is almost the equivalent of having your teeth pulled without anesthesia, it can be quite excruciating.

I didn't start doing comedy to become famous or rich, I just wanted to tell jokes and make people laugh. I had been invited by my instructor to perform at a showcase contest for new comics at a playhouse in Orange County. I invited a couple of close friends and a few people from my class to attend the event with me for support. The theater was fairly large and there was a mixed crowd of about 50 people in attendance. I waited patiently backstage and practiced my material along with a few other comics.

I soon realized that many of the comics had a lot more experience on stage than I did. I wasn't deterred but I knew that I had to bring my "A-game." Once I hit the stage, I paced around the elevated platform and delivered my material with the alacrity of a polished, veteran comic. My comedic style has often been described as conversational, I would often ask rhetorical questions of the audience as a segue to my next punchline. One of the jokes that received the best crowd response was a routine I did about the brainwashing of young black kids. I had seen a documentary about inner city black kids who were asked to choose between a black doll and a white doll and the black kids overwhelming chose the white doll almost every time. My joke went as follows, "So I saw this documentary about black kids and how they prefer to play with white dolls over black dolls. You know whose fault this is, right? Barbie's! In case you guys don't know; there's a black Barbie but you *never* see black Barbie driving a Corvette, no, no, no...black Barbie drives a Chevette! You never see black Barbie chillin' out in her Malibu mansion, oh no...black Barbie has a baby and a two bedroom apartment over in Compton."

The crowd really loved my routine but unfortunately I didn't win the competition. The winner was a black guy who told stale jokes like, "Hey do you have any black in you? Well do you want some?" Afterwards, several people walked up to me and wished me the best. They told me that they really loved my performance. A local club owner also invited me to perform at his club the following week.

The feeling of doing a good comedy show is simply nirvana. The adulation and the attention that you receive as a comic can be intoxicating and addictive. I wasn't sure if I wanted to do comedy full time, at the time it was really a hobby but people were encouraging me to continue on.

So I decided to sign up for an open mic at the world famous Laugh Factory on Sunset Boulevard. The Laugh Factory was the place where famous comics like Richard Pryor, Rodney Dangerfield and George Carlin got their start. Every Wednesday night, they would host an open mic for new comics and the owner, Jamie Masada would always be in attendance. If Jamie liked you, he would invite you to return the following week to do a showcase in front of a real audience.

On my first show at Laugh Factory, I opened my set by saying, "Thank you guys for coming out to my five minute HBO Special." I immediately took control of the crowd, I made fun of Japanese people's love for Adidas and I also talked about some of my strange dates in LA.

"The other day I met this girl and she asked me to take her to 'that place' in Hollywood where she could see all of the celebrities' handprints. So I decided to take her to the Hollywood police station."

The crowd loved it!

After the show was over, Jamie invited me to return the following week. While I was hanging out after the show, I started receiving a lot of attention from the other comics. They were wishing me well and I also noticed a brunette girl who was well dressed lingering a few feet away. She saw the commotion and the buzz surrounding me and she casually approached me and introduced herself. She told me her name was Emily Meador and that she was an agent for comics. Emily started asking questions about how long I had been doing comedy and where else I had performed. She was surprised to hear that I had only been doing comedy for a few weeks. She admitted that she did not see my show but she gave me her card and I gave her my number. A few days later, she invited me to lunch at the famous Greenblatt's Deli located next door to the Laugh Factory.

I had given her a couple of my scripts to read prior to our meeting and when we met for lunch, she told me that she liked my writing and then we talked about an opportunity to appear on the Chelsea Handler Show and maybe become a writer for her show.

I was really excited about the possibility of appearing on her show and meeting with Chelsea. I always liked her sarcastic and witty sense of humor. I was feeling ecstatic about my future as a comic because I had only been doing comedy for a few weeks and I already had an agent. I still wasn't completely convinced that I wanted to be a comic, it was still a hobby for me and I knew that the life of a comic was not always filled with laughter.

Emily asked me to send her video tape of my performances, so I had to go out and perform at different venues in order to build up a reel. While I was out performing at different clubs, Emily had arranged for me to perform at a new comic showcase at the Laugh Factory. She had a great relationship with Jamie, and she was able to pull some strings and get me on the lineup. I couldn't believe how fast things were progressing for me. I invited a few of my friends to see me perform and I worked on some new material for my Laugh Factory debut.

On the night of my show, I waited patiently in the VIP area along with Emily. I was really nervous, I knew that this was the "big time" but I tried not to show my apprehension. The opening act that night was Tom Arnold and he was well over his allotted time as he continued to tell·stories about his marriage to Roseanne and his friendship with Arnold Schwarzenegger. Janice Dickinson, the model, was also in attendance, she was drunk and laughing out loud at almost everything Tom said. It was quite a spectacle to behold. .

Finally, Tom was done and the new comic showcase was ready to begin. As Tom exited the stage, Janice shouted out, "You killed it man! You killed it!" After waiting for the first two comics to finish, it was finally my turn. I was·pumped but still very nervous.

When I finally hit the stage, I tried a joke that fell flat. I opened with, "Hope you guys are doing alright, I just got pulled over by a cop on the way here tonight. Yea, he pulled me over and gave me a speeding ticket. I said, 'Officer can't you see I'm riding on the bus?'" The response was muted but I quickly recovered and went into my more familiar material. Within a few minutes, I had the crowd laughing hysterically at my impression of the Spanish TV hosts who always shouted, "Sabado Gigante! Sabado Gigante!" and how I couldn't understand what they were saying, but the girls were hot and it always seemed like a dance party would break out at any time.

Once I was done, I walked off the stage near Janice Dickinson's seat and she yelled out, "You killed it man! You killed it!" I knew that I hadn't "killed it" but I thought it was a good show for my first time on a big stage. Several people congratulated me on a good show but when I approached Emily, she had a look of disgust on her face. I knew right away that she was not happy. She had never seen me perform and I think she was expecting me to be the next Eddie Murphy. I took a seat as she sat quietly staring ahead for a few minutes. Finally, she spoke to me and gave me some advice on my material and then a few minutes later she abruptly left the club. I was perplexed about her attitude, I was still reeling from my first performance and here she was, chastising me shortly afterwards.

We mutually agreed to void the contract that I had signed with her. She told me that I was "too green," which meant that she was looking for comics that she could make money off of right away. There was no further interest in helping me develop my career and so I decided to stop doing comedy for a while and focus on other things. I still occasionally get the urge to do stand-up and hopefully with the success of this book, I'll have an opportunity to travel around the country and do a few shows.

Chapter 25

Advice for Bachelors

As a lifelong bachelor, I have a lot of knowledge to share with fellow bachelors. Here are just a few:

- Don't get married too soon. I personally feel that most men are not ready to marry until they're at least 35 years old. This gives a man enough time to establish himself and generate a decent income without the obligations of a wife and kids.

- Don't have kids with the wrong woman. If you're having unprotected sex with a woman that you're not in love with, then expect to deal with the consequences of raising a child with her.

- Be Interesting. Read up on different subjects and enhance your knowledge of the world.

- Don't lie about your height or your income on your dating profile. (The truth will come out.)

- Learn a different language (Something I'm currently working on).

- Forget the three day rule; send a "Nice to meet you," text within 24 hours of meeting her.

- Learn to cook at least one really good dish.

- Always be nice to waiters and leave a generous tip on your first date.

- Open your date's car door and pull out her chair for dinner.

- Don't go broke trying to impress a lady that's not that interested in you.

Chapter 26

The Future

I have a lot more stories to share but my fingers are hurting and I think I'm getting carpal tunnel so I will conclude with this part of my story.

I wish that I could say that I've met the woman of my dreams while writing this book but unfortunately, I'm still waiting. I wonder sometimes if I've overlooked a few good women along the way but I'm a believer in fate -- and I still have hope that the right woman will come into my life. I definitely want to have children, which means that I need a woman who's sincerely interested in being a mother.

Some may criticize my choices and my lifestyle but I know who I am and I'm at peace with everything that's happened in my life. I know that I will be an "older" father but that's okay because I'll have a lot more time to spend with them, guiding them and encouraging them to be the best that they can be.

I'm still a vegetarian (actually a pescatarian), I eat seafood occasionally but I love my fruit and veggies. I also enjoy an adult beverage every now and then but I'm not a big drinker and I no longer indulge in any type of drugs.

My faith is very important to me, I try to meditate and fast on a regular basis. My dream is to travel to India and visit Gandhi's homeland to pay respect for his impact on my life and the life of others.

My ideal woman is someone who's educated, loves to laugh, can cook at least one amazing dish, likes to wear dresses, doesn't use profanity (at least not around kids), believes in a higher power and respects others beliefs, likes to travel, owns a bike, a decent tennis player and comes from a stable family.

Thanks for taking the time to read my memoirs.

Fade Out: —

African Proverb: A man without a wife is like a vase without flowers.

© 2014

PLEASE leave AMAZON REVIEW ! (handwritten)

Acknowledgments

Special shout out to my good friends and family --
Matt, Karl, Carol, David, Jack, Mom, Ahlee, Lutrell,
Lawrence, Christian, Kristine, Sharon, Edwin, Jay, Brian,
Bryan, Clancy, Billy, Eric P., Ted, Dennis, Shedrick,
Dereck, F. Gary, Tyrone, Lamont, Mike, Cordova and all
of my aunts, uncles and many cousins.

Twitter
@ 40 Confessions